IT'S NEVER TOO LATE
TO START OVER
By Jo Danna, Ph.D.

IT'S NEVER TOO LATE
TO START OVER

By Jo Danna, Ph.D.

Published by:

Palomino Press
86-07 144th Street
Briarwood, N.Y. 11435

Copyright © 1983 by Jo J. Danna
First Printing November 1983
Printed in the United States of America

Library of Congress Cataloging in Publication Data
Danna, Jo

It's Never Too Late to Start Over
Bibliography: p. Includes Appendix, Index
1. Personal & Practical Guides
2. Occupational & Educational Information
ISBN 0-9610036-1-8 Paperback

ACKNOWLEDGEMENT

Many thanks to the following persons for their generosity in providing information and/or encouragement: Claude Pepper, Augustus F. Hawkins, and John Burton of the U.S. House of Representatives, Select Committee on Aging; Burt S. Barnow, Employment and Training Administration, U.S. Department of Labor; Lenora Cole-Alexander, Women's Bureau, U.S. Department of Labor; Josephine Lerro, Temps-America; Cynthia E. Duran, the Institute for Management Competency, American Management Association; Sarah White, Academy for Educational Development; Annette Klippensteen, Institute of Lifetime Learning; Tanya L Beshgetoor, National Council on the Aging; Mary Bradley Brown, Senior Community Service Employment Program; Fred Z. Hetzel, Senior Aides; Lois L. Tate, Senior Services of Snohomish County; Mrs. Wilhelmina V. Hetzel, and the many others. I also wish to thank the wonderful people at the Career Opportunities Institute, University of Virginia at Charlottesville for opening up new worlds of opportunities. My gratitude, also, to Herb Ahrend of Arhend Associates for his invaluable advice and criticism. And a gold medal to my family and friends for their encouragement, patience, and fortitude during the years I researched and wrote this book.

ABOUT THE AUTHOR

Jo Danna is a social scientist, writer and educa-
tor. She graduated from Hunter College and Columbia University in New York City and from the
Career Opportunities Institute, University of
Virginia. She has, as she puts it, been "through
the wringer" in the fluctuating job market. She
has also experienced the exhilaration and frustration of changing careers several times. This is
the type of book she needed, but couldn't find,
when universities were dispatching tenured and
nontenured professors onto the unemployment lines
-a book to save the busy job seeker and career
changer many months of time and many headaches in
gathering the essential facts; a book that will
make them feel good about themselves again, and
help them to understand that the problems they are
experiencing are not of their own making.

TABLE OF CONTENTS

Laws which protect women workers
Where to go for help and advice
    Advocacy groups   Law schools
    Civil Liberties Union   Working Woman
    Grey Law
    Equal Rights Advocates
    American Bar Association
    Legal Services For the Elderly
    National Employment Law Project
    Equal Employment Opportunity Commission
    National Legal and Defenders Association

Education and training
Interests and leisure activities
Personal factors
Interest inventories
Aptitudes tests
Occupational Outlook Handbook
Other occupations which utilize your abilities
Career counseling services
    What they can and cannot do for you
    How to select a good one
    How to avoid getting ripped off

All-purpose resume   Targeted resume
Chronological resume   Functional resume
Cover letter   Tips for women
How to write a good resume
How to deal with your age
How to make it stand out from the crowd
Tips for professionals who are changing careers
Why more employers prefer an informational letter
Tips on how to write a letter
Mass mailings - Are they worth the expense?
What to do after you've mailed it

Why you should prepare weeks in advance
    Know yourself
    Believe in yourself
    How to practice cognitive therapy
Improving your job interview skills
    Job rehearsal
    Other sources of help
Two main things employers look for
Personality traits that make age irrelevant
Major causes for dismissal
Traits the ideal, mature candidate possesses
Employers' most frequent excuses for not
    hiring older persons
Why your leisure activities are important

How to dispel negative age stereotypes
How to show that you are a winner
If you are changing careers
How to explain dismissals and long gaps in the
    work record without lying
You don't have enough formal education?
How to overcome the interview jitters
The job application form
    Should you lie about your age/ formal education?
    The way you answer can make or break you
    The most important questions
Questions interviewers ask
    Probing questions: What's behind them?
    The stress interview
    Which questions can make or break you?
    How to deal with personal questions
    Illegal questions: how to deal with them
Questions you may wish to ask
Most frequent mistakes made by mature job seekers
What to do after the interview
Passing the second hurdle - Psychological tests
    Why too high a score can disqualify you
    Why a below average score may not matter
    How to reduce test anxiety
    Tips on how to improve your score

    How to beat the competition
    Is moving out of town the only way to save
        your career?
    Which companies have a good record of
        hiring mature persons?
    Occupations where age discrimination is
        MOST/LEAST severe
    Jobs that won't be hurt by high technology
    Opportunities created by the over 55-population
        explosion
    Occupations with the best job prospects
    Emerging occupations
    Why it's poor policy to base a career choice
        on forecasts alone
    Why the computer industry may not be the
        best choice for you
    How to get up-to-date information on the job market
    The fastest growing industries
    How a 2-year certificate or less can help you land
        a better paying job than a 4-year degree in
        computer science
    Industries that need people with writing, teaching,
        sales, marketing and management skills
    Word processing
        High pay for part-time and at-home work
        How to get free training in less than 7 days

Health industry
        Best and worst prospects
        Occupations which don't require a certificate
            or diploma
        Occupations where maturity is an asset
    The emerging industries (ceramics, fiber optics,
cable TV, lasers...)

        Advantages of working for yourself
        Do you have what it takes to be a success?
        Some business ideas that have worked
        How to brainstorm for good business ideas
        Questions to ask after selecting an idea
        How to make a business plan
        How to reduce start-up costs
        How to raise money without asking for a loan
        Getting a loan
        How to do your own market research
        Free/low cost professional market research
        How to attract clients
            Space ads   Classified ads
            Direct mail   Promotion
            Telephone sales
            Free/low cost advertising
        Problems you may encounter after starting
        How to reduce the risks
        The Small Business Administration

THE REASON FOR THIS BOOK

A job is more than a means for earning a living. It's also a means for self-expression, for making a contribution to society and, in return, of earning respect as a valued member of the community. It doesn't matter whether you're an assembly line worker or a nuclear physicist, a high school dropout or a Ph.d. If you're like most people, you measure your own worth by the most important criterion used in our society to evaluate us. What kind of work do you do? Why aren't you bringing home a paycheck?

In October 1982, the U. S. Labor Department counted 13.7 million Americans out of work. This figure doesn't include the millions of workers who dropped out of the labor market because they had lost hope and the retirees who wanted a job because they couldn't make ends meet. It doesn't express the tragedy of many workers who, through no fault of their own, have suffered joblessness more than once because of the recurring cycles of recession. Time magazine reports the case of a 54 year old engineer, father of eight, who had endured it three times; first as a child during the Great Depression when the family home was lost, and later during the 1958 and 1980 recessions when the companies he worked for closed down.

The days when a well "packaged" job hunter can fast-talk his or her way into a job are coming to an end. The invasion of robots in the workplace and stiffening foreign competition leave little room for slack in our economic system. The job market is changing and so are employers' attitudes. They can't afford to select new workers on the basis of who is the best looking, the most persuasive, and who has high class credentials. All they want to know is, "Can you do this particular job and do it well?"

The entire Western world is in the throes of a scientific-technological revolution which is changing the way we live and work. Some experts say up to two thirds of all jobs will be affected. Already in this country, some gas stations have robots which take your money, give you change and fill up your tank.

Yet, to look at the continuing popularity of advice which dangles the promise of a good job, at high pay , if you only would learn the tricks of resume writing, apple polishing and "packaging" your assets as if you were a tube of toothpaste, you wouldn't know this is happening.

I wrote this book because I, too, was a discouraged, displaced, older worker. The old fashioned "make 'em feel good and teach 'em positive thinking" advice didn't work. It didn't prepare me for the changing job market. Nor did it reveal the many new opportunities waiting for someone with my skills.

It's amazing that with all the media coverage on the technological revolution, there are people who still don't understand the extent of what's happening or know what to do in order to get plugged back into the mainstream. In 1982, the steel mills of Pennsylvania shut down, throwing many people out of work. The state set up programs to help them train for new jobs. But, many failed to take advantage of the opportunity. They expected the good old times would soon return.

It's not the generation gap that's hurting mature job seekers. It's an information and skills gap. Even occupations which take years of training are vulnerable to obsolescence. Half of what a physician knows becomes obsolete after five years. No wonder adult education is one of the fastest growing industries today.

In life you have to be lucky; but luck tends to favor the well prepared.   - A. Edward Friedmann, who became a professor after spending most of his life in the diamond business.

"DO YOU HAVE THE CAREER FLEXIBILITY YOU NEED?" This is how a help wanted ad placed by an electronics firm put it. Today, employers expect to see several changes on a resume. (The average American worker holds ten different jobs before retirement, cites a 1980 report by the National Bureau for Economic Research.) Anyone who has stayed on the same job for 20 years or more is suspected of lacking adaptability, a quality that is much in demand in times of overwhelming change.

Change is good for us. Current research shows that our personalities and capacities continue to develop well into old age. But it doesn't happen automatically. It happens only when we accept the challenge of change. A study by Dr. Suzanne Kobasa, of the University of Chicago, indicates that people who thrive on change are more likely to be healthy.

Most young whippersnappers in their sixties want the free and easy life on a pension. - Frank Wheaton, still active as chairman of Wheaton Industries, two weeks before his 100th birthday.

WHEN IS A PERSON "OLD?" What is "old?" People of 65 or 70, very vigorous, do a great day's work. We have a couple of candidates running for office who aren't terribly young. We have prime ministers of nations who are older. They do a good job. I remember Golda Meir of Israel. No one questioned her age. There are many others. - Mario Biaggi, U. S. House Select Committee on Aging

Another reason why I wrote this book is that I came head on with age discrimination. We go on pretending that we are perpetually 35 years old until a single event, like being told "You're overqualified," brings the truth crashing in on us. It's an unhealthy social attitude. It's much less ego crushing to know that we didn't get the job because of discrimination based on ignorance than it is to think we failed because we don't have what it takes.

It all depends on what you have to contribute that society values. In primitive hunting societies, a man was considered "old" at 30, when his physical strength began to wane. But, his usefulness wasn't over. He settled down to the new responsibilities of governing his tribe and raising a family.

In many contemporary societies, too, the "old" are accorded greater prestige than in our own. It was the "old" people of Irish villages at the turn of the century who made the important political and economic decisions. In fact, some European critics wonder whether America is going to lapse into senility after a prolonged period of adolescence.

In our own pre-industrial days, age discrimination and mandatory retirement did not exist. Most people worked until they could no longer hold a job.

In 1890, two our of every three men age 65 and older were working. By 1980, only one in five did so. Age discrimination emerged in the late 1800's when factories began to supplant the farm as America's breadbasket. Since many Americans were employed at heavy manual labor in the manufacturing industries, the belief that after 40 a person's usefulness to society is over, no matter what the occupation, became firmly established. This was followed by compulsory retirement rules. It wasn't long before everyone believed it's "natural" to retire by the age of 65. Soon, a host of negative age stereotypes spread to support this belief.

We feel that older Americans have a great deal to offer the country. They are an important source of information, experience and knowledge. They . . . should not be forgotten, overlooked, or ignored.
          - U. S. House Select Committee on Aging

When a person loses a job or retires, the psychological impact can be devastating. Long before recent medical findings, sociologist Talcot Parsons wrote that the problem of joblessness isn't the financial loss involved, it's isolation from the mainstream of life. He believed this was the cause of the increased incidence of heart disease, hypertension and memory loss. He recommended a gradual relinquishing of responsibilities with advancing age instead of sudden retirement.

Our society goes to extremes in emphasizing the contrasts between the activities of youth and those of our later years, wrote anthropologist Ruth Benedict. We demand an overnight switch from the non-responsible role of childhood and adolescence to the responsible role of adulthood. Then, at an arbitrary age in later life, we expect a person who has held a responsible position for 40-plus years to adjust easily into the play loving, dependent posture of childhood.

The so called "primitive" societies had customs and rituals which eased the psychological stress of passing from one stage of life to another. In some, there was a gradual lessening of responsibilities. In others, there was a public "graduation" with all the pomp and circumstance of a college graduation.

We discard teenagers and older, unemployed workers into the dust bin of social limbo. No wonder, writes psychologist James Anthony, each age group shows similar psychological problems - a high incidence of suicide and drug and alcohol abuse. And, what appears to be senility among the elderly is often a case of severe depression.

According to Harvey Brenner, of Johns Hopkins University, every 1% increase in unemployment brings a 2% increase in the nation's mortality rate, a 5% to 6% increase in homicides, a 5% increase in imprisonment and a 3% to 4% increase in first admissions to mental hospitals. High unemployment also sickens the entire community and causes a hemorrhaging of valuable skills and experience from the nation's economy.

I believe it won't be long before the old chronological division between the "young" (economically useful) and the "old" (economically useless) will disappear. The nation has entered a post-industrial era in which the heavy labor performed by blue collar workers will be done by robots, and onerous office tasks will be eliminated by talking computers. The muscle power of youth will no longer be in demand. Specialized knowledge, up-to-date skills, and good work attitudes will be needed. These qualities are not limited by age.

Besides, chronological age is a poor indicator of a person's ability to do a job, says Robert N.Butler, of the National Institute on Aging. Ability and performance should be the only criteria used in hiring, promoting, and firing decisions. Performance, or age-free, criteria may well show a 55 year old machinist or truck driver scoring higher than a 35 year old.

A five year experiment which replaced chronological age with performance criteria showed that mid-life and older workers have the capacity to do very well on jobs they would ordinarily have been denied on the basis of age. And, the companies involved in the study showed increased productivity as a result of matching each worker to the demands of the job. The study was hailed as a giant step toward changing industry's attitude toward older workers.

The older the fiddle, the sweeter the tune.
                                    - Australian saying

The youth kick of the sixties is passing. It was only a decade ago that men under 45 were looked upon with favor by employers for high level jobs.

The Wall Street Journal recently reported that 45 to 50 year old persons are being given closer attention for middle management positions. For top management positions, it's persons 55 and over.

There are also signs of an improvement in the attitude toward retirement age workers. A survey by the National Clearinghouse on Careers for Older Americans showed that 57% of the California firms which responded showed an interest in hiring them and 97% reported positive results with post re-tirement workers.

In fact, pension plans may soon be altered in order to lure more retirees back to work. This is because many firms which hire retirees for part time or temporary, full time jobs are reporting good results. Another reason is the rapid increase in the number of older Americans at the same time that the Social Security fund and the number of 16 to 24 year old workers are shrinking. In early 1981, there were almost 26 million Americans age 65 and over. They represented more than 11.4% of the nation's population. By the year 2000, this figure will rise to more than 13.1%. The Bureau of Labor Statistics predicts a severe shortage of skilled workers by the end of this decade. All of these factors add up to brighter opportunities for mature workers.

The United States can't neglect its resources of brain power any more than it can neglect energy, capital, or other factors of production. Employ-ment, productivity and, ultimately, our humanity hangs in the balance. - A. W. Clausen, presi-dent of the World Bank.

No stone was left unturned to gather the informa-tion you'll need to help you find satisfying work. If you can't what you need in this book, the appendix will show you where you can get it. Every attempt was made to get the most current and accurate information available. Since publication, however, employment and training programs may have come and gone, addresses and phone numbers may have changed, and organizations may have been restructured and new ones created. Such changes will be noted in the annual revisions of the book. As it is impossible to name all the sources of help that are available, the inclusion of certain programs and organizations does not imply that they are recommended over others which have been omitted. Good Luck!

1

IT'S NEVER TOO LATE

> By "work" I mean...something very
> different, what people used to call
> a "vocation" or "calling," some-
> thing so worth doing for its own
> sake that you would gladly choose
> to do it even if you don't need or
> get any money from it...To find
> our work, in this sense, is one of
> the most important and difficult
> tasks that we have in life, and
> that even if we find our work once,
> we may later have to look for it
> again, since work that is right for
> us at one stage of our life may not
> be right for us at the next.
> — John Holt[1]

LOSING YOUR JOB CAN BE A GOLDEN OPPORTUNITY TO START A MORE REWARDING CAREER.

Others have done so in their mid-life and vintage years, and so can you. Many people have gone back to the classroom to learn new job skills or burnish rusty ones. Others have turned a lifelong hobby or interest into a profitable business, and several have even become millionaires. Wayman Presley had only $1,000 to his name when he retired as a rural postman in Illinois. During the years he delivered mail, he spent his weekends touring local scenic spots with groups of children. Retirement gave him the opportunity to transform a pastime into a tour business which today grosses millions of dollars yearly.

Instead of feeling sorry for yourself, think how lucky you are to be living in a time of exciting, new career opportunities. New jobs are being created which are begging for workers who have the right skills, and the current boom in adult education makes it easier than ever to learn these skills. The computer revolution and the exploding population growth of older Americans creates unbounded opportunities to start your own business.

The stigma of age is gradually disappearing in the job market. Many occupations are becoming age blind as the result of a growing shortage of trained, young workers. Furthermore, the strenuous and monotonous aspects of certain blue and white collar jobs will soon be done by robots and computers, making it possible for workers to stay on the job long after the traditional retirement age. In fact, retirement may come to mean a pause between careers rather than an end.

SO LONG 9-TO-5, HELLO FLEXIBLE WORKSTYLES.

The variety of flexible workstyles is increasing as the nation turns away from manufacturing to the service and information processing industries, predicts the Work in America Institute of Scarsdale, N.Y. You now have a choice of work schedules which are better suited to your lifestyle than the traditional 9-to-5 grind, or you may prefer to work full-time in the comfort of your own living room. Part-time and temporary job opportunities are increasing, and instead of being confined to low level, low paying jobs, they will spread to professional, administrative and middle management levels.

Labor experts predict that by 1990 more than 50% of workers will be involved in one or more of the new workstyles, and many will be past the traditional retirement age. Flexible work schedules will give people more time to study, travel, do volunteer work, and engage in leisure pursuits.

Even when I was younger, the end of the day was always better than the beginning. I took that to mean that life would be that way, also. I see this coming true for myself. - John Cowley, who published his first novel, The Chrysanthemum Garden, at the age of 57.

THERE HAS NEVER BEEN A BETTER TIME TO BE A "MATURE" AMERICAN.

People 55 and older now comprise over 20% of the population, and their numbers are growing twice as fast as the overall population. They are also healthier, better educated, and more politically influential. This means better protection for the older worker's interests. Already there has been an increase in the number of older persons in positions of political power in the past few years.

Recently, at the age of 68, Josephine Oblinger ran for her first term in the Illinois House of Representatives. At 82, Claude Pepper was chairman of the U.S. House Select Committee on Aging. At 80, John C. Stennis was elected to his fifth term as senator from Mississippi. And, at 72, Millicent Fenwick entered the race for the Senate. On the international scene, there were more than 30 elder heads of state in 1982. Among them were 85-year old Sandro Pertini of Italy, 81-year old Urho Kekkonen of Finland, 78-year old Deng Xiaoping of China, 75-year old Benjamin H. Sheares of Singapore, and 77-year old Felix Houphouet-Boigny of the Ivory Coast.

I guess I'm getting old. - Dora Spangler, age 103, who stopped bowling a few years back and is now afraid she'll have to drop golf and take up crocheting.

THE FOUNTAIN OF YOUTH HAS BEEN DISCOVERED.

Today a man of 60 is still young, and 70 is no longer considered old. Diseases such as arthritis, arteriosclerosis, hypertension and cancer are being wiped out, and most of us will maintain a Shangri-La youthfulness until we are in our eighties. Scientists are on the verge of reversing the aging process itself. Already, they've learned to synthesize a youth hormone which our bodies stop producing by late middle age. They're also learning how to slow down aging by diet, drugs, lowering body temperature, and by eliminating the major crippling diseases of aging.

The time when people become "old" will no longer be measured by the calendar. It will be determined, instead, by our physical and mental health, and certain psychological characteristics which include acceptance of change, adaptability, and the ability to keep up-to-date with advances in knowledge. The bottom line will be not how old you are but how strong is your desire to learn the skills and knowledge required in this new era.

Jeannette Piccard was ordained in the Episcopal Church when she was 79 years old. Phillip J. Wingate became a successful writer after he retired from DuPont's Photo Products department, and at 71, Ray Heatherton, former bandleader and television's "Merry Mailman," accepted the Democratic designate for Presiding Supervisor of Hempstead,

13

New York.

IT'S NEVER TOO LATE TO START A NEW CAREER, or to find an exciting new job, and live a new life. The years beyond 50 need no longer be the years when many people find themselves trapped in a job they hate, when all they have to look forward to is early retirement. Life once began at 40, as the old saying goes. Today, it can begin at 50, 60 and older. At the age of 67, Lillian Carter, mother of the president, joined the Peace Corps and went off to a village in India to work as a nurse. James Michener would still be scraping along on a retired teacher's pension if he hadn't turned to writing novels at the age of forty. Now in his seventies, he's a Pulitzer Prize winner, a millionaire, and is still writing blockbuster novels.

"All my life I worked too hard to enjoy life," said Victor, an 80-year old retired waiter turned actor. "Now my days are so full of activities I don't even have time to go to sleep." For many people, the opportunity to do the kind of work they really enjoy comes after retirement, when they are finally free from the responsibilities of youth. A second, even a third, career which comes after retirement can be the most enjoyable and, for some, more lucrative.

Ray Kroc, a high school dropout and former salesman, established MacDonald's food chain when he was only 52; and Harland Sanders, a former gas station operator, was 62 when he started the Kentucky Fried Chicken chain. Mary Kay Ashe started her famous cosmetics company after she had retired.

I remind you that the Middle Ages were followed by the Renaissance.   - Senator Edward M. Kennedy

BELIEVE IN YOURSELF. FORGET THE FALSE, NEGATIVE
AGE STEREOTYPES.

People used to think that after the growing pains of adolescence are over, our personalities also stop developing. Our minds and hearts become set in concrete, so to speak. Psychologist Erik Erikson produced evidence that psychological growth continues well into old age, but only in response to accepting and learning to solve life's inevitable challenges. Without the challenge of change there is stagnation.

14

As a mature worker, you have acquired special qualities which make you a better employee, contrary to what the negative age stereotypes would have you believe. It won't hurt, and it will probably help, if you mention some of the following research findings during a job interview.

OLDER WORKERS ARE LOYAL WORKERS. They aren't constantly on the lookout for a better job, and are more likely to be happy doing the best they can right where they are. A study by the Work in America Institute found that young workers are more loyal to their own careers instead, and 70% of those interviewed said they didn't have to take orders from a supervisor if they didn't want to.

America's values have changed, say social scientists. A sense of loyalty to outside forces has been replaced by loyalty to one's self. There is a greater unwillingness to sacrifice today for tomorrow and more questioning of authority. Teamwork was as valued prior to the Sixties as is the exaggerated Me-First ethic of today. Workers who grew up during the Depression learned its value the hard way.

At a 1978 hearing before the House Select Committee on Aging, it was pointed out that the baby-boom workers who tend to hold these new attitudes will comprise one quarter of the workforce by 1980. On the positive side, these young workers will probably bring about more worker participation in decisions affecting their jobs, greater flexibility in work schedules, and a redesign of the workplace to meet human needs.

OLDER WORKERS ARE RELIABLE. As far back as 1957, a U.S. Department of Labor study found that older (45-plus) employees not only were absent less frequently than younger workers, their turnover rate was lower, adding more stability to the company workforce.

More recent findings support this study and shed further light. For example, the number of days lost from work tends to decrease as age increases. One study found that older workers are more apt to come in on weekends to finish a job if need be. Another reported that older workers involved in a training program were more likely to remain with their employer than younger trainees.

Many employers say that work attitudes such as punctuality, responsibility, carefulness, cleanliness, and meeting deadlines are much harder to teach than work skills. These attitudes have been instilled in persons who grew up under the influence of the old-fashioned work ethic, who experienced the hardships of the Depression. In fact, social scientists believe the work ethic is dying.

Senator Chiles: "From the point of view of a non-profit employer who certainly has to be concerned about costs, do you see hiring older persons as more expensive, or is it less expensive, or is there no difference?"

Dr. Jeffrey Solomon: "There is no significant difference in terms of expense per se....What we see is a higher rate of productivity. We are getting more bang for the buck in what we are paying with the older person than with the younger person."[1]

OLDER WORKERS ARE AS PRODUCTIVE AS YOUNGER WORKERS. Individuals differ widely in productivity, but the difference is not significantly related to chronological age, reports Dr. Warner Schaie, director of the Gerontology Research Institute, University of Southern California. And - surpise! surprise!- where a correlation between age and productivity has been found, it has generally been in favor of the older, more experienced worker.

In white collar jobs the performance of older workers is as good as, and often better than, that of younger workers, reports the Andrus Gerontology Center of the University of California. Many studies report findings such as the following.

- At Bankers Trust and Casualty Company, 4% of the 1977 workforce were over 65, and the majority of them held clerical jobs. According to the managers, these workers had better attendance records, stayed on the job longer, and did as much work as the younger workers.

- Employees age 60-plus, who comprised 20% of the sales force of the Texas Refining Corporation, had the highest sales average, stayed on the job longer, and were easier to work with.

- Studies conducted by the Department of Labor in 1956, 1957 and 1960 found that clerical

16

workers age 65 and older had the best performance record. Even the productivity of
older factory workers did not vary significantly from that of younger workers. The
investigators concluded that a worker should
be evaluated according to his or her potential rather than by chronological age.

- In a 1977 Labor Department study, supervisors
were asked to rate some 3,000 employees age
60 and older in 81 organizations. The older
workers were rated as good as, or superior
to, the average younger worker on quality and
quantity   of work, absenteeism, dependability, judgement, and human relations.

Some studies find, however, that as the physical
demands of a job in heavy industry increases,
there is some correlation between age and de-
creased productivity. Other studies report that
when older workers are placed in more suitable
jobs, they have little or no decline in productivity and fewer accidents.

Dr. N. Williams reports findings which show no
decline in productivity until after age 65, and
the decline is dependent on a variety of factors
other than age. Productivity in office workers,
for example, was best after age 65. Surprisingly,
one study found that even in jobs requiring substantial physical effort, age didn't matter much.
Apparently, older workers have learned how to work
at a more measured pace and with less effort.
Productivity depends a lot on work habits and
attitudes, and many studies show older workers
excel in these qualities.

In a recent survey by the William M. Mercer consulting firm of New York, a significant number of
senior corporate executives who were interviewed
said they believe older workers are more valuable
than their younger colleagues. Among the reasons
given is that they are more committed to company
objectives.

The employers of 21% of manufacturing firms surveyed in 1981 said labor costs would decline if
large numbers of older workers postpone retirement. Lower absenteeism was given as a major reason since in some manufacturing industries the
rate of absenteeism among young workers has been
alarmingly high.

The superior qualities of older workers has led some companies to give preference to retired job applicants. The age range of workers at a Burpee Seeds subsidiary of General Foods in 1977 was 55 to 85, and much of the company's success was attributed to a flexible work schedule which brought out the best in these workers. The United Bank of Illinois solved a problem of young worker dissatisfaction and high error rates in its check filing and records department by hiring a unit of retirees. The error rate shot down to zero.

The American Council of Life Insurance reports older workers in 1980 stayed home sick less often. The average for workers over age 45 was 3.1 days compared to 3.7 days for workers 17 to 44 years of age.

People are like fruitcake. The more they age, the better they get.

Health specialists say the majority of the sick elderly are well into their eighties, not the "young-old" (persons in their sixties and seventies) as Bernice Neugarten of Northwestern University calls them. She suggests using the terms "young-old" and "old-old" to differentiate older persons who are still vigorous and healthy from those who are more likely to be in decline. And yet, there are many vigorous, active persons who are in their eighties and older.

- At the age of 100, Sir Robert Mayer, British patron of music, sets off on an American lecture tour.

- At 96, Elizabeth Craig of England publishes another of her many cookbooks.

- At 95, Catherine Bramwell-Booth, of the British Salvation Army, addresses Army meetings, appears on British television and radio, writes her fifth book, and is voted "best speaker of the year" by the guild of professional toastmasters.

- At 90, Sir Adrian Boult, conductor and founder of the BBC Symphony Orchestra, publishes another book.

- In his nineties, Professor Joel H. Hildebrand is still active in the chemistry department of the University of California.

- At 88, Dr. Karel Steinbach retires as gyneco-
logist with the Brooklyn Fort Hamilton induction
station so that he can devote more time to private
practice. The doctor who replaces him is 76 years
old.

- At 86, Ellen Mitchell retires as a supervisor
at Chase Econometrics/Interactive Data Corporation
in New York City. However, she can still be seen
dancing regularly at the Roseland Ballroom.

- At 86, Eubie Blake comes out of retirement to
resume his career as composer and pianist of rag-
time music.

- At 84, Susan B. Anthony organizes the International Women's Suffrage Alliance.

- At 82, Richard Gatling invents the motor dri-
ven plow; Winston Churchill writes a four volume
history of the English speaking people; Leo Tol-
stoy completes another book; and Armand Hammer is
busy as chief executive of Occidental Petroleum
Corporation and the nation's ombudsman to the
U.S.S.R.

- At 76, guitarist Andre Segovia becomes a father. At 90, he slows down a bit. Instead of
playing 30 concerts a year, he plays only 23.

Scientists predict that in the near future, disease will no longer be a major factor in reducing
the work capabilities of older persons. Some of
the physical changes which occur as we grow older
can now be corrected, and others eased by making
changes in the workplace and scheduling, says Dr.
Schaie. He believes large individual differences
and widely differing job demands suggest that
these physical changes will be trivial for most
older workers in most jobs.

OLDER WORKERS HAVE GOOD SAFETY RECORDS, say labor
experts. Several studies find older workers have
fewer accidents in addition to getting more work
done in a day. This is true even when older workers have no more experience on the job than younger workers. One reason is that younger workers are
more likely to take risks, whereas older workers
have learned to avoid accidents by using judgement
based on experience.

Older workers are less likely to be injured in
misusing machinery. While they tend to have fewer

accidents than the young, there are some work settings in which they face a greater hazard. For example, when quick, evasive action is necessary, older workers are less likely to avoid an accident. But this can be corrected by adapting the tasks and pace of work to their capabilities.

One of the studies involved a group of workers ranging in age from 55 to over 75, who had not held a job for two or more years.[3] After they had been placed in a job, their employers were asked to rate them on learning ability, attendance, ability to get along with co-workers and supervisors, ability to follow instructions, and accident proneness. The following results were found.

- On overall job performance, 53% of the workers were rated better than average to outstanding, and only 3% were rated unsatisfactory.

- On accident proneness, 98% were rated as no more accident prone than younger workers.

- On attendance, 68% were rated average to outstanding. (Only 8% of the older workers had above average absenteeism due to health reasons.)

LITERACY IS STILL ALIVE AMONG OLDER WORKERS. Some employers in California were recently asked to choose the skills they value most in new employees. They named the ability to read manuals, write reports and do the basic arithmetic needed for simple record keeping. This response would have been considered ludicrous a generation ago, when schools emphasized the three Rs, and any student who failed to master them was not promoted to the next grade. Even older persons who had to drop out because of the Depression, have been educated more rigorously.

The problem of semi-literacy among young workers today is a national disgrace. One large insurance firm, for example, reported that about 70% of dictated correspondence has to be redone at least once because of errors. A 1982 survey of over 2,000 employers found that about two fifths reported reading deficiencies among office workers, and over half found poor mathematical skills among technical workers, supervisors, and bookkeepers.

Many job applicants can barely write a complete sentence, let alone spell and punctuate properly. "We mist you wile you wer out" is the caliber of literacy employers must contend with these days. There are even college graduates who can't write a coherent report or memo. As a result, colleges are offering remedial English and math courses to their incoming students.

Studies show that semi-literate and illiterate workers have lower productivity and more industrial accidents. A Westinghouse Electric Company plant had to fire several workers because they couldn't read the instructions on how to handle dangerous equipment. In 1975, a herd of prime beef cattle was killed because a feed lot worker misread the package label, and gave the cattle poison instead of feed.

Because secretaries can't write complete, grammatical sentences, machinists can't read equipment manuals, and executives can't write a coherent business report, at least 35% of U.S. companies in 1981 had to give remedial education to their employees.

Employers complain that schools are also failing to instill the attitudes and work habits needed to compete for a job and keep it. Probably even worse is the decline in problem solving ability in the nation's high schools, as reported by the National Assessment of Educational Progress in 1983.

OLDER PERSONS ARE MORE FLEXIBLE AND ADAPTABLE THAN MOST PEOPLE THINK. One of the biggest prejudices faced by older workers, said a young placement counselor, is the belief that they have less patience, and are less willing or able to adapt to change. Regardless of studies which attest to the higher productivity of older workers, this prejudice still exists in the minds of many employers.

Chronological age has less to do with how old you are in terms of adaptability than the rocking chair myth would have us believe. In fact, said the late anthropologist Margaret Mead, adults over 60 have had to adapt to more overwhelming changes than have younger persons - to at least three wars, a dramatic change in customs and values, and a radical change in family and community relations. No other generation has had to face more tests of its ability to adapt.

Adaptability is a personality trait, not a physiological fact. It is shaped in early childhood by the values learned from the family, church and community. Individual variations in adaptability among the over-50 generation are probably greater than among the peer-following youth generation. A senior executive officer said, "Many older executives remain receptive to new ideas and exhibit immense vitality."

The 1982 television documentary, "America Works When It Works," showed how differently automobile workers in Detroit responded to a lay-off. One group of workers, which included persons nearing retirement, realistically assessed the gloomy job prospects in the region. They learned about job opportunities in the Sunbelt states, read out-of-town newspapers, answered job ads, put their houses up for sale, and piled into their U-Haul trucks for a new life elswhere.

The other group, which included some of the younger men, decided to remain because, "There's always someone to lend a hand when you need it." As one of them explained, "I'm not the kind of person who takes to change, being a stranger in a new job, with new neighbors. I'd rather be where I grew up, even if it means going on welfare for a while."

OLDER PEOPLE ARE RELATIVELY FREE OF THE SERIOUS PROBLEMS FACED BY THOSE IN THE EARLY STAGES OF THEIR CAREERS, AND ARE LESS LIKELY TO BE DEPRESSED, writes Gail Sheehy in her book, Pathfinders.[4] Through the years they have learned how to cope with stress and the inevitable life crises. They have come to terms with themselves and are more likely to accept what life has to offer. Consequently, they're more relaxed and tolerant. The older persons she surveyed generally had the highest sense of well being. And a tension-free worker is a better worker.

There are other, job related personality factors which have been overlooked by employers because they're more difficult to assess. For example, the prevalence of neuroses declines with age, several studies find. In one study, workers over 40 reported significantly fewer psychiatric symptoms than those under 40. Also, it is generally recognized that older persons have learned valuable skills in getting along with others, coping with frustration, and general problem solving. These characteristics should also be considered in hiring and firing decisions, say the experts.

I don't know quite yet what it feels like to be 90, but whatever it feels like, I don't feel it....I swim just about every day, make a speech or two every week, see a steady stream of visitors. And I'm working on a book about the Truman years.
                    - Averell Harriman, elder statesman

INTELLIGENCE AND LEARNING ABILITY REMAIN UNIM-PAIRED among healthy, active, older persons. On tests which assess creative intelligence and problem solving ability, many actually show gains in scores.

It's now known that earlier studies which reported a decline in I.Q. scores as we grow older confused speed of response with the ability to solve problems. Current studies show the average, healthy, 70-year old performs as well as, and in many cases better than, younger persons on power intelligence tests. These are tests which allow a person to take a much time as needed to solve a series of increasingly complex problems.

Many studies show that judgement, vocabulary and general information either continue to improve from the age of 60 on or, at the very least, do not decline. A study which compared persons age 60 to 82 with much younger persons found insignificant differences in learning, and many of the oldest persons were still learning very well. One study of creativity found that 80% of the best, new ideas were produced by employees who were over 40 years of age. According to the researchers, younger employees tended to re-invent the wheel.

Another study compared groups of men ranging in age from 20 to 53 on tests of reading comprehension, mental agility, and mechanical comprehension.[5] The most striking finding was that the scores were generally very similar across the age groups. The scores changed significantly with age in only one test, and the change was in favor of the older men. With advancing age there was only an insignificant decline in reading speed and comprehension. The problem seems to be, say the researchers, that as employees grow older, they tend to believe in the negative age stereotypes and unconsciously perform according to everyone's expectations.

Often, what appears to be a decline in memory, learning and problem solving ability is actually a symptom of emotional stress, poor health, poor nutrition, and/or a lack of exercise. Studies with animals often provide clues to what's bothering humans, and the results of several suggest the brain shrinks with inactivity and understimulation just as the muscles do. There is some evidence that older people who exercise their bodies and minds have a lower incidence of senility.

Actually, senility affects fewer than 10% of persons age 60-plus. In at least half of the cases, it's due to metabolic disorders, chronic alcoholism, strokes and hardening of the arteries. Most of these physical problems are now treatable with miracle drugs, by surgery, or by a simple change in diet.

Soon, we'll be able to buy substances which improve memory and learning ability. Scientists have already synthesized a brain hormone, vasopressin, which significantly improves memory and learning, and there are other substances which show similar effects such as acetylcholine and strychine sulfate adrenaline. Already on the market as aids to memory and learning are vitamin B, folic acid, the cholines found in egg yolks, and the lecithin in soybeans.

1. Reprinted from Psychology Today magazine, copyright 1980 (APA)

2. Senator Lawton Chiles and Dr. Jeffrey Solomon, who is associate director of the Miami Jewish Home and Hospital for the Aged at Douglas Gardens. This excerpt was taken from the July 9, 1980 hearings before the Special Committee on Aging, U.S. Senate.

3. Borzilleri, Thomas C., "Evaluation of the Senior Community Service employment program: New enrollee characteristics, job performance after permanent hiring, and the costs and benefits of permanent placement." American Association of Retired Persons and the National Retired Teachers Association, February 15, 978.

4. Sheehy, Gail. Pathfinders, William Morrow & Co. Inc., 1981.

5. Thumin, Fred. "Performance on tests of power and speed as related to age among male job applicants," Aging and Work, Spring 1981.

2

BEFORE YOU TAKE THE PLUNGE

WHAT DO SUCCESSFUL CAREER CHANGERS HAVE IN COMMON?

CHANGE DOESN'T FRIGHTEN THEM. Many mid-life and older persons have a youthful flexibility which helps them to adapt successfully. You can, too, if you concentrate on the ways change can improve your life rather than on your fear of the unknown.

Of all the "isms" that have plagued this century, ageism is the most stupid. It's time to declare war on the mindless youth cult that has our time in its grip, demoralizing our people, weakening our system...wasting our experience, betraying our democracy and blowing out our brains. Garson Kanin.

When the time comes to take action, they don't freeze with fear. Sometimes, the fear stems from an uncritical belief in society's myths about aging. Though you may have better qualifications for a job or for success in a new career than many young persons, you could be brainwashed into believing you're "too old" for the job, or that "it's too late" to make a change.

THEY KEEP THEIR BODIES AND MINDS IN TIP-TOP CONDITION.

THEY'RE NOT AFRAID TO TAKE CALCULATED RISKS. At the start, they are willing to accept a lower income, a lower level job, even a financial loss for the sake of gaining greater job satisfaction, more money or leisure time, and a better lifestyle later on.

THEY PLAN CAREFULLY AND GET THE FACTS. Dr. Paula Robbin's study of 91 men who made voluntary mid-life career changes found that the more carefully they planned the move, the happier they were with the outcome. The unsuccessful men had hastily accepted a new job without making a preliminary study of the job market, without thinking about their priorities in life and whether they had the skills or expertise to succeed in the new career.[1]

IF THE CHANGE REQUIRES GOING BACK TO SCHOOL, THEY DO IT. They don't think of themselves as "too old" to learn something new.

SOME QUESTIONS YOU SHOULD CONSIDER

WHICH OCCUPATIONS AND INDUSTRIES CURRENTLY OFFER THE BEST EMPLOYMENT OPPORTUNITIES? Some of the new occupations require little prior work experience, but they may require going back to school for a period of several weeks to several years. Some careers, such as going into business for yourself, require only some reading on the subject and several visits to the Small Business Administration for free advice.

WHICH COMPANIES ARE MORE LIKELY TO HIRE SOMEONE WITH YOUR SKILLS AND EXPERIENCE?

WHICH COMPANIES HAVE A GOOD RECORD OF HIRING OLDER WORKERS?

WHAT RISKS ARE INVOLVED IN CHANGING CAREERS? HOW CAN YOU MINIMIZE OR AVOID THEM?

WHICH OCCUPATIONS ARE YOU BEST SUITED FOR IN TERMS OF YOUR SKILLS, APTITUDES, INTERESTS, TRAINING AND EXPERIENCE?

ARE YOU COMPATIBLE WITH THE NEW CAREER YOU'RE CONSIDERING? Your personality and energy level must also be considered in choosing a career. Does the work involve more standing, sitting, bending, walking or talking than you can take? Let's suppose you spend a lot of time and money learning word processing and, after you get the job, you discover that your eyes can't take staring for hours into a lighted screen. Learning more about the physical demands of the new job before you invest time and money preparing for it can save you a lot of heartache.

Will you mind working with employees who are young enough to be your children or grandchildren? Will you be working with lots of people around or will much of your workday be spent in relative solitude? What about the noise level in the office or factory? One woman quit a good job because the clattering electric typewriters were driving her crazy.

Companies have "personalities" just as people do. They vary considerably in the pace of activity, the rate of changes that occur, and their command structure. Before you decide on a career in one of the new, space age industries, for example, consider whether you would like to work in their highly charged, fast-paced work settings.

"We believe in open lines of communication, flexibility and teamwork...Share your ideas with top management," said a help-wanted ad for a computer company. Which style of management and decision making harmonizes with your personality? Many firms in the more conservative industries, such as banking, oil and insurance, continue to rely on the top-down management style in which orders issued from above go "down the line" and are expected to be carried out to the letter. There's a sense of security in knowing exactly what your responsibilities are, but you'll have less freedom to decide how to carry them out or to question management directives.

You may be happier, on the other hand, working for a firm that is in the forefront of technological and scientific change. Generally, these have a command structure in which decisions are made on the basis of consensus among all levels of employees, in which workers have more freedom to decide how and when to carry out their assignments. Some labor experts predict this management style is the wave of the future in the nation.

WHAT LEVEL OF SKILLS, EDUCATION AND TRAINING ARE REQUIRED?

WHAT ARE THE DUTIES AND WORKING CONDITIONS, WHAT IS THE SALARY RANGE, AND HOW GOOD ARE THE OPPORTUNITIES FOR ADVANCEMENT?

HOW IS YOUR HEALTH? It takes a lot of time and energy to prepare for a career or job change. How much energy you have depends on the state of your health as well as your attitude toward change. Important life changes, such as losing a job, retiring, or making a voluntary career change increase the level of stress which, in turn, increases your chances of becoming ill. It also lowers your energy level and diminishes your appeal to a prospective employer. Knowing how to minimize stress during this period will improve your chances of making a successful career or job change.

WHICH TOWNS, CITIES AND REGIONS OF THE COUNTRY OFFER THE BEST OPPORTUNITIES FOR THE TYPE OF JOB YOU WANT?

WHOM CAN YOU TURN TO, WHERE CAN YOU GO IN ORDER TO GET HELP IN FINDING A JOB?

DO YOU HAVE ENOUGH SAVINGS? If not, a part time or temporary job can tide you over while you work to achieve your goal. If the job is in the firm or industry you eventually hope to work for, your transition to the new career will be smoother.

HOW DO YOU NORMALLY REACT TO CHANGE? Are you the kind of person who is afraid to take risks? When the time comes to take action, will you freeze with fear? No one ever climbed the heights without taking a risk. Some people are so afraid to take a risk that they trade achievement and job satisfaction for boredom, security, and staying in a rut. If this is your problem, read David Viscott's book, Risking. It could change your life.

Sometimes, people delay taking the plunge by planning too carefully. At some point in your fact finding, ask yourself, "Am I doing all this unnecessary research as an excuse to avoid making the final decision? Am I scared?" Next to hasty and inadequate planning, failure to take action when the time is ripe is a major reason for failure, as any executive worth his or her salt knows.

DOES THE CAREER CHANGE REQUIRE GOING BACK TO SCHOOL? If so, do it! The idea of being too old to learn something new never occurs to successful, mature career changers. The day James Petrie showed up for classes at a merchant marine academy, with scholarship in hand, the college administrators thought they had made a mistake in admitting a 71-year old student, and they tried to expel him. At last report, he was planning to sue the academy on the grounds of age discrimination, and was looking ahead to another fight when he graduates and applies for a job on a merchant ship.

I simply have to pass the bar because I have to strike a blow at the shibboleths and stereotypes against old people. You are expected, at my age, to do whatever you want, as long as it has no impact on the world, to fill time instead of use it. I hate it! - Jacob Landers, who earned his law degree at the age of 69 from New York University.

HOW WILL YOUR FAMILY REACT TO A JOB OR CAREER CHANGE, ESPECIALLY IF IT INVOLVES A MOVE TO ANOTHER CITY? Your family is more likely to go along with your wishes if you first discuss the proposed change with them, and allow them to express their fears and needs. Asking for suggestions on how to make the change generally makes everyone, or at least the majority, happy.

It might be wise, before revealing your plans, to make a list of all the benefits to them resulting from the change. Learn about the schools, clubs and social activities in the new community. Try to discover at least one irresistible lure about it. This will help them to see your point of view.

Some people find the transition to a new career devastating, worse than they anticipated. That's why planning and research are important. One horror story involves a woman who quit her job as executive secretary to become a full time college student in librarianship. Before she was able to graduate, her savings ran out, and she had to take a full-time, entry level job at lower pay and transfer to evening school. Finally, she graduated, but then she discovered to her dismay that jobs in her town were scarcer than hen's teeth.

All this trouble could have been avoided if she had first learned about the market for librarians in her state and, assuming she was willing to relocate, where the best opportunities are nationwide. Despite the general overall shortage of jobs in this field, some places have more openings than others. She should also have done a careful self assessment to determine whether her interests and temperament match those of successful, happily employed librarians.

The following questions can help you decide whether you and your family are cut out for a change of job or career which entails a move to another community.

1. Do I make friends easily?

2. When I go on vacation, do I prefer to travel to new, exotic places? Or, do I prefer places that are as similar as possible to my own community?

3. Do I like to try new recipes, or do I prefer to stick to the tried and true?

4. Am I comfortable with, do I find it stimulating to be with, persons of a different nationality, race, or religion?

5. Do I like to try new TV shows, even though I'm content with what I usually watch?

If your answers to three or more of these questions are "No," you might be better off if you do several of the following.

- Choose a job or career that's as similar as possible to your present or last one.

- Transfer to a new position in the company or industry you work for. If you're a switchboard operator or bookkeeper, for example, you might train for a job as computer technician or word processor. Most companies nowadays are computerizing their office and factory operations, and jobs in this field are relatively plentiful.

- Stay in the city where you now live, no matter how gloomy its job prospects. Be prepared, however, for a longer period of unemployment. You can take a part-time or temporary job while you're waiting for something better.

- Start a business of your own.

- Learn the techniques of job hunting.

- Learn how to detect age discrimination and what to do about it.

- God helps those who help themselves. Find out what others in your situation are doing in your community. Get together and form your own job bank and referral service. Plan a campaign to win over the employers in your community to the idea of hiring more older persons. See the appendix for references on how to do this.

These are some of the questions you need to answer in order to select a job or career in which you'll be happy. The alternative is simply finding a job, which implies accepting anything, regardless of whether it suits you.

1. Robbins, Paula. Successful Midlife Career Change, American Management Association, 1980.

3

HOW TO FIND A JOB:
INFORMATION SOURCES

The following sources of information provide all
you need to know in order to find a job or change
careers. Don't be scared off by the enormous a-
mount of information that's available. You don't
need to explore every one in depth. Just concentrate on those you need the most.

.The Y's
.Libraries
.Chamber of Commerce
.Job Placement Services
.Voluntary Associations
.Conventions,Job Fairs
.Adult Education Centers
.Special Interest Groups
.Religious Organizations
.Newspaper Help Wanted Ads
.Career Counseling Services
.Direct Contact With Employers
.Federal Job Information Centers
.Personal Contacts ("Old Boy" networks)
.Community Social Service Organizations
.City, County and State Agencies On Aging
.Unions, Trade and Professional Associations

LIBRARIES

YOUR PUBLIC LIBRARY has much of the information
you need. Look in the card catalogue for books and
periodicals on the occupations and employers you
are considering.

Trade and professional newsletters and journals
generally contain more up-to-date information than
books. Some have classified ads that list a wide
range of job openings in the industry. For example, INFOWORLD, a newsweekly for microcomputer
users, also lists openings for non-computer specialists,such as sales representatives, writers,
and teachers,who have a layman's understanding of
the technology and can train new users of computers, sell computers and write about them without
using hard-to-understand jargon.

Education and Job Information Centers (EJIC) can
be found in the public libraries of some states.
They enable you to get information and professional advice with the least amount of time, money and
effort. They were established recently as a public
service because of the high unemployment rate. If

your library doesn't have an EJIC, ask the librarian for a list of other educational and career counseling services for adults in your state.

For example, almost all of New York State's 22 public library systems have at least one EJIC where it is possible to obtain the following information.

JOB OPENINGS
- Local and out-of-town help wanted ads.

- Civil service lists and announcements.

- Job newsletters such as <u>Federal Jobs, Federal Research Service, Federal Times, and The Chief.</u>

- The State's Job Bank on microfiche.

- Directories of employment agencies.

- Overseas and out-of-state job openings

- Business directories, magazines, newsletters

JOB FINDING INFORMATION: Resume preparation, interview techniques and other tips.

CAREER CHANGE INFORMATION: Administration and interpretation of psychological tests; books on careers; and tests on interests, skills and aptitudes which can be self-administered and scored. Career Counselors are available in some EJIC centers. Other centers will refer job hunters to appropriate services for testing, counseling or job placement.

PRIOR CIVIL SERVICE EXAMINATIONS are available for many civil service jobs as well as guides on how to prepare for the tests.

EDUCATIONAL RESOURCES: Catalogues on a wide variety of vocational schools, colleges and home study programs; information on how to apply for financial aid. In many centers, specially trained librarians help job hunters select the most suitable educational programs.

Each center also has information useful to the older job hunter and offers services which are tailored to the special needs of the community.

The only difference between a gentleman and a derelict is a job.   - William Powell in <u>My</u> <u>Man</u> <u>Godfrey</u> (Universal Pictures, 1936)

COMMUNITY AND FOUR YEAR COLLEGES have career counseling and job placement offices which maintain a library of career publications. Some have videotapes and audio-cassettes which demonstrate how to do an interview and write a resume. Others have the equipment for videotaping a practice interview session so that you can see yourself in action. In many communities, you don't have to be a registered student or alumnus in order to avail yourself of these services.

NEWSPAPERS

Although only a small percentage of job openings are advertised in newspapers, many job hunters swear by them. Surveys show such ads rank well below personal contacts and direct contacts with employers as a source of jobs.

How helpful they can be depends on the type of job you're looking for. Ads for high-skill, executive, managerial and professional job openings are worth looking into. A 1979 survey by the Bureau of National Affairs showed that over 80% of the employers who responded used newspapers to advertise their technical, managerial and professional openings, and about 70% used them for white collar and sales openings.

ADS FOR "GAL OR GUY FRIDAY" and other low-skill, low paying, entry level jobs are more likely to result in disappointment. You're better off by simply walking into a company's personnel office and filling out a job application form.

BLIND ADS which give only a box number (The employer's name and address are omitted) are also said to be a waste of time. Some companies place blind ads in order to get information on the labor market and salary levels or to test the loyalty of their employees.

OMNIBUS ADS which list a huge smorgasbord of job openings at pay that seems too good to be true are often used as lures to get your name added to their list of clients.

ADS THAT SAY "NO EXPERIENCE NECESSARY" should be viewed with caution. The employer may be having difficulty filling the vacancy because of poor salary and/or working conditions.

CITY NEWSPAPERS which have a large circulation are more likely to have a special Sunday supplement which is devoted exclusively to help-wanted ads. Although many of the job openings are local, quite a few are located in other cities and states.

THE WALL STREET JOURNAL issues a National Business Employment Weekly which lists job vacancies paying over $25,000, mostly at the executive, managerial and professional levels. A monthly feature article, "Business Offerings," discusses some of the best opportunities to start your own business. Single copies can be purchased at newsstand for $3.00. An 8-week subscription costs $32. Write to The Wall Street Journal, 420 Lexington Avenue, New York, N.Y. 10170 or telephone (212) 808-6792.

THE NEW YORK TIMES claims to advertise over 100,000 vacancies a month. On Mondays through Saturdays, job openings are advertised in the Classified Section. In addition, there are the following special weekday sections.

Monday's Sports Section lists job vacancies in various fields. Tuesday's Science Section lists openings in the fields of education, health, library services and high technology. Wednesday's Business Section has a career marketplace for executive, managerial and professional openings. Elizabeth Fowler's column, "Careers," gives information on industries and occupations which have a favorable job outlook, as well as job hunting tips and in-depth descriptions of emerging occupations.

On Sundays, there is the huge Sunday Help-Wanted Supplement. Additional job listings are in the Business Section which lists openings at the professional, technical, management and executive levels. The Week in Review Section lists openings in education, library and health services.

It's important to know that the library subscription copies of out-of-town newspapers generally arrive several days after they appear on the newsstand. Since every minute counts, find out when they usually arrive and get to the library as early as possible. Better yet, order a subscription if you can afford it. The librarian can give you information on subscriptions to the major city newspapers. (The Washington Post is another excellent source.)

OUT-OF-TOWN NEWSPAPERS are an excellent source of employers you can contact by mail or long distance phone call. The Washington Post's Sunday edition, for example, contains ads placed by high technology firms which list their toll-free phone numbers for the convenience of interested job hunters. You can follow up a phone inquiry with a resume or informational letter.

Some job hunters have had success in making an interview appointment by phone. When they arrive, they make a tour of the community in order to get a first hand look at the living conditions and further information on unadvertised job leads. Other sections of these newspapers contain information on the cost of living and quality of life in the community. News articles, especially those in the business section, often give clues to which industries and companies are thriving and, therefore, in a hiring mood.

A PROBLEM IN USING NEWSPAPER ADS is that you're competing with hundreds, maybe thousands, of other job hunters who have seen the same ad. So, in order to be the early bird that gets the worm, buy the newspaper as soon as it's issued. Stay up till midnight or get up at the crack of dawn, if need be, and answer the ads without delay. Have a stack of resumes and cover letters ready for such opportunities. Some job hunters send their resumes and letters by special delivery mail. Others send a second copy a day later just in case the first one gets buried beneath the pile.

DO YOUR OWN "MARKET RESEARCH" on local job market conditions. A simple tally of advertised job vacancies will give you a general picture of occupations and industries that are thriving as well as their salary range. You may discover job opportunities you hadn't even considered.

SOME PEOPLE PLACE THEIR OWN "JOB WANTED" AD in the local newspaper. This is useful mainly to self employed persons who have specialized skills, such as tutors, repairmen, and typists and to executives and professionals who have impressive credentials.

OTHER PUBLISHED SOURCES OF INFORMATION, like the ones listed below, can be purchased or are available free in public libraries, guidance and placement offices of colleges and universities, in state employment offices and in women's centers.

JOURNALS AND NEWSLETTERS OF TRADE, UNION AND PROFESSIONAL ORGANIZATIONS

These carry information on job openings which the newspapers don't usually carry. Look in the appendix for directories which have information on the various associations and their publications. The public library may have a file of association publications. All you have to do is ask.

BUSINESS MAGAZINES

The library also has a periodical index of magazines which give up-to-date information on the national job market. These include MONEY, Time, Forbes, Fortune, Business Week and others.

FEDERAL GOVERNMENT PUBLICATIONS

These can generally be found in the library and in the Federal Job Service offices (formerly known as Federal and state employment offices). See the appendix for details on how to order a subscription.

JOB OPENINGS, is a monthly newsletter put out by the U.S. Department of Labor's Employment and Training Administration. It lists occupations that have the largest number of current openings, where they are located nationwide, their salaries, and phone numbers to call. It also gives information on local job vacancies, wage rates, and training and skills requirements. The publication was formerly known as Occupations in Demand. Apply for promising job openings without delay since there are thousands of people across the nation who are doing just as you are doing. Other U.S. Department of Labor Publications include:

THE 1982-83 OCCUPATIONAL OUTLOOK HANDBOOK describes in detail hundreds of occupations. It includes their job responsibilities; skills, training and education requirements; salary range; and where jobs are in greatest supply. It also tells about advancement opportunities and where to go for more information. Names and addresses of professional societies, trade associations, labor unions, corporations, and educational institutions which also provide free or low cost information on careers are also given.

THE OCCUPATIONAL OUTLOOK QUARTERLY describes new occupations and their training requirements, salary range, and long term job prospects. It also gives information on how to choose an occupation and find a job.

DICTIONARY OF OCCUPATIONAL TITLES gives job descriptions for over 35,000 occupations. Unlike The Occupational Outlook Handbook, however, it does not give information on outlook, salaries, education, training and employers

INFORMATION ABOUT GOVERNMENT JOBS AND PRIVATE AGENCIES AND ASSOCIATIONS WHICH DO BUSINESS WITH THE GOVERNMENT can be found through the following sources.

Federal Career Opportunities lists Federal openings in this nation and overseas. A six months subscription costs $52.50 and can be obtained from the Federal Research Service, Inc., 370 Maple Avenue West, Box 1059, Vienna, VA 22180.

Federal Jobs is another privately published monthly newsletter which lists civil service jobs throughout the nation. It covers a wide range of occupations including senior executive positions and overseas jobs. A subscription to six biweekly issues costs $29.00 and can be obtained from Federal Jobs Digest NE, 325 Pennsylvania Avenue SE, Washington, D.C. 20003.

The Congressional Staff Directory and The Congressional Directory are good sources of persons in Congress to contact. These books include congressional staff biographies as well as the key persons of executive departments and agencies, international organizations, diplomatic representatives and consular offices.

Federal Career Guide gives a general description on government jobs and agencies and how the jobs are filled.

The Washington Information Directory is a guide to Congress, the Executive branch, and private asso-

ciations located in Washington, D.C. It gives
addresses, phone numbers and names of persons to
contact.

*One of the ways to avoid hardening of the arteries
is to feel you still have a lot to learn about the
world.*   - Kingman Brewster

HOW TO CONTACT GOVERNMENT EMPLOYERS AND AGENCIES
WHICH DO BUSINESS WITH THE FEDERAL GOVERNMENT. If
there are branch offices of the department or
agency near you, write to them rather than to the
Washington headquarters for more prompt service.
You can phone Federal Information Centers which
are located outside your state by using the toll
free, long distance phone numbers provided by the
Civil Service Commission. You can look this up in
the phone book.

COMMUNITY SERVICE JOBS

Community Jobs is a monthly newsletter which lists
job openings and volunteer opportunities throughout the U.S. These don't pay much, but they can be
fascinating, and they help improve the quality of
life in our communities. For 10 yearly issues,
send $12.00 to Community Jobs Clearinghouse, 1704
R Street NW, Washington, D.C. 20009, or phone
(202) 387-7707.

Good Works is a directory of organizations across
the nation which are involved in public interest
work. If you can't find it in the library, write
to: The Center for the Study of Responsive Law,
P.O. Box 19367, Washington, D.C. 20036. Include a
self-addressed, stamped envelope.

Environmental Opportunities lists job openings in
this field throughout the nation. A single issue
costs $3.50, or you can order a 12-month subscrip-
tion by sending $40.00 to: Environmental Opportu-
nities, Box 450, School Street, NH 03608 or phone
(603) 756-4541.

JOBS IN PRIVATE INDUSTRY

Information on employers in private industry can
be found in the following sources. A more complete
list of sources is in the appendix.

COMPANY MANUALS of major corporations describe the
firm's activities, its divisions and branches, and
give the names, addresses and phone numbers of key

persons you can contact. Various occupations within the firm are described, together with their education, training and skills requirements and instructions on how to apply for a job. The manuals give an insider's look at the business activities of the firm and what it's like to be an employee.

Each company also issues an annual report which gives facts on its major business activities and how well it's doing. This is a clue to whether it will expand and, therefore, hire more workers.

SUPER-DIRECTORIES list all the employer directories that are available for various industries. There are also directories on associations and publications in every field. See the appendix.

DIRECTORIES of business firms and of trade and professional associations are an important information source for the serious job hunter. Private industry directories, for example, give brief descriptions of each company's major activities and the names, addresses and phone numbers of persons to contact.

Dun and Bradstreet, for example, lists about 31,000 businesses which have a net worth between $500,00 and $1 million. The American Bank Directory lists about 18,000 banks and gives their addresses and phone numbers and names of executives. See the appendix for more.

The Encyclopedia of Associations lists thousands of associations which can provide the facts you need in such general areas as business, agriculture, law, science, education, social welfare, health, and public affairs. Specific areas are also included, such as direct marketing, data processing, and energy. It lists addresses and phone numbers, employment exchanges, reports and bulletins, newsletters and other services. You'll probably be able to find it in the public library but, if you can afford $160 plus shipping, you can order your own copy from Gale's Research Company, Suite N, Book Tower, Detroit, MI 48226.

The 1982/83 Occupational Outlook Handbook has a list of professional societies, trade associations, labor unions, government agencies, private corporations, and educational institutions.

<u>Who's</u> <u>Who</u> <u>In</u> <u>America</u> - If you're aiming for an off-beat job, such as research assistant, secretary or butler to a famous person, this is the place to find the address you'll need. It lists thousands of well known persons in the theater and arts, in science and education, and in government and community service. Make sure you get the volume for the specific field you want.

<u>Literary</u> <u>Marketplace</u> lists book manufacturers, publishers, editorial services, magazines, newspapers, public relations services, and radio and television stations. It's a must for freelance writers, researchers, editors, word processors and typists.

STOCK MARKET TRENDS

You can find this information in the financial pages of newspapers, the local brokerage firm and in business newsletters and magazines. If you want to work in a particular company or industry, study its recent stock price trends. An increase generally means the company may be expanding, and this means more employees will be hired.

PROFESSIONAL AND TRADE ASSOCIATIONS AND UNIONS

These provide up-to-date information on job openings, salaries and wages, and their training requirement. Generally, the main office maintains a job bank for members. Job openings are also listed in their newsletters and journals. If you meet the membership requirements and pay a fee, you can have your name registered in the central job bank and receive the newsletter or journal.

If you are not eligible for membership, you may be able to find their publications in the library. Not all the job openings listed require a license, certificate or degree in a particular field. For example, there is a universal demand for secretaries, janitors, computer specialists, and administrators which cuts across industries. Such openings may also be listed. Their publications are also the best source of up-to-date information on job market conditions in the industry.

THE CHAMBER OF COMMERCE

If you're thinking of moving to a distant community, write to its Chamber of Commerce for information on housing costs and the job market. You might learn, before it's too late, that the community is actively discouraging job seekers from out of town.

FEDERAL JOB INFORMATION CENTERS

The U.S. Office of Personnel Management has offices in ten regions of the nation which give information about job opportunities with the Federal government. (There is no upper age limit to Federal Civil Service jobs.) Look in the phone book under "U.S. Government" for the office nearest you. (Note: Funds for this service have been drastically reduced by the Reagan administration.)

PERSONAL CONTACTS

They used to be known as the "old boy" networks without which no ambitious person could hope to reach the top of the ladder. They are the modern equivalent of the old family, school, political club and church ties which have made the careers of many prominent men. They are still extremely important.

Personal contacts include relatives; friends; neighbors; former co-workers, employers, teachers and classmates; clergymen; your family physician and lawyer; your bank officer; the local cop; elected and appointed town and city officials; members of voluntary associations, and anyone else who can give you job leads or introduce you to someone who can.

Preferably, they should know about your experience, capabilities and job interests. If they work in the same industry, company or occupation you are interested in, so much the better. If not, they may be able to refer you to someone who does. All you have to do is ask. One career changer, who was enrolled in a computer programming course, introduced himself to a guest speaker who was a manager in a local firm. He asked about job opportunities, and six months later he was offered a job.

"Misery loves company," as the saying goes, and people you meet on unemployment benefit lines and in job placement offices often have leads to actual job vacancies which they don't want. Be friendly.

Present or former employers, co-workers and teachers are often the best persons to give references to an employer, especially if they are in the same field. They can describe your qualifications more objectively than a relative or a friend, and their recommendation carries more weight.

A survey by the Bureau of National Affairs found that most of the companies which responded recruit new workers through their own employees. Several companies, in fact, award bonuses to employees who refer qualified job applicants.

An earlier study by Mark S. Granovetter showed that about 74.5% of professional, technical and managerial jobs were obtained through personal contacts. Compare this with the 8.9% obtained through employment agencies, 9.9% through classified ads, and 6.7% through civil service, unions and other channels.

Your contacts can also let you know when job openings are about to come up in their organization before these are advertised. They can also give you inside information about the organization which can be of value during an interview.

If you're thinking of moving to another community or state, someone you know who lives there may be able to provide information about the local job market, cost of living, and the quality of life. Your friend may even be able to make the initial contact with an employer for you or let you know of appropriate job openings advertised in the local newspaper. Newspaper accounts of laid-off automobile workers who migrated to the Sunbelt states regularly report how someone from Detroit got his wonderful, new job through a friend or relative who lives there.

OFFICE PARTIES, writes Elizabeth Fowler, whose column, "Careers" regularly appears in The New York Times, are excellent occasions for making contacts, especially if you have recently received a dismissal notice. She cautions against putting someone on the spot by asking if there are any openings in his or her department.

As any anthropologist worth his or her salt knows, timing is crucial for gaining entry into a new community, and joyous occasions are among the best of times. You can also ask key persons you meet at conventions, association gatherings, and the like for advice and information on existing openings.

CONVENTIONS AND TRADE SHOWS

These are also opportune occasions to make contacts and get valuable information. Some admit only members and their guests. Others accept any interested person who pays the entrance fee. You can look up the dates of such gatherings in the newspaper, in the publications of the industry, and by telephoning the local Chamber of Commerce.

If you're a freelance writer, for example, you can attend any of the numerous computer industry gatherings where you'll have the opportunity to meet representatives from high technology firms. At present, there is such a critical shortage of persons who can write coherently and who demonstrate, by their presence at the gathering, an interest and knowledge of the industry and its jargon, that it's possible to land a job or interview right on the spot. Medical and dental conventions are another good hunting ground for writers and skilled office workers.

JOB FAIRS

These are fun, and they save employers and job seekers alike lots of time. Job fairs are often held by companies in an industry where there is a shortage of workers with special skills. Business People, Inc., of Minneapolis, for example, arranges open house events in cities across the nation for high technology firms which are looking for skilled employees. At each event, a company often hires three to seven applicants. A complaint heard about these fairs is that many of the job seekers who attend are only qualified for entry level jobs, whereas the firms are generally looking for highly skilled persons.

If you have a high level, non-technical skill, such as writing, editing, word processing or secretarial, you can also make your pitch for a job. Be sure you know the buzzwords (jargon) of the industry. Such skills are also in demand in every industry.

Annual job fairs are also sponsored by municipal and community service organizations for the benefit of older residents. See chapter 6 for more information.

You can learn about forthcoming events in the local newspaper or by phoning the appropriate municipal agency or Chamber of Commerce.

VOLUNTARY ORGANIZATIONS

These are excellent sources of job contacts. Many were founded with the specific purpose of helping persons who are considered disadvantaged because of sex, race, age, physical handicap, religion and other reasons. Don't hesitate to contact them. If you're not a member, join. Even better, volunteer your services. They are often eager to help, and some of them wield mighty political clout.

THE Y's (Young Men's/Women's Christian Association, Young Men's/Women's Hebrew Association) may also offer services to unemployed persons or career changers. Some have professional social workers who do personal counseling and provide information on jobs and community resources. Seminars, workshops and courses are also offered on how to start your own business, on job search techniques, and similar topics. Many Y's have Women's Centers which offer workshops and courses designed to help women find jobs, change careers, start their own business, and advance in their careers.

WOMEN'S GROUPS provide the support and self-help functions that the "old boy" networks provide. They can help you get job referrals, promotions, and legal assistance where there is sex and age discrimination. They also provide social activities, emotional support, educational services, and friendship. There are hundreds of women's organizations. There is probably one in or near your community. The nice thing about them is that they go out of their way to help.

Some women's organizations cater to a specific age group or occupational level. Others serve as umbrella organizations for a variety of ages and interests. The following is a small sample to show you the variety and extent of services provided. See the appendix for their addresses and phone numbers and a more complete list.

9-to-5, NATIONAL ASSOCIATION OF WORKING WOMEN, helps women office workers below the executive level.

OWL (Older Women's League) is a relatively new organization which was founded by Tish Sommers and Laurie Shields, who also founded the Displaced Homemakers. Whereas the Displaced Homemakers' main function is to help older women who haven't held a job in years, OWL is presently focussing on political issues which affect women. These include combating age and sex discrimination in employment, making more jobs available to women, eradicating unflattering stereotypes in the media, and other issues. There were 78 chapters nationwide in 1982. To become a member or learn how to start a chapter in your community, contact Older Women's League, 3800 Harrison Street, Oakland, California 94611.

CATALYST and THE DISPLACED HOMEMAKERS - See chapter six for details.

SPECIAL WOMEN'S PROGRAMS IN COLLEGES AND UNIVERSITIES - New York University, for example, has WISDOM, a program for women in their late fifties and older, which offers workshops, courses, counseling and a supportive network of peers. Another program, WATCH, helps women in their thirties and forties decide on careers and select an appropriate program of study or training. There are also workshops which help women who are already employed to advance in their careers.

RELIGIOUS AND COMMUNITY ASSOCIATIONS are good networks of potential job contacts, and some of them provide career counseling and job referral services for their members. A 1979 survey by the Bureau of National Affairs found that many companies recruit for new employees among community associations. Who knows, you may meet your future employer at the next barbecue or tennis outing.

Civic and social service associations, tenant's and ethnic groups are found in most communities. There are voluntary associations for almost every conceivable area of interest which can serve as an excuse to get gregarious, like-minded persons together, such as SCROOGE (Society to Curtail Ridiculous, Outrageous and Ostentatious Gift Exchange.)

Local associations are listed in the Yellow Pages
under social (or community) associations. National
associations, such as the Lions, Knights of Columbus, Elks, and Kiwanis, are listed in Gale's Encyclopedia of Associations.

SCHOOL ALUMNI ASSOCIATIONS Contact your alumni
association for a list of names and addresses of
former classmates, even if it's been years since
you graduated and some of the names are unfami-
liar. The old school bonds never die and, who
knows, at least one of your old classmates may
have risen to the top of the corporate ladder.
Nothing ventured, nothing gained.

The more lists your name is on, the larger your
network of contacts, and the better your chances
of obtaining invaluable help.

HOW TO GET AND USE JOB REFERENCES

Your contact persons can also write job references
for you or give you permission to use their names
as references. Generally, job seekers give the
names of friends and relatives, but the best person to use as a reference is the one who is able
to describe your qualifications for the job objectively. Such persons include former employers, co-
workers , teachers, and members of organizations
in which you worked as a volunteer.

It's generally more difficult to refuse a request
for a reference that is made in person rather than
by mail or phone. Get permission to use someone's
name as a reference, even if the person is a close
friend or relative. Better no reference at all
than a negative or lukewarm one. If a valuable
contact person is so busy that he or she is likely
to say "no" to your request, ask if it would be
more convenient to have the employer phone for a
recommendation.

Make sure you have the correct spelling of the
names of persons you give as references and their
current addresses and telephone numbers. Make it
easier for them to write a letter of recommendation by giving them a copy of your resume and/or
telling them about the job you are applying for
and why you think you're the best person for it.
This helps them to be more specific about your
qualifications for the job. If the contact person
is frequently out of town, try to get the schedule

and phone number where he or she can be reached. Give this information to the employer. Should the employer call when the person is away, it could be the fatal flaw in your application for a job where there is much competition.

When you want something, go back and go back and go back, and don't take "No" for an answer. And when rejection comes, don't take it personally. It goes with the territory. Expose yourself to as much humiliation as you can bear, then go home and go do it all again tomorrow. - Betty Furness' advice to women attending the Midlife Conference, Marymount Manhattan, February 4, 1983.

PERSISTENCE PAYS OFF

Before the recent recession, the rule of thumb was that it takes one week of intensive job searching for every $1,000 annual salary a person expects to receive. In hard times, however, nothing is certain except that persistence, plus the right skills and contacts, pay off. If you don't make an outright pest of yourself, a demonstration of indomitable persistence when the right opening occurs will more likely win over the employer's heart.

This happened to a woman who wanted a job as copywriter, despite the fact that she had no college degree and no experience in that field. All she had to go on was the assurance provided by the results of aptitude tests which showed she had high potential in this occupation. It took about 14 phone calls to an employer before she finally wore down his resistance. If there was one thing about her he was sure of, it was that she wanted to work for his firm.

A college graduate applied three times for a management trainee job at Macy's in New York City. Each rejection spurred her to try again. On the fourth try, she decided to substitute a one page, well written informational letter for her resume. She got the job.

MONEY magazine describes another form of persistence which was demonstrated by a recent college graduate who wanted to be a television news reporter. Knowing she faced formidable competition, she took a low paying receptionist job at a local TV station, and spent hours after five o'clock doing odd jobs on a voluntary basis. While she was acquiring good will with her employer, she gained a lot of valuable experience which helped her land her dream job.

You can look at life in two ways: You can say, "Isn't this a dreadful circumstance!" or you can turn it around and say, "I'm going to learn something from this."...You have to consciously and determinedly make things work to your advantage. That's an art at any age.
- 93 year old Ruth Mills, radio broadcaster of "The Art of Being Your Own Age."

Don't be discouraged if you get rejections, lots of them. It happens to everyone, even young, highly skilled, well educated persons. As one 32-year old college graduate put it, "The more I get turned down, the harder it gets. I've got to keep reminding myself that as one door closes, another will open." The 50-plus job seeker may have to endure many outright rejections before striking oil.

If you are a woman returning to work after many years as a homemaker, you're more likely to call it quits early in the game. Don't do it! One woman who had invested two years and considerable money on a computer programming course received eight job rejections before finally landing a job. A man who quit a high paying job as stock market analyst in order to start his own interior design business had to make about 600 phone calls before he found the opportunity he needed. Each had seriously considered giving up.

Improve your job search techniques and work harder instead. A study of unemployed women over 45 showed that one of their biggest handicaps was that they used fewer job finding strategies than younger women. They were less likely to use personal contacts, employment services and newspaper ads. They were more likely to just walk in cold and ask for a job. Today, just about every high school and college offers workshops and seminars to their senior students on how to find a job. This puts the unsophisticated older person at a greater disadvantage.

I can't get old; I'm working. I was old when I was 21 and out of work.
                                        - George Burns

PLAN YOUR JOB FINDING STRATEGY.

It takes more time than you realize to get the information you need. A good plan will help you save time and effort, and your data will be in a more usable form.

TIMING IS CRUCIAL Follow up job leads immediately. As soon as you learn about an opening, send in your resume or informational letter without delay. Then follow it up with a phone call to ask if it was received.

If you lose your job just before the holidays, don't wait until they're over to start job hunting, advises Elizabeth Fowler. Use the vacation period to prepare your resume, get more information on employers to contact, and sort out your job priorities. You'll be ready to go into action right after the holidays and be several steps ahead of the hares who went to sleep. Apply for vacancies immediately since companies which advertise during the holidays need to fill an opening quickly. Personnel departments get fewer letters of application at this time, and there are more vacancies to fill since employees generally wait to retire at the end of the year.

FOCUS YOUR ENERGIES ON THE GEOGRAPHIC AREA AND INDUSTRY YOU WANT, and look for job openings there. One man looked up the names and phone numbers of all the employers listed in the classified ads and Yellow Pages who matched these categories, and began phoning. Five months, and a $1,250 phone bill later, he found the job he wanted.

Making a pitch to employers by phone works for some job seekers. It's more expensive in the short run, but you'll be able to cover more territory.

WHEN YOU GO TO THE LIBRARY, take along some index cards or a looseleaf notebook with dividers. Keep a separate section for each occupation, industry and employer you're interested in, one page or card for each. As you read, jot down the facts under one or more of the following headings. You may think of others that are more relevant to your needs.

- Pay range
- Persons to contact
- Working conditions
- Current need for workers
- Buzzwords of the industry
- Where and how do I fit in?
- On-the-job training opportunities.
- Where the best opportunities are.
- Education and training requirements.
- Miscellaneous ("personality" of the company, areas where you can be an asset, etc.)

On the page for each employer you plan to contact, reserve another section for recording the dates of resumes sent, phone calls made, letters received, and persons contacted. Also, leave some room for recording dates of interviews and ideas on how to improve your next interview.

IRS REGULATIONS allow you to deduct the expenses of looking for a job, whether you are employed or not. Be sure to keep a record of all expenses involved in travel, meals, phone calls, resume preparation and printing, employment agency fees, parking meters and postage. If you land a job which requires moving out of town, these expenses are also deductible.

KEEP A FACT FILE of articles from newspapers and magazines about the industry, occupation, and companies which interest you. It will be of great help during an interview. You'll make a better impression by displaying your knowledge about the company and the industry. Furthermore, the more you know, the better you'll be able to describe how your background will be an asset to the firm.

JOT DOWN THE BUZZWORDS used by insiders in the occupation and industry, and memorize them. Use them, discretely, in your letters, resume and interviews, wherever they are appropriate. Even if you aren't applying for a managerial, technical or professional job, the judicious use of saavy terminology such as "bottom line," "systems analysis," or "software" makes you appear up-to-date. This is especially important for the older job seeker. Be careful not to overdo it, or appear to be overqualified for the job.

Walk-Ins are where you simply walk into a company's personnel office and fill out a job application form. They are more effective for clerical and unskilled and semiskilled jobs. If you plan to make such contacts, learn the best time and day of the week to apply for a job in this manner.

DON'T PUT ALL YOUR EGGS IN ONE BASKET. Send resumes or informational letters to employers you hope to work for, answer newspaper ads, register with employment agencies, use your personal contacts, and enroll in courses which update your skills. Do all these things concurrently, not one at a time.

Keep your eyes fixed on alternative career goals in case one doesn't work out. A 1982 Department of Labor study showed that many persons who train for one field either end up using their skills and knowledge in an entirely different field or take jobs where these skills aren't even used. Very often, they are happy in their unanticipated career

If you can't find a job as a history teacher, for example, consider other fields where your skills can be transferred. There are private firms and municipal agencies which hire people with advanced degrees to work as historians, as editors on in-house publications, and as librarians. Retired police officers take jobs as private chauffeurs and security guards. I know one who lives on a magnificent estate and drives around in a Cadillac which is equipped with a bar and a television set.

DON'T ACCEPT THE FIRST OFFER THAT COMES ALONG, unless it's the kind of job you want or a stepping stone in that direction. If you need income, try to manage on part-time work which gives you more time for job hunting. It makes you look good to an employer, and it usually provides more job leads. Often, a part-time job becomes a full-time one.

I don't like the word, "retirement." The challenge of retirement is to put ourselves in a position where we are a part of the national resource, where we continue to make significant contributions to the welfare of our fellow citizens.
Arthur Flemming, chairman of the U.S. Commission on Civil Rights, at the age of 76.

BE FLEXIBLE ABOUT THE JOBS YOU WANT. This is especially important if you're at the retirement age. Even if you held a high level position before retiring, you've got to prove yourself to a new employer. It's easier to get promotions after you shine in a lower level job than to apply for a high position and get turned down because of age. Although it's more difficult for a person past 60 to start at a lower level and work himself up to a management level position, it has been done. Such persons must have tremendous drive.

If you've been at the management level and you're offered a job at a subordinate level with no management involvement, however, you are compromising your experience, especially if the company is in the same field in which you had previously worked, advises Josephine Lerro, director of human resources at TempsAmerica.

The jobseeker must know as much as possible about the company and how he fits in, how many years he has left within the workforce, and then decide if it's possible to achieve his goal within that time frame. The issue must be handled on an individual basis. You can't give a blanket answer that fits all candidates in that category.

If you've been retired for several years or if you are a homemaker returning to the job market after many years, consider offers in an entirely different field, or an entry-level job if it's in the industry or company you want. Entry-level jobs often lead to promotions to a better position within a company.

Regarding retirees who are returning to the labor market, a Federal Jobs Service counselor says,

Older job hunters often create their own barriers. They won't accept the realities of the current job market, such as the fact that they will, in all probability, have to start at a lower salary level. They don't realize that they're also competing with younger persons who have more up-to-date training and will work for less.

Another self-imposed barrier is created by the person who restricts his options by saying he wants a job that's only on a main bus line or near the subway. Some even say they want a job within walking distance of their home. Others refuse to consider jobs where they may have to work late.

An official of the Florida Department of Labor adds:

*Sometimes they get the feeling that younger people
are...smarter and are always breaking records.
Nevertheless, if some believe it, it can be a
barrier....I don't think the elderly are any different from others in that the more skills you
have to sell, the more employable you are.*

At 95, George Abbott directs the hit Broadway
musical, "On Your Toes."

At 94, philosopher Bertrand Russell leads international peace drives.

At 93, George Bernard Shaw writes "Farfetched
Fables," and Ruth Moore is the oldest practicing
attorney in the United States.

At 91, Eamon de Valera is president of Ireland and
Adolph Zucker is chairman of Paramount Pictures.

At 89, Michelangelo designs the church of Santa
Maria Degli Angeli; Albert Schweitzer is director
of a hospital in Africa; Artur Rubinstein gives
brilliant piano recitals; and Mary Baker Eddy is
director of the Christian Science Church.

At 88, Pablo Casals still performs cello concerts,
and Konrad Adenauer is chancellor of Germany.

At 85, Coco Chanel is director of a fashion design
firm, and Arabella Williams wins her eighth polar
bear trophy as the oldest water-skier to brave the
frigid waters of Mission Bay in San Diego, California on New Year's Day.

At 82, Elisabeth Seifert continues writing two
novels a year, and already has 82 books published.

At 81, Johann Wolfgang Von Goethe finishes his
masterpiece, "Faust."

As he approaches 80, Giuseppe Verdi writes three
of his greatest operas.

In 1983, at age 76, United States Navy Captain
Grace Hopper is the oldest uniformed military
officer and is a pioneer in the computer industry.

At the age of 65, Lillian Ryan graduates highest
in her class at Fairleigh Dickinson University's
Edward Williams College.

4

SO LONG, 9-TO-5

Flexible workstyles include job sharing, flexitime work, temporary full-time and part-time work, permanent part-time work, compressed week, month or year, and work-at-home. You can get these assignments through temporary placement agencies. Office work, sales, accounting, word processing, drafting, engineering, computer programming and research are some of the skills that are suitable for such work.

FLEXITIME WORK replaces the traditional 9-to-5 routine with a more flexible schedule. It allows you to choose your own hours to start and stop working, often without prior notification to your boss, as long as you and your co-workers are present during a certain period of the day, usually from ten in the morning until three in the afternoon.

The beauty of this arrangement is that YOU, and not some higher authority, select a schedule which best suits your living arrangements. You can shop for that great bargain, go to the dentist, and wait for the repairman without worrying about losing your job. Employers who have tried flexitime schedules report happier workers and lower absenteeism.

COMPRESSED WORK WEEK OR MONTH - In this arrangement, a 5 day, 40 hour week is compressed into four days of 10 hours each or even three days of 13.3 hours each. This gives you three or more weekend days to do as you like. A compressed month works on the same principle except that the longer workdays are credited towards a shorter month or year, so that you can take off on a world cruise or attend school full-time and still keep your job.

THE FLEXIYEAR CONTRACT is popular in Europe but relatively unknown in this country. In this system, you and your employer work out a plan for the entire year which determines how much time you want to put in each day on the job and how much vacation you'll have. The proportion of work time and vacation time doesn't matter as long as you complete your yearly quota of work. You may both agree on an overtime work week for only eight months a year, giving you four months of vacation. Or, you may decide on five hours of work each workday all year round, or any other variation which suits you both.

FLEXIPLACE involves working full or part-time in the comfort of your own home or in a nearby office. This is one of the predicted outcomes of the computer revolution, and another may well be the elimination of mandatory retirement altogether. The computer is making it possible for retirees, handicapped persons, and homemakers to earn a living at home without putting up with the hassles of commuting and an externally imposed work schedule.

An increasing number of persons are employed in full-time, work-at-home jobs which are made possible through advanced communications systems and computerized office work. For example, an employer with headquarters in New York City, such as the Satellite Data Corporation, is able to assign word processing and data-entry work to employees living in Kalamazoo.

Some companies have a policy of hiring retirees and/or the handicapped for at-home work. The company installs the equipment in the workers' homes and may also provide training. American Express in New York City has such a cooperative arrangement with the Private Industry Council.

The price of home computers is now within the reach of many Americans. Software is available which can help you learn the essentials of word processing and programming. Many low cost adult education courses are also available. In some communities, unemployed residents can take such courses at reduced or no charge. There are also inexpensive workbooks in the local book store. Learning these valuable skills will vastly increase your job opportunities.

JOB SHARING is permanent, part-time work in which the duties and income of one, full-time job are shared by two persons. The partners determine their own schedule which can range from splitting each workday or working half a year each. Generally, it works best when they have complementary skills rather than similar skills. It's especially suitable for highly skilled persons, because few part-time jobs at this level are available at this time, although experts predict it will become widespread soon.

Job sharing has been tried with success by teachers, administrators, coordinators, program developers, secretaries, receptionists, clerical workers, counselors, social workers, psychologists, researchers, and technicians. Other occupations where it has been tried include bank tellers, editors, therapists, ministers, physicians, librarians, and food service workers.[1]

The Federal Job Service and private placement agencies in your community can tell you where such jobs are available.

The obvious advantage of flexible workstyles is that you have more leisure time to do what you want. The less obvious ones include the elimination or reduction of boredom and job "burn out."

Some critics fear that workers in such arrangements can be exploited to handle peak work loads and frequent, heavy deadlines. They may also be denied access to training programs, promotions and other fringe benefits. Others predict that flexible workstyles are the wave of the future and, as they become more widespread, such drawbacks will be minimized.

PART-TIME WORK involves working less than eight or seven hours daily. It can be done on a permanent or a temporary basis. Permanent part-time work has certain advantages over the temporary kind. The pay is better and workers receive fringe benefits which temporary workers do not ordinarily get. Also, while temporary, part-time jobs are usually low paying and at the entry level, permanent, part-time jobs are more often available at the management and professional level.

Currently, part-time work is the most popular form of flexitime work among retirees. Employers in government and private industry plan to increase the number of opportunities for part-time work in order to lure more retirees back into the workforce and distribute work more equitably in the event that an overall shortage of jobs occurs as a result of technological change.

Another advantage of part-time work is the freedom from worry about age discrimination. This is because older, displaced workers and retirees are especially valued as temporary employees. Another advantage is that you can work whenever you like for as long as you like. You'll also meet more people and experience a greater variety of work settings than you would in a full-time job.

If you're planning to take adult education courses in order to brush up your job skills, or set up a small business, you can earn some "pin-money" and still have plenty of time to prepare for your goal.

If you are planning to change careers, or if you haven't had a paid job in years, you'll be able to test the waters, so to speak, by trying out different companies and work settings before you make a more permanent commitment. You also have an opportunity to make valuable job contacts and learn about full-time openings elsewhere.

If you're having difficulty getting the kind of full-time job you want because of age discrimination or some other reason, a temporary job in a firm which has such openings offers the opportunity to prove yourself. Then, when a full-time opening occurs, you're more likely to be asked to stay on than if you were to apply for the job as a stranger.

This happened to a retired marketing person in his mid-seventies who was placed by Mature TempsAmerica on a temporary assignment to do an analysis of a company's sales force. In addition to completing his assignment, he prepared a written report on ways to improve the productivity of the sales force. The report, which was not expected of him, demonstrated his sharp mind and valuable expertise. The employer was so impressed that he offered the man a full-time position.

PRIVATE, TEMPORARY PLACEMENT AGENCIES.

The large firms have branches throughout a region or the nation which deal with a wide variety of occupations. Among the best known are TempsAmerica; Manpower, Inc.; Kelly Services, Inc.; Staff Builders, Inc.; The Olsten Corp.; and Personnel Pool of America.

Some have separate divisions which specialize in certain industries or occupations. For example, TempsAmerica has a division, Mature TempsAmerica, which specializes in placing older workers in office jobs. Manpower, Inc. has divisions for office work, health care, technical work, and industrial assignments.

There are also agencies which deal exclusively
with a certain industry or occupational family.
For example, Volt Information Sciences[2] places
engineers and technicians on temporary jobs. United Engineers, Inc., of Holyoke, Massachusetts,
specializes in placing draftsmen, engineers and
technicians. Accountemps, which has 80 offices
throughout the nation, places accounting, financial and data processing workers. Upjohn places
nurses, nurses aides, home health aides, companions and other health workers. There is also an
Association of Part-Time Professionals.[3]

These for-profit agencies generally operate as
employment contractors. This means that, in addition to assigning you to a job, they also pay you,
and some train you in needed skills. In other
words, you would be employed by them, not by the
company you are sent to work for.

In 1982, in the New York metropolitan area, their
pay scale ranged from the minimum wage up to $19
an hour for high demand skills, such as nursing,
and $12 an hour for word processors. Many also
offer fringe benefits such as vacation and holiday
pay, bonuses, and hospital benefits. This enables
companies to hire their own retirees for special
assignments without stepping on the union's toes.

The length of assignment may vary from one day to
several months. During the course of a year, it's
possible to be given scores of assignments by a
single placement agency. By registering with more
than one agency, you'll be able to keep busy for
as long as you like. Since the agencies vary in
their wages, types of jobs and fringe benefits, it
pays to shop around and compare a few.

Look in the classified ads of the newspaper or in
the Yellow Pages for the names of the nearest
temporary placement agencies. See chapter 6 for
tips on how to deal with a for-profit agency.

For a close-up view of how these operate, let's
look more closely at one of the large national
agencies and one of the small, local agencies.

TEMPSAMERICA Inc. has 13 offices located in New
York City, Los Angeles, Downey, Pasadena, San
Francisco, Denver, Dallas, and the following Pen-
nsylvania communities: Bala Cynwyd, Malvern, Ply-

mouth Meeting, and Philadelphia. A division,
Mature TempsAmerica, specializes in finding temporary, full and part-time jobs for older persons.

In some of their marketplaces, you would receive a
paid vacation, the length of which varies according to the number of hours you put in. You would
also get free training in transcription typing and
word processing, if that's what you want, and you
would have the use of their office equipment for
brushing up your rusty skills.

Before assigning you to a job, you'll undergo
several hours of skills evaluation and an in-depth
interview. For example, a secretary is evaluated
on speed, accuracy, dictation, letter set-up,
spelling, grammar and punctuation. All recruits
are evaluated on their grooming, work attitudes
and aptitudes, and previous work history. The firm
has an excellent reputation among the Blue Chip
corporations because it takes care in evaluating
new recruits and placing them on assignments that
are appropriate to their skills and experience.

SENIOR RESOURCES, INC., of 60 East 42nd Street,
New York City, is a small agency which specializes
in finding permanent, part-time jobs for mature
persons in the New York metropolitan area. It has
placed persons ranging in age from their late
fifties to late seventies. A few who were approaching 80 years of age and had been placed ten
years earlier were still on the job in 1983. The
founder, William V. Lyons, says because his service pays the workers' wages, companies are able
to take a totally age-blind approach to hiring,
since this frees them from union objections.

The agency deals exclusively with office jobs, and
persons are often placed in jobs that are totally
unrelated to their occupations before retirement.
For example, a man who had worked 40 years as a
rug salesman is now a bank teller. A former accountant is a librarian in a financial firm, and a
retired government employee operates an in-house
bowling facility for a large insurance firm.

Senior Resources specializes in job sharing. This
type of permanent, part-time work is popular with
companies the firm does business with. "It's a
superior way to staff routine office jobs which
have repetitive tasks, and the company benefits
from the resulting higher productivity," says Mr.
Lyons.

"As for age discrimination," Mr. Lyons adds, "we don't have a problem because any employer coming to us knows he is dealing with seniors. He prefers them because they can be more productive, reliable and stable, especially in jobs with limited career potential."

He advises persons who held a relatively high position before retirement to "try not to overwhelm the interviewer with your former achievements." He cites the case of a former stock market analyst who failed to get the job because he was too anxious to make an impression. Consequently, he was viewed as overqualified and likely to quit as soon as something better comes along.

WHO HIRES TEMPORARY AND PART-TIME WORKERS?

For many years, corporations have been rehiring their retired executives and professional employees as consultants. Recently, in response to an unexpected shortage of skilled workers, such as technicians, some skilled blue-collar workers and engineers, some companies have started work pools of retirees at lower occupational levels. Most of the rehiring, however, is for white collar jobs.

Don't despair if you are not a former employee of one of these firms. It may still be possible to get your name on their roster of badly needed, skilled, older workers. The following are some of the companies which have benefited from the skills of retired workers.
- American Express
- Burger King
- Burpee Seed
- Continental Illinois Bank & Trust
- Deer & Company
- General Electric
- Grumman Aerospace
- MacDonald's
- M.D.Anderson Hospital
- Polaroid Corp.
- Standard Oil
- Travelers Insurance
- Woodward & Lothrop
- Yankelovitch, Skelley & White

Yankelovitch, Skelley & White, a prominent market research firm with branches in major cities, employs a Senior Council of retired executives, managers and professionals who work as permanent, part-time interviewers. "The work is fascinating," says an unemployed college professor in her fifties who was a member of the Council. "One day you're interviewing the president of a major corporation and the next day it might be a high level government official." In 1982, in the New York metropolitan area, they were paying $25 per interview plus transportation, meals and other costs.

Grumman Aerospace also keeps a list of retired employees for on-call assignments. Among these was an 84-year old former secretary who one day received an urgent call to come back to work. Blue collar retirees with special skills, such as sheet metal work, are especially needed to instruct new employees.

Woodward & Lothrop, a retail firm in Washington, D.C. with over 13 stores and 8,000 employees, has seasonal hiring periods during which older workers are badly needed. Many of their own retirees come in on a part-time, mid-day schedule or for full-time seasonal work. These older workers are considered special assets for their dependability and their tact and patience in dealing with customers. (Retailing is a very good field for part-time work.)

FEDERAL, STATE AND LOCAL GOVERNMENTS also need part-time workers. The Census Bureau, for example, needs people who can read maps and drive a car to do special, one-time surveys. The Teacher Corps needs retired teachers to serve as teacher aides in disadvantaged areas on a voluntary or paid basis. You can get information on these and other part-time job opportunities at the Jobs Service office.

GETTING YOUR FOOT IN THE DOORWAY THROUGH
VOLUNTEER WORK

Public charity has never been sufficient to support all our private social service agencies. The result is that schools cut back their extracurricular programs, and cities cut back their housing services and cancel planned development of parks and recreational programs. The direct outcome of these unresolved issues is a deterioration in the quality of life, especially in our cities.
Lawrence H. Mirel, founder of the American Association of Emeriti, which serves as a clearing house of information on volunteer work.[4]

Many persons go on to better, paid jobs as a result of the experience and expertise gained through volunteer work. Often, personnel recruiters carefully evaluate a candidate's volunteer work along with his or her paid work experience. Some volunteers become so proficient and valuable that they are offered a permanent, paid job by the agency in which they serve. Volunteer work is an excellent way to develop job skills and meet people who are in a position to help you find the kind of paid job you want.

Many women who have been out of the job market for years are able to develop skills which they later use to get paid jobs in management, public relations, research, writing, training and counseling. About 29% of the women respondents in one survey said they were able to use the personal contacts made in volunteer work to get a paid job. Many had been out of the job market for years.[5]

Women have more opportunities to develop management and other higher level skills in volunteer work than in paid work because there are fewer sex barriers than in private and public industry. One study found that women without a college degree are able to exercise skills in research, writing, teaching and counseling.

Volunteer work can also be a stepping stone to a professional career. A volunteer in a social work agency, for example, can enroll in an 2-year Associate Degree program of study which can lead to a paid job as social work aide. A 4-year Bachelor's Degree program (shortened by using the volunteer work experience to acquire college credit) can lead to a career as professional social worker. A volunteer legal aide who takes a few adult education courses can become a legal secretary. A 2-year program leading to a diploma or certificate in paralegal studies can lead to a career as paralegal professional.[6] A volunteer nurse's aide can become a medical secretary after taking a few adult education courses, or a practical nurse with a 2-year diploma or certificate, or a registered nurse with a 4-year college degree. See chapter 9 for additional information on how to use volunteer work experience to obtain a paid job.

Volunteer work is becoming more widely recognized as a bona fide credential. A 48-year old homemaker who had done volunteer work for years in community organizations, including setting up a Head Start program for disadvantaged pre-schoolers, used this experience to obtain a paid job as director of the Day Care Council in Long Island, N.Y.

New York State is considering a new policy which requires part-time and full-time volunteer work to be given credit along with paid work experience in applications for civil service jobs. This is the result of a sex discrimination lawsuit filed by a woman who was denied a job with a State agency because of its policy of crediting only paid work experience. The sex discrimination charge was based on the fact that more women than men do volunteer work for the community. The woman had listed as work experience two years as president of the PTA and the founding and directing of a day care center, activities which required as much as 50 hours a week of her time. If this isn't bona fide work experience, than what is?

The biggest sin is sitting on your ass. - Florynce Kennedy

GOVERNMENT SPONSORED VOLUNTEER PROGRAMS

ACTION is a Federal agency which administers several volunteer programs that accept older persons, VISTA (Volunteers in Service to America), RSVP (Senior Volunteer Program), AUXILIARY AND SPECIAL VOLUNTEER PROGRAMS, FOSTER GRANDPARENTS, and the PEACE CORPS.[7]

THE PEACE CORPS, for example, recruits Americans of all ages to serve up to 27 months in developing countries. At the age of 67, Lillian Carter, mother of the former President, went to a village in India to serve as a nurse. Among the projects the Peace Corps is engaged in are agriculture, education, vocational training, business and public administration, health, home economics, and natural resource development. Although the work is hard and the hours are long, more than 9 out of 10 volunteers say they would do it again.

There is an orientation and training period of 4 to 10 weeks in the country of service which includes learning its language and culture. Transportation to and from the country is provided as well as a monthly allowance for food, rent, medical needs, and travel within the country. Generally, this amounts to about $300 a month. Upon completion of service, the volunteers receive a readjustment allowance of $125 a month for every month served. All volunteers are covered by the Federal Employees Compensation Act for any disabilities incurred during service. A Peace Corps medical officer and/or a dispensary which is part of the U.S. Embassy are available in the assigned country.

Persons with practical experience as well as those with degrees are needed. If you don't have a special skill, the Peace Corps will teach you one or develop the rusty skills you already have. There is no upper age limit for eligibility. Volunteers should be in good health. Married couples are accepted as long as both serve as volunteers. Handicapped persons have also served successfully. For information, contact The Peace Corps, Washington, D.C. 20525 or telephone toll-free (800) 424-8580 ext. 93.

.At 79, "Odi" Long, a retired lumberjack from Illinois, receives a medal from the president of Sierra Leone for his contributions to that country. In his 13 years of service in the Peace Corps, he has helped design and construct schools, bridges and a sports pavillion in Gabon, Togo and Sierra Leone.

.At 87, Mabel Patton celebrates her 70th year as a volunteer nurse's aide at a veteran's hospital in Los Angeles.

THE VISTA PROGRAM needs persons of all ages to serve for one year or more in depressed communities in the United States. For this reason it has been dubbed the "domestic Peace Corps." Volunteers serve in education, day care, drug abuse, health, legal aid, and city planning agencies. They may work with migrant families in Florida, on an American Indian reservation, or in an institution for the mentally handicapped. They receive a weekly allowance for food, housing, transportation and other necessities during their period of service and a readjustment allowance of $70 a month afterward.

CITY AND COUNTY GOVERNMENTS AND SCHOOL SYSTEMS also sponsor voluntary programs to assist youth groups, museums, schools, local government agencies, hospitals and institutions for the handicapped and elderly. New York City, for example, has a Second Careers Voluntary Program which assigns volunteers to projects which utilize their particular skills and interests. These assignments may include helping agencies in accounting practices, doing research on such issues as health and aging and setting up museum displays.

PRIVATELY SPONSORED VOLUNTEER PROGRAMS

COMMUNITY COLLEGES need adults to serve in a wide range of assignments within the college or in the community. At the College of Extended Studies, of San Diego State University, for example, volunteers do clerical work, help staff classes, and write public relations materials. The Center for Continuing Education for Women at Valencia Community College in Orlando, Florida, uses volunteers in its Displaced Homemaker Program to do counseling, research, public relations, clerical and other work.

The University of Maryland at College Park has a volunteer service corps of retired professionals who teach, serve as student advisors, assistants to professors, and administrative consultants, among other activities. Often, a new job is created when a person with special skills volunteers. One volunteer, for example, helped establish the Office of Disabled Student Services. The volunteers range in age from 50 to past 80, and some of them have used the program as a way station to paid jobs.

At Santa Fe Community College in Gainesville, Florida, volunteers work in local community agencies to help in poverty areas. They also are enrolled as full-time students in the human services program of the College. Upon graduation, they can use their Associate Degree to get paid jobs.

Contact your nearest community college for information about any existing volunteer programs.

RELIGIOUS ORGANIZATIONS offer many opportunities for volunteer work. The Federation of Protestant Welfare Agencies, Federation of Jewish Philanthropies, Catholic Charities, and individual places of worship are all involved in upgrading the quality of life in their communities.

For information on these and other volunteer programs in your community, look in the phone book

for your local volunteer bureau, which is listed
under the city and/or state governments and social
service organizations. You may also wish to contact the Association of Volunteer Bureaus, 801
North Fairfax Street, Alexandria, Virginia 22314,
or phone (703) 836-7100. Also contact the Lawrence
Mirel, c/o Association of Emeriti (see below).

1. Meier, Grete A., Job Sharing (W.E. UpJohn Institute for Employment Research, 1979)

2. Volt Information Services, 1221 Avenue of the
Americas, New York, NY 10020. Phone number: (212)
764-0700.

3. Association of Part-Time Professionals, 4848
Mauri Lane, Alexandria, VA. Phone number: (703)
370-6206.

4. Association of Emeriti, 918 16th Street NW,
Washington, D.C. The phone number is (202)463-
7880.

5. Hybels, Judith H. and Marnie W. Mueller.
"Volunteer Work: Recognition and Accreditation."
Report given to the U.S. House of Representatives,
Select Committee on Aging, December 1978.

6. The author learned, just as this book was going
into publication, that computerized legal data
files will eventually eliminate or reduce the
number of jobs for paralegal aides, law clerks and
recent law school graduates. How soon this will
happen, if it really does happen, is anybody's
guess. A good way to keep one step ahead of these
changes is to add one or more computer courses to
your program of study.

7. The future of these programs was uncertain at
the time of publication, since the Reagan Administration favors private, rather than government,
sponsored programs. In 1982, it planned to eliminate VISTA, which is our domestic Peace Corps.
More than 5,000 volunteers have served in this
program, helping neighborhood agencies obtain
improved public services and upgrade literacy.

For current information about the programs,
contact the Director of Personnel, ACTION, 806
Connecticut Avenue NW, Washington, D.C. 20525.

5

JOB PLACEMENT SERVICES

You can save lots of time and energy by registering with one or more job placement services. Private placement services, in particular, have access to the "hidden" job market (jobs that aren't
advertised in the newspapers or registered with
the Federal Job Service offices) than any other
source. Just one visit may lead to several promising job interviews which would probably take you
months to arrange on your own.

An employment service which has nationwide
branches or affiliates is an excellent source of
out-of-town jobs. It can obtain for you information on living costs, housing, and the quality of
life in a distant community. The counselors can
also give you expert advice on how to improve your
"image" and your interview techniques. However,
you may be charged for such advice. They can also
give you valuable inside information about a company, such as its management style and other matters which can be helpful during an interview.

HOW TO GET THE MOST FROM AN EMPLOYMENT SERVICE.

Bring your resume and any other information you
would take to a job interview. A good employment
service needs this in order to refer you to jobs
that suit your qualifications and interests. It
should not send you on a wild goose chase just to
grab a fee. The counselor should interview you on
your work experience, qualifications, and job
interests before even suggesting a job opening.

Be prepared to answer questions on such matters as
long periods of unemployment or hospitalization,
why you quit or were dismissed from a job, and
whether you have a handicap which will interfere
with your work performance. This information is
needed in order to help you find a job that's
right for you, and to advise you on how to deal
with these issues if they come up during an
interview. The counselor serves as an ombudsman
between you and a potential employer, so you
needn't fear discussing such matters openly. Make
it clear, however, that you have surmounted any
serious problems and are the better for it.

Such advice from the experts generally works during normal periods of unemployment. What has not

been resolved, however, is whether in times of high unemployment your best interests are served by disclosing a serious problem which will not obstruct your job performance. You have to play it by ear. A job seeker who discloses, for example, a period of alcoholism or imprisonment should dispel any doubts about his or her present ability to do the job.

Another reason for coming prepared is to make the most of your time with the counselor. Register only after you've done a thorough assessment of your job related assets and interests. If you are not sure about the kind of job you want, you may end up paying extra for career counseling or, even worse, placed in a job you don't like.

Read the contract carefully before signing it so that you won't be shocked by the extra charges for advice you assumed would be part of the package. For example, if you hand the counselor a draft of your resume or if you ask for advice on how to improve your finished resume, it could cost you plenty.

Don't put all your eggs in one basket. Register with more than one employment service and, at the same time, carry on with your own job hunt.

PRIVATE, FOR-PROFIT PLACEMENT FIRMS

Generally, when a placement firm refers you to an employer, and you are hired, the employer pays the fee. In cases where you must pay the fee, it is based on a percentage of your monthly or yearly salary. If you are offered a job which is not fee-paid, it's perfectly proper to ask the employer to split the fee with you or give you a refund after you have proven yourself on the job. Many job seekers prefer to tell an employment agency they are only interested in fee-paid jobs.

Some states limit the amount of fees an employment agency can charge job seekers. If you are asked to pay a fee that seems exorbitant, check with the local Better Business Bureau or the state's licensing bureau before you sign anything. Before you accept a job which requires a fee, ask for a copy of the agency's refund policy and fee plan.

A reputable service will bill you only after you accept a job. It will not charge for interviews that are arranged for you. If you are asked to pay a fee for an interview referral, walk out the door. If the job does not turn out to be as it was described, you have the right to ask for a refund. In order to get a refund after you have been on the job for a while, you must have a valid reason for quitting, one that is not your fault. You must also make your request within the time limit specified in the contract you signed. If your request for a refund is valid, but it is not granted, contact the Better Business Bureau or your state's licensing bureau.

All these conditions should be described fully in the contract which you will be asked to sign in advance. Take home a copy and read it carefully before signing it. A reputable service will take the time to explain anything that is not clear to you and will not pressure you into signing before consulting with you, nor will it try to persuade you to accept a job that is far below the level of your qualifications.

If you find a job through your own efforts while you are registered with an employment agency, you do not have to pay a fee. If it refers you to a secretarial job, for example, and during the interview you are offered a job as trainee word processor, you do not have to pay a fee even though the agency arranged the interview for you. Nor are you required to pay a fee if, during the course of the interview, you learn of a job vacancy elsewhere.

A top notch agency will follow up each interview it arranges for you, and advise you on how to improve your techniques. It won't send you on wild goose chases by exaggerating the conditions of the jobs recommended to you.

If you obtain a job lead on your own, don't mention it, otherwise you may discover later on that the agency has advertised the vacancy and referred another client to it before you've had an opportunity to look into it.

Employment agencies must be licensed by the city and state in which they operate. It does happen, however, that unlicensed firms continue to operate regardless of the law. Investigations in the past have turned up cases of false advertising and discrimination based on age, sex, and race. Because such practices give the entire industry a black eye, the National Association of Personnel Consultants makes an effort to weed out these unethical operators. If you have a question or complaint about a placement firm, write to the Association at Two Skyline Plaza, Suite 400, 5203 Leesburg Pike, Falls Church, VA 22041, or telephone (703) 820-4700.

Here are some tips on how to check the reputation of a for-profit placement agency before you sign a contract:

   - Contact the state's licensing agency, the local Better Business Bureau, or the consumer protection organization.

   - Ask people you know who have used its services whether they are satisfied with the results or if they have any complaints.

   - Ask the agency how many of their listings are fee paid. If many are, this is a good sign because employers generally avoid registering their job vacancies with disreputable firms.

   - Contact the National Association of Personnel Consultants, 1432 Duke Street, Alexandria, VA. 22314; phone number - (703) 684-0180.

Private employment agencies are listed in the Yellow Pages, in the help-wanted section of newspapers, and in trade journals.

The computer era has arrived in this industry as well. Career Placement Registry, Inc. (CPR) has a computerized listing of job applicants for over 400 different kinds of jobs. It claims that about 8,000 employers use its registry to find suitable employees. To register, you fill out a mini-resume form. Then, if an employer is interested in learning more about you, a more complete resume is forwarded within 24 hours.

CPR operates as an exchange through which employers and job seekers are able to contact one another; therefore, it doesn't do a preliminary interview of job seekers. Fees for having your name and resume placed in the database range from $15 to $40, depending on your salary level. For information, write to CPR, 302 Swann Avenue, Alexandria, Virginia 22301 or phone toll-free, (800)-368-3093 if you live outside Virginia or (703) 683-1085 if you are a resident of that state.

If you own a home computer with a modem (a phone-like device which enables two computers at a distance to "talk" to each other), you can phone CLEO (Computer Listings of Employment Opportunities) at (213) 618-8800. Indicate which job categories, companies and geographic location you want, and CLEO calls up the appropriate classified ads on your screen. You can even apply for a job right from your terminal. CLEO is an electronic publishing service of the Copley Press, Inc.

Federal and state governments have been the biggest users of computers to list job vacancies and screen candidates to date, but more private placement firms are expected to use this medium. See below for information on the Job Bank of the Federal Job Service. In 1983, the Federal Job Service offices in some states were experimenting with resume presentations made by unemployed residents which are televised through regular news channels as a public service. For information, phone your local Job Service office.

During the recent period of high unemployment, local radio and television stations in some cities began advertising job vacancies and the phone numbers of employers to contact as a public service. In April 1983, WPIX's "Mission: Employment" began a series which is broadcast every weekday morning between ten and eleven on channel eleven. The program is coordinated by the Departments of Labor and Commerce of New York State.

RECRUITING FIRMS

These firms are paid by employers to find a special type of person who is, generally, already employed. There are management search firms which find persons for professional and middle management level positions paying from $30,000 to $50,000 yearly, and there are executive search firms which specialize in filling top-level management openings which pay over $50,000. As a rule, they seek you out; you don't go to them. They are known as headhunters because they often raid rival companies for their most talented employees.

You're not out in the cold if you haven't been tapped on the shoulder by a recruiting firm. Some are known to keep a file of resumes sent to them by promising job seekers in order to have a talent

bank to draw upon as needed. It won't do you any
harm and it might lead to something good if you
send in your resume and follow it up with a phone
call to ask for a meeting. Better yet, ask someone
you know who is in management to make the initial
contact for you.

You can get a list of recruiting firms from the
Association of Executive Recruiting Consultants,
Inc., 30 Rockefeller Plaza, New York, NY 10020.
(Don't let on that you are looking for a job.)
Many place ads in the business section of large
city newspapers. The best source is Gale's Direc-
tory of Associations.

NON-PROFIT EMPLOYMENT SERVICES

These are operated or sponsored by Federal, state
and municipal departments, religious organizations, social service agencies, community service
societies, community colleges and special interest
groups. Although they generally have job listings
at the lower end of the pay scale, high-level
openings are available.

THE FEDERAL JOB SERVICE is funded by the U.S.
Department of Labor, and its services are free to
the public. It is said to have more job listings
and more information on the local and national job
market than any other source. Referrals to job
training programs and information on apprenticeship opportunities in your area may also be offered. It also maintains national registries for
some professional groups, such as engineers, librarians, economists, statisticians, and data
processors.

In large cities the Job Service may have separate
offices which deal with different industries. Get
the address of the office which deals with the
jobs you want before wasting a trip to the central
office. You can find the phone number in the White
Pages, listed under "Federal" or "State" governments.

Job-Flo is a monthly, computerized listing of
vacancies and where they are located nationwide,
which is issued by the Job Service. If you're
looking for an out-of-town job, this is a good way
to find one. You should be able to obtain a copy
for the asking, but you may have to be persistent
about it because of recent cutbacks in funding.

In 1982, there were more than 2,500 local Job Service offices throughout the nation. Several states, however, did not list their vacancies with the Service, because they lacked the funds or because they didn't want a flotilla of out-of-town job seekers landing on their shores.

Be sure to get to your local Job Service office as soon as the doors open and go regularly, because most of the vacancies are filled almost as soon as they are listed. In order to get the best service possible, be prepared to tell the counselor exactly what you want. Bring all the information that you would ordinarily take to a job interview.

You may have heard the Job Service is good only for placing people in entry-level, unskilled or semi-skilled jobs. This is not true. The law requires civil service jobs at all levels to be listed. In occupations where there is a shortage of workers, such as nurses, engineers, and computer specialists, employers in private industry do list their vacancies with the Service. But, not all vacancies in the private sector are listed. This is because the law requires employers to list only vacancies that are below a certain salary level and higher paying jobs in firms which have a government contract.

Your local Job Service office may also provide free career counseling which includes the administration and interpretation of tests which assess your aptitudes and interests. You must ask for this service. Don't expect it to be offered to you.

Special services are also provided in some states to certain categories of job seekers such as persons over 45, displaced homemakers, veterans, and the handicapped. Workers who have lost their jobs because of imports also qualify under the Trade Readjustment Allowance Act. Unemployed executives and professionals are also considered to be in need of special help because they often lack knowhow on how to find a job, and finding an appropriate job is often more difficult for them than for white and blue-collar workers. New York State's Professional Placement Center, for example, offers free seminars on resume writing, interview techniques, and other job search activities.

In 1982, because of a cutback in Federal funds, some states were on the verge of scraping their Job Service system. The public's outcry over the timing of these cuts, coming in a period of severe unemployment, led to partial restoration of funds. However, many states were expected to have difficulty providing for the huge increase in the demand for its services. The workload at the local level has doubled due to staff reductions, and this is causing a delay in placing job seekers.

THE U.S. OFFICE OF PERSONNEL MANAGEMENT, formerly known as the Civil Service Commission, deals with full and part time Civil Service jobs in a wide range of occupations. The job vacancies are located throughout the nation, in Washington, D.C., and overseas.

Most of the jobs require that you take a civil service test and then wait your turn on the basis of your score and other qualifications. Many professional and management level openings, however, do not require taking a test. These are filled on the basis of training, education, and work experience. The tests are given several times a year in cities throughout the nation. You can get information and application forms at your local Job Service office and at the post office. You can also write to the U.S. Office of Personnel Management, Washington, D.C., 20415.

PRIVATE INDUSTRY COUNCILS - In 1982, the Jobs Training Partnership Act was passed to enable states and local communities to continue the training phase of CETA after it was abolished.[2] It requires each state to supervise local programs and provide for the retraining of workers who have lost their jobs due to technological change and the recession. This is to be accomplished through classes and on-the-job training. Local Private Industry Councils are made up of representatives from private industry, labor organizations, and the Federal and local governments. They jointly sponsor and operate the job training program.

Although the focus is on disadvantaged youths, state and local councils are free to use part of their Federal funds to retrain older workers who have lost their jobs through industry shut-downs and high technology. The training programs are tailored to specific local labor needs such as office work in brokerage firms, food preparation, sewing machine operators, welders, bank tellers, computer repairers, and word processors.

The employers provide the technical expertise (such as market research to find out which job skills are needed by local industries) and training equipment. They also hire and pay the salaries of instructors. (In New York City, for example, the Council hires retired machinists, upholsterers, diesel engine mechanics, cable TV technicians, and other skilled tradespersons. The retirees may earn up to $25,000 annually.)

The services include retraining, during which trainees receive up to $30 per week to help cover expenses, and job placement. (The author was assured by a Private Industry Council representative that trainees are actually placed in jobs.)

Who is eligible? The main target of the Job Training Partnership Act is the hard-core poor, persons whose total family income in the previous tax year fell within the poverty range, who lack the skills needed by local industries, and/or are disabled. (This included persons who have learning and mental disabilities.) Ph.D.s who can't find jobs in their field and need retraining, and other displaced workers are also eligible, as are women who want training for jobs which have been traditionally held by men. All must pass the income needs test.

The goal of the Private Industry Council is to stimulate local economic development and help the unemployed find jobs. In 1981, for example, a severe shortage of skilled workers for the new, high technology industries of Long Island, N.Y. threatened to stall the region's economic growth. A group of Long Island firms and government agencies got together to do something about it.[3] The County screened eligible persons who were receiving unemployment insurance or welfare benefits, and the firms provided the training needed to hire them for existing vacancies. This joint effort helped improve the region's economy, and reduce the number of persons on public assistance.

WHERE TO GET INFORMATION ON THE PRIVATE INDUSTRY COUNCIL IN YOUR AREA.

- The elected official in your area should be able to give you up-to-date information on this new program (which was still in a state of formation in early 1983).

- Unemployment insurance offices

- State or area agencies on aging

- Mayor or county commissioner's office

- Local Federal Job Service office

- Office (or department) of human resources (or human development, manpower resources, or some other variation of the title)

- The U.S. Department of Labor (Look in the White Pages under "U.S. Government")

THE SENIOR COMMUNITY SERVICES EMPLOYMENT PROGRAM (SCSEP) offers career counseling and job placement in part-time and temporary full-time jobs in the public sector to low income persons who are 55 and older. (Some SCSEP offices give job leads to persons who do not meet these eligibility criteria if they cannot fill vacancies with their own clients.) Several of its sponsoring organizations provide intensive training which helps the recruits to find permanent jobs in private industry.

Among the jobs SCSEP has found for older persons are recreation supervisor, park and museum guide, tribal historian, energy auditor, home repair aide, day care assistant, crime prevention counselor, paralegal aide, housing advisor, mobile library driver, vocational counselor, casework aide, clerical worker, and assistant to the handicapped.

SCSEP is administered by the U.S. Department of Labor in association with state governments and the following sponsors. All except the last two have their headquarters in Washington, D.C. Green Thumb, Forest Service, National Farmer's Union, National Council on Aging, U.S. Department of Agriculture, National Council of Senior Citizens, state and regional agencies on aging, National Urban League of New York City, American Association of Retired Persons, National Caucus and Center on the Black Aged, and the National Association for Spanish-speaking Elderly of Los Angeles

THE NATIONAL COUNCIL OF SENIOR CITIZENS (NCSC) operates a part-time Senior Aide Program which has served as a stepping stone to a full-time job in private industry. Many Senior Aides have found better paying jobs with the experience and skills acquired in community service work.

Persons have been placed as teacher's aides in classes of mentally retarded children, information assistants in libraries, drivers for day care centers, aides in mental health centers, office workers, home repairers for the elderly, and writers. There is even a senior "disk jockey," Jack Beauvais, who works on a program for senior citizens at the WJUL-FM radio station of the University of Lowell in Massachusetts.

Cities with crime prevention programs utilize Senior Aides in legal research and in crisis intervention programs. Aides also serve as police dispatchers, investigators in the District Attorney's office and in city fire prevention programs. The National Council on Senior Citizens has a legal research and services program which trains persons to work as paralegal aides to assist the elderly with their legal problems. Many communities provide this service.

Among the organizations that are involved in this program are municipal agencies, religious organizations, AFL-CIO Central Labor Union Council, state technical colleges, Council of Older American Organizations and Senior Citizen Services.

To be eligible, you must be over 55 and physically and mentally capable of at least part time work. However, jobs are often tailored to a person's particular capabilities. Priority is given to persons age 60 and older who are in greatest need. Unemployed persons who do not meet the eligibility criteria are referred to other agencies which can help them find a job or make ends meet

Senior Aides are covered by Social Security, state worker's compensation, and unemployment and health insurance. Paid vacations and holidays, sick leave and other benefits are also provided.

THE AMERICAN ASSOCIATION OF RETIRED PERSONS, in conjunction with the National Retired Teachers Association, operates a program which places persons in need of job training in non-profit agencies. These include the Red Cross, day care centers, Goodwill Industries, nutrition centers, schools, senior centers, veteran's hospitals and environmental agencies. They help in education, recreation, parks and forests, public works and transportation, social services, outreach and referral, and housing rehabilitation projects.

While training for a new job, recruits may work up to 20 hours a week at the minimum wage level. After training, they are helped to find permanent, full or part-time jobs. They have been placed as hospital aides, employment counselors, arts and crafts aides, receptionists, typists, day care workers, secretarial assistants, teacher aides, maintenance men, security guards and other occupations.

For information on how to apply for these programs, write to the Employment and Training Administration, U.S. Department of Labor, 601 D Street, Washington, D.C. 20213. You can also look in the phone book for the address of your state agency on aging or any one of the above mentioned sponsors.

STATE AND AREA AGENCIES ON AGING

These, together with the Federal government and non-profit social service organizations, also sponsor and administer job placement and related services. The minimum age for eligibility varies from 45 to 60 or older. Some offer their services only to low income persons in that age category.

These agencies are a storehouse of information on job openings, job training and educational opportunities elsewhere in the community. New York City's Department of Aging, for example, often gets calls from local employers who are looking for workers. The Nassau County (N.Y.) Department of Senior Citizen Affairs has its own job placement service for persons age 55-plus. In hiring their own full and part-time staff, preference is given to qualified persons age 60 and older.

The main offices of these agencies are in the state capitols, and within each state there are local planning and service areas, each with its own agency. In 1981 there were 56 state units (including U.S. territories) and 665 area agencies on aging. In order to illustrate how these operate and the diversity of services they provide, the following are described in some detail as they existed in 1982.

SENIOR SERVICES OF SNOHOMISH COUNTY has successfully placed a variety of job applicants, including women who have never worked outside the home and executives whose salaries had been in the upper income range. They are placed in full and part-time jobs in various occupations. It is located at 3402 112th Street SW, Everett, Washington 98204.

The bottom age limit for eligibility is 45, and priority is given to persons whose income for the previous six month period was below the Federal poverty level. Despite the recent recession and cuts in Federal support, the agency has been able to maintain a high level of service in providing on-the-job and classroom training through its Job Resource Center. They have been able to do this through local fund raising events. One of their new goals is to expand community awareness of the benefits of hiring older persons.

OPERATION ABLE (Ability Based on Long Experience) is a network of more than 35 organizations which include local training institutions, the Forty Plus Club, and the local Senior Community Service Employment Program (SCSEP). Employers in private industry also serve on the board and are involved in its projects.

ABLE maintains a job bank which matches older persons with local job vacancies. When an employer places a job order, ABLE calls upon its network of organizations to find someone with the appropriate skills and experience. It also provides education and training for persons who need skills and knowledge updating and career counseling for those who have been out of the job market for a long time.

ABLE's success has made it a model for the creation of similar programs in Boston, New York City, San Francisco, Little Rock, Omaha and other cities. Its headquarters are at 36 South Wabash Avenue, Chicago, ILL 60603. The phone number is (312) 782-3335.

NEW YORK CITY also has a program which is a joint endeavor of the Job Service of the State's Department of Labor, private industry employers, community service agencies, the City's Department for the Aging, and the Chamber of Commerce and Industry.

Every year it sponsors an "Ability is Ageless" fair which brings together employers and job seekers on a face-to-face basis. If an applicant cannot be placed right away, the resources established at the Fair are used throughout the year to help that person find a job. Workshops are also held on such topics as resume writing, job interview techniques and how to dress for success.

SKILLS AVAILABLE, in Cleveland, Ohio, is administered by the state's Vocational Guidance and Rehabilitation Services Department. It offers job counseling and placement. A unique feature of this program is its branch offices, which are situated in community centers, city halls, libraries and other places on major bus lines to make it easier for older persons to attend.

It, too, conducts a citywide job fair which brings together employers, job seekers, representatives from education and training institutions, and social service agencies. Throughout the year, the Cleveland Press assists with its regular Friday column which describes the qualifications of several Skills Available clients for all potential employers to read. Over half of the persons placed in jobs have been 55 and older.

PROJECTS WITH INDUSTRY
This helps persons 50 years of age or older who have a disability find jobs. It is designed to serve clients of state vocational rehabilitation agencies, although applicants may apply directly to the program. There are no fees involved. Its services include on-the-job training, apprenticeship, training in job search skills, job placement, and follow up services to ensure that the client remains happy and productive while employed.

The program has an advisory council which is made up of experts from business, labor organizations, vocational rehabilitation agencies, and agencies on aging. Contact your state department of vocational rehabilitation or write to the U.S. Department of Education, Rehabilitation Services Administration, in Washington, D.C. (see appendix for address)

MUNICIPAL OFFICES AND AGENCIES in many states have programs which offer job training and placement for older persons. For example, the City Council of Torrance, California has created part-time jobs in city agencies. Contact the mayor's office, the city council, or the local area on aging in your community to find out what is available.

PRIVATE, NON-PROFIT EMPLOYMENT AGENCIES

The following is a small sample of agencies which primarily help older persons find jobs. The purpose of including these is to illustrate the range of services available. More are listed in the appendix.

THE FEDERATION EMPLOYMENT AND GUIDANCE SERVICE, of 114 Fifth Avenue, New York, N.Y. 10011, has branches located in New York City, Westchester and Long Island. Its free services include counseling on second career planning and mid-life change. An employment preparation program includes counseling, career planning, skills assessment, job placement and, if needed, job training in such fields as business skills, jewelry manufacturing and home appliance repair. High school equivalency classes are available for adults who were unable to complete high school. These some of the many services provided.

FORTY PLUS CLUBS are self-help associations of unemployed executives who are looking for new positions which utilize their high level of skills and experience. Once accepted, each member agrees to share in all expenses and office responsibilities. In order to ensure high standards, only about half of those who apply are accepted.

In order to be eligible, you must be at least 40 years old, in good health, a U.S. citizen, and recently employed in a position with executive responsibilities and salary. At least six references from former employers and business associates are also required.

Among the benefits members receive are these.

- Help in assessing skills and expertise that are transferable to new careers or industries.

- Workshops on job finding techniques such as interviewing, resume writing, and job finding.

- Use of the club as a base of operations in the job search.

- A committee to help place members in appropriate jobs (although most members are able to find jobs on their own). There are no fees for this service. Some Clubs distribute the resumes of members to potential employers.

- Group therapy sessions are provided by some Clubs to help resolve or prevent family and psychological problems which often accompany unemployment

There are currently Forty-Plus Clubs in eleven cities: Chicago, Denver, Honolulu, Houston, Los Angeles, Oakland, San Diego, Philadelphia, Washington, New York, Raleigh and also in London. If you do no find one listed in your telephone book, write to the executive offices at 15 Park Row, New York, N.Y. 10038 for the address of one nearest you. The phone number is (212) 233-6086.

THE SENIOR PERSONNEL EMPLOYMENT COUNCIL, at 158 Westchester Avenue, White Plains, N.Y., finds full and part-time jobs for persons age 60 and older. A retired dentist, for example, was placed as supervisor of a clerical unit, and a former window dresser was hired to teach automotive maintenance to the employees of a local company. Most of the placements have been in sales at the minimum wage level, but some high wage placements have also been made. There are branches in Yonkers, New Rochelle, Greenburg and Mount Kisco.

THE JOB RESOURCE CENTER at Village Hall, 169 Mount Pleasant Avenue, Mamaroneck, N.Y. was originally established to help residents whose jobs were destroyed by the recession. It now provides counseling and job placement for low income persons as well, and has had much success in keeping the local welfare rolls low.

JOB FINDERS, INC., in San Mateo, California, has a three week job search training program. It has a 95% placement rate for jobseekers over age 50 who complete the workshops.

THE ASSOCIATION OF PART TIME PROFESSIONALS is a nationwide organization which has the purpose of promoting part-time job opportunities for professionals of all ages, to upgrade the status of part-time work and to promote flexitime employment. It also serves as an information resource center. For a copy of their brochure, A part-timer's Guide to Federal Part-Time Employment, write to P.O. Box 3419, Alexandria, VA 22302 and the phone number is (703) 370-6206.

THE RETIRED OFFICERS' ASSOCIATION is an employment service for any former military officer. Write to Officer Placement Services, 1625 Eye Street, NW,

Washington, D.C. 20006.

THE VETERAN'S EMPLOYMENT ASSISTANCE PROGRAM, NON-COMMISSIONED OFFICERS ASSOCIATION (NCOA) offers free services to veterans and their surviving spouses. It hires retired persons for its own staff and maintains a roster of resumes which it sends to employers in private industry. For information and a resume form write to: Veteran's Employment Assistance Program, NCOA Headquarters, P.O. Box 33616, San Antonio, TX 72833.

THE JOB NETWORK INFORMATION SERVICE, is operated by New York State's Office of Occupational Education Special Programs (OESP). It maintains a list of names of qualified job candidates for the use of employers who want to meet affirmative action goals. OESP regularly receives announcements of administrative openings.

A special effort is made to encourage the employment of women in managerial positions. If you are a New York State resident, write to Job Network Information Service, New York State Education Department, 99 Washington Avenue, Room 1610, Twin Towers, Albany, NY 12230, or phone (518) 474-0097. If not, contact your state's Job Service or Labor Department to learn if there is a similar program.

WOMEN'S CENTERS

They generally provide one or more of the following services: job placement, psychological counseling, and career testing and guidance. They also serve as valuable networks of job contacts and social support. Some serve certain categories of women only: professional and executive, older women, displaced homemakers, and women who head families. Others serve women at all levels of occupational skills and experience. A few charge a fee which varies according to the services provided and ability to pay. Often, if a woman is unable to pay, the services are free of charge.

Women's centers are located in community and 4-year colleges, adult education divisions of public school systems, churches, and voluntary community organizations such as the YWCA and B'nai B'rith. In addition, many states, cities and counties have special commissions or councils to promote women's employment and career opportunities. Some operate counseling and/or job placement services as well.

The following is a small sample of the various kinds of services and activities they provide.

CATALYST sponsors over 220 counseling centers nationwide. Its services include aptitudes and interests testing, career counseling, a career resource library and, in some centers, job placement. It also furthers the advancement of women in management and executive level positions. It maintains dossiers of qualified women candidates which company chairmen have access to in order to find women to serve on their boards and for their top level positions. Catalyst's headquarters are at 14 East 60th Street, New York, NY 10022.

W.O.W. (Wider Opportunities for Women, Inc.) provides training for jobs traditionally held by men, career counseling for managerial and professional women, and job placement. (Some centers charge a nominal fee.) It also publishes a National Directory of Employment Programs for Women which you can purchase if your library doesn't have a copy. Its headquarters are at 1511 K Street, NW, Suite 700, Washington, D.C. 20006.

DISPLACED HOMEMAKER PROGRAM: A displaced homemaker is

"usually a woman between 35 and 64...who falls between the cracks of our income security program. She has never had a job or may be a professional woman who decided to stay home to take care of her children...and suddenly, either as a result of a divorce or widowhood, has lost her means of support. She often has no financial resources to fall back on...is not eligible for unemployment insurance or Social Security unless she is disabled and has young children, or for Welfare assistance."[3]

The program started as a voluntary effort of Tish Sommers and Laurie Shields, and has grown into a nationwide program which is now under the umbrella of Action, state departments of labor, and other government programs. As an example, the Women's Survival Center of Tampa, Florida, has had a job placement record of over 76% of the women who complete its job counseling and placement program.

One of these was a 57-year old nurse who was widowed, and whose feelings of uselessness had led to a suicide attempt. The Center provided emotional support, helped boost her self-confidence, and gave her the information and advocacy that resulted in her becoming the supervisor of a wing of a 240 member nursing home. About one third of the Center's clients are women over 50-years of age.

The services provided by the Displaced Homemaker program include the following:

.Psychological counseling

.Social support and friendship

.Job referrals

.Education seminars and workshops on such topics as job readiness, how to be more assertive, how to deal effectively with your lawyer, money management, and more.

.Referrals to adult education courses

.On-the-job training

Generally, there is no fee for these services, although some centers may charge a fee based on ability to pay. For information on a program near you, contact any one of the following:

- The Displaced Homemakers Network, Inc., c/o Business and Professional Women's Foundation, 755 8th Street, NW, Washington, D.C. 20001.

- Your state department of labor.

- YWCA

- The Women's Bureau, U.S. Department of Labor, 200 Constitution Avenue, NW, Washington, D.C. 20210. Ask for a free copy of <u>Job Options for Women in the 80's.</u> Enclose a stamped, self addressed envelope.

VOCATIONAL AND BUSINESS SCHOOLS, COLLEGES AND UNIVERSITIES

These have traditionally offered career guidance and job placement for their students and alumni, even years after graduation or attendance. If you have recently taken courses as a part-time student, you may also be eligible to receive their services. If you attended many years ago, it's not too late to have your dossier updated and registration reactivated. For a small fee your name will be placed on their active file which entitles you to receive regular announcements of job openings in your field.

They also offer aptitudes and interests testing, career counseling, and advice on how to improve your resume and interview techniques. Some offices provide videotaped practice interviews which enable you to see yourself in action. And some have computerized, do-it-yourself career guidance. All have a well stocked reference library which contains directories of employers in private industry and government, guidebooks on how to write a resume and improve your interview techniques, and reports on the job market.

Drop in frequently so that you will get to know the counselors on a first name basis. Then, when a suitable vacancy comes up, your name will be among the first they will recall.

Recently, as a result of the severe recession, some colleges and universities began offering counseling and job placement services to all unemployed residents of the community, regardless of whether they are, or have been, enrolled as students. More are expected to do so as the Federal Job Training Partnership Act, which requires each state to provide matching funds for retraining older, displaced workers, gains momentum.

In the mid-West, some schools have joined with labor unions and private groups to counsel and train displaced automobile and steelworkers for new occupations. These include the University of Illinois in Chicago and Wayne State University in Detroit.

Some schools help the hard core unemployed by offering special job training and remedial courses in the three-R's. The program at New York City Technical College, for example, prepares them for jobs in clerical work, repair of heating and air conditioning systems, building maintenance and as home health aides and companions.

Many schools offer free or reduced rate enrollment in career related courses. At Massachusetts' 21 colleges and universities, for example, persons who have exhausted their unemployment insurance benefits can take one credit each semester, or 11 credits if they are still receiving benefits. Florida's colleges and universities offer free enrollment, without any academic prerequisite, to all older residents. Texas offers career training courses for persons age 55 and older. Some offer courses on an audit basis (without credit towards a degree or certificate), others for credit towards a degree or certificate.

THE OLDER AMERICANS PROGRAM was established in 1978 by the American Association of Community and Junior Colleges. Its purpose is to help two year colleges work with local governments, senior advisory groups, and private industry employers to establish special programs, job training courses and workshops to help older persons find jobs or establish themselves in new careers. The following are some of the services provided.

- Job Development and Training. Many community colleges have established relations with local employers to increase their hiring of older persons and help develop job training programs.

- Career Counseling.

- Job Placement.

- Educational Counseling to help clients who want to learn new job skills or upgrade present skills select appropriate courses and training facilities.

- Skills Banks (Talent Banks, Ability Banks, or Swap-A-Job) which maintain a list of older persons' talents and skills, and help community residents exchange services in lieu of money.

- Women's Centers which provide career and psychological counseling, job training, and/or placement.

OTHER PLACES TO GO FOR HELP

The following organizations and associations in your community may also provide free or inexpensive job placement and career counseling. They can also refer you to other places which offer these services.

RELIGIOUS ORGANIZATIONS in many communities sponsor free counseling and job placement services. In areas hard hit by unemployment, local churches have set up job banks or placement services for their parishioners. Reverend William J. Bausch of St. Mary's Roman Catholic Church of Colts Neck,

N.J, for example, prints mini-resumes of unemployed parishioners in the Church bulletin and maintains a file of job leads.

STATE VOCATIONAL REHABILITATION AGENCIES

SOCIAL SERVICE ORGANIZATIONS, such as community action groups, senior centers, and senior citizens' councils.

GOVERNMENT AGENCIES AND DEPARTMENTS often provide special services to older job seekers and career changers and to the hard core unemployed in their communities. They are also a good source of information on other sources of job training and placement and how to establish yourself in a new career. These include the following.

- Federal Job Service offices
- Mayor's office
- County or state manpower commission
- Department of human resources
- Commission on economic development
- Department of employment services
- State department of labor

Look in the White Pages of the phone book under the name of your city, county or state government for the address and phone number of the appropriate agency.

Look in the Yellow Pages under the following: employment agencies, community service organizations, senior citizen's service organizations, religious denominations, social service organizations.

Ask your local librarian for information. The library is a huge repository of information on community resources. Ask to see The Directory of Educational and Career Information Services For Adults, published by the National Center for Educational Brokering. It lists over 200 service centers throughout the nation which are located in community and government agencies, libraries, and other places. Make sure it is not out of date.

Eat a lobster, eat a pound of caviar - live! If you are in love with a beautiful blonde with an empty face and no brains at all, don't be afraid. Marry her! Live! Arthur Rubinstein, at age 75, when asked to explain his youthful vitality.

1. Education and Health Career Services, 142 Ridgewood Avenue, Glen Ridge, NJ 07028.

2. The CETA (Comprehensive Employment and Training Act) program provided funds to states and smaller communities for the training and placement of disadvantaged persons. This included workers age 55 and older. State and local governments operated the programs themselves or contracted xwith other organizations to provide the services. In 1981 these organizations, called "sponsors," included the National Council on Aging, the Urban League, Green Thumb, and the Steelworkers Old-timers Foundation.

3. As defined by Representative Yvonne Burke of California at a hearing of the U.S. House Select Committee on Aging.

7

HOW TO MAKE A GOOD IMPRESSION

"Shiny shoes show you care," said the recruiter. In October 1982, at a newly opened hotel in Long Island, 4,508 job applicants showed up for the 296 advertised vacancies. Among those weeded out first were men with beards and persons who were considered unkempt for jobs involving guest contact. The qualities the employer was looking for - attitude, appearance, and energy level - could easily have made up for lack of job experience.

We are a nation of strangers. One reason is that the average American changes residence more often in a lifetime than any other national. No wonder employers prefer to recruit new workers through known and trusted channels. It's the next best thing to hiring a relative or an old school chum.

Because it's so difficult to know one another well before making a commitment, Americans rely a lot on surface appearance. As a result, some persons earn a good living by applying the latest packaging and marketing techniques to the "selling" of personalities as if they were tubes of toothpaste. Sad, but true, in job hunting, as in running for political office, the total package often substitutes for genuine knowledge of a person. The right image often compensates for insufficient credentials, and the best qualified person may not get the job because of a poor image.

What does my hairdo have to do with my husband's ability to be president? - Jacqueline Kennedy

Have you taken a good look at yourself lately - your grooming and wardrobe, your speech and body language, the degree of self-confidence you express, your apparent vitality and state of health? All these combine to create an image of your true self. "Image" has such a powerful impact in this nation of strangers that corporations pay consultants on "image enhancement" as much as $400 a day to create the look of success for their executives.

You don't have to spend a fortune to learn how to enhance your image. Common sense and some good books on the topic can work miracles for you. Creating the right image is even more important for the older job seeker. This is especially true for women, since they are evaluated more on the basis of physical appearance than are men.

The image you project can shout, "Look at me. I'm
the best person for the job." It can reinforce
positive age stereotypes - Wise, Stable, Understanding, Efficient, and Reliable. The wrong image
can shout, "I'm a nobody. I don't have confidence
in myself, so why should you? Hire me at your own
risk." It can reinforce negative age stereotypes -
Old Timer, Bossy, Irritable, Frail, Rigid, etc.

Two main aspects of your personality comprise your
total image:

>   1. THE VISIBLE ASPECT
>   Wardrobe
>   Grooming
>   Speech
>   Body Language
>
>   2. THE LESS VISIBLE ASPECT
>   Intelligence
>   Energy Level
>   State of Health

Let's begin with tips on how to enhance the visible aspect.

Question:

*On a scale of one to ten, where does personal
appearance rank among the criteria used to rate an
older job applicant?*

Answer:

*I would say it ranks between eight and nine.
Appearance is very instrumental in determining the
quantity and quality of job opportunities job
seekers have. They don't have to be expensively
dressed, but they should wear proper business
attire - a skirt, jacket and coordinated blouse.
There are many companies which want to present a
specific image, and they look for the type of
person who projects that image. It's not just at
the level of articulation and skills. I'm talking
about clothes, about a stylish haircut. People can
get jobs without a stylish appearance, but it goes
a long way in getting placements.* - Josephine
Lerro, Director of Human Resources, TempsAmerica.

WARDROBE AND GROOMING TIPS FOR THE JOB INTERVIEW

KNOWING THAT YOU'RE PROPERLY DRESSED can do a lot to boost your self confidence. Almost everyone knows the cardinal rules of good grooming - clean, pressed clothes, polished shoes with no scruffy heels, hair neatly trimmed and combed. Apparently, there are many persons who don't know how to achieve the look of success, otherwise books such as The Woman's Dress For Success Book, by John Molloy (Warner, 1982) wouldn't be best sellers.

This was apparent at a 1982 job fair for senior adults which was held in New York City. Representatives from several large companies were there, eagerly anticipating hiring a few seniors in order to demonstrate their sense of social responsibility. Unfortunately, only a handful of persons in the large crowd of job seekers were dressed as if they were seriously looking for work. Most looked like they were headed for the beach, wearing tight, polyester pants and loud, Hawaiian print shirts, no stockings, and open-toed sandals. Some were even carrying oversized shopping bags!

THE MOVERS AND SHAKERS OF WASHINGTON DO NOT WEAR POLYESTER - Barbara Blaes, consultant on Image Enhancement, Washington, D.C.

Like it or not, the corporate "uniform" exists, and anyone looking for a good job would be wise to adhere to the corporate rules of dress and grooming. Even intelligent, well educated people, like Margaret, a 54-year old Ph.D., can be ignorant of this. She showed up for an interview wearing eyeglasses that made her look outdated; a polyester, flower printed, lavender dress (her best outfit); and open-toed sandals with no stockings. (It was 99 degrees outside.) She was flatly told no one in the business world would hire her in such an outfit. Apparently, few people bother to see beyond the "emperor's clothes."

The experts advise both men and women to wear a dark, tailored suit that is well made, with a good fit. Preferably, it should be of pure cotton or wool - never pure polyester! The suit should have a dull or mat finish and should not shine like a new penny.

The best colors are navy, medium to dark gray, and brown, in that order. Black is okay, but it's best for formal or after business occasions. If you

want to look like a shaker and mover, avoid plaids
and greens. A bargain basement suit which fits
poorly is no bargain. Get a custom tailored one if
you can afford it. If you can't, have the local
tailor adjust one that is modestly priced.

The fashion gurus now say that career women may
wear tailored dresses at the office. However,
until this new fashion dictate becomes widespread,
it's safer to stick to the classic, tailored suit,
softened with feminine touches such as pockets
placed on the slant to emphasize a narrow waist,
and blouses with ruffled or lace collars or bow
ties. A good quality pantsuit may be substituted
for a skirt and jacket. Never, under any circumstance, wear anything resembling resort wear.
Steer clear of spike heels, open-toed shoes,
plunging necklines, naked legs, and tight sweaters, skirts or pants.

As we grow older, our skin and hair lose pigmenta-
tion. A cream or light colored shirt or blouse
will offset this and make you look more alive.
Wear stark white only if you want to look like
Count Dracula, since it tends to drain color from
the face. Dark suits go best with light colored
shirts and blouses, whereas light, summer suits
look best with a softly contrasting shirt, blouse
and tie. Avoid cheap, flashy jewelry at all cost.
Steer clear of sweaters and blouses in loud patterns and brassy colors.

How strictly should you follow such advice from
the experts? It depends on the industry in which
you hope to find a job. The conservative industries (such as banking, law, insurance and oil)
tend to follow more closely the conservative dress
code. The newer, high technology industries (electronics, cable television, information processing,
bioengineering, etc.) have a higher proportion of
young executives and managers who follow the more
relaxed dress code of the Sixties. They've even
been seen wearing blue jeans and flowing beards at
the office.

Older persons who hope to find work in one of
these younger firms have to decide whether to
follow the newer dress code in order to look
"cool" or stick to the traditional code. On the
one hand, the traditional dress might make them
look like old timers. On the other hand, a paunch-
y, 65-year old who wears tight jeans in order to
appear younger creates the opposite impression.

The safest bet is to visit the firm at lunch time or at 5:00 P.M. several days before the interview and observe how employees of various ages are dressed.

He's still...going strong, and sexier than most men half his age. - Playgirl Magazine, which selected George Burns, at age 87, as one of the nation's 10 sexiest men.

SHOULD YOU DYE THOSE GRAY HAIRS? Until recently, the answer would have been an unqualified "Yes." Now, however, changing political forces are introducing new slogans, such as "Older is better." Witness the surging popularity of beautiful, silver haired fashion models like Carmen. Notice the growing number of male public figures, like Dan Rather, who sport silver streaks in their hair like diamonds on a lapel. Hair stylists say more young men are asking to have silver added to their locks. If you must dye your hair, remember that the skin and eyes tend to lose color with age, so a softer shade than your original hair color will be more flattering and make you look younger.

Hair softened with a coloring that conforms to the mature woman's natural hair pattern is more flattering than brassy red, blonde, or blue-black hair. The lacquered, bouffant hairstyles of the Fifties make her look outdated and older, as does hair that's flat on top, or too straight, or either too long or too short. The experts recommend ear length or chin length hair, styled to softness. If you wear a wig, make sure it's of good quality. Dime store wigs are aging and almost anyone can tell when you're wearing one.

MAKEUP that is subtle and natural enhances a youthful figure and softens wrinkles. Soft shades, applied lightly, are more flattering than either no makeup at all or makeup applied with a heavy hand. The rule to follow in selecting your clothes makeup and hair style should be, AVOID OVERDOING AND UNDERDOING IT.

THE WAY YOU SPEAK RANKS WITH GROOMING IN IMAGE
IMPACT

And each can diminish or reinforce the other. Careless speech habits and a poor voice quality have wrecked the careers of several glamorous movie stars when "talking pictures" were introduced. Handsome John Gilbert, the idol of millions of women, was done in by his squeaky, thin voice. The musical comedy, "My Fair Lady," celebrates the transformation of a Cockney speaking urchin, Eliza Doolittle, into a debutante with the help of a speech professor, 'Enry 'Iggins.

Voice tone is an important component of speech. The finishing school tones of Jackie Kennedy Onnasis, soft and low pitched, compliment her exquisite sense of style to produce an overall smashing effect. It's the result of training and practice, not of genes. Contrast this with the high pitched, loud, nasal tone of "Dingbat" of "All In The Family" which heightens her dowdy image.

You can easily improve your voice and speech pattern by tape recording a job interview rehearsal with the help of a friend. The first time you listen to your voice, you'll probably be shocked. Most people are. Is your voice too high pitched? Is it too loud? Does it sound harsh or nasal? Don't despair. It can easily be improved.

Even if you like the sound of your voice, try lowering it a bit and you will notice an immediate improvement. Voice experts say most people pitch theirs too high, especially when they are under stress. And what is more stressful than a job interview? Just being aware of this will help you to modulate your voice. Women, especially, are advised to lower their voices and slow down their rate of speaking, because they have a tendency to speak too rapidly and in too high a pitch when they are under stress.

Men and women have different ways of communicating which reflect their traditional status in society (MALE = dominant; FEMALE = submissive) and social roles (MALE = provider, achiever; FEMALE = dependent, nurturer).

A woman with impressive credentials can apply for a management level job, but if she uses a female mode of communicating, her audience will subconsciously devalue what she says. This was observed in a study of male-female differences in communicating while in a courtroom situation. Both male and female jurors, without being aware of it, listened more closely when a man gave testimony than when a woman did. In fact, the woman's comments were more often ignored.

Dorothy Sarnoff, author of <u>Speech</u> <u>Can</u> <u>Change</u> <u>Your</u> <u>Life</u> (Doubleday, 1970) and <u>Make</u> <u>the</u> <u>Most</u> <u>of</u> <u>Your</u> <u>Best:</u> <u>A</u> <u>Complete</u> <u>Program</u> <u>for</u> <u>Presenting</u> <u>Yourself</u> <u>&</u> <u>Your</u> <u>Ideas</u> <u>With</u> <u>Confidence</u> <u>and</u> <u>Authority</u> (Double-day, 1981), says many women don't know how to communicate their ideas in a way that commands attention and respect.

They subconsciously employ a woman's language and tone of voice which makes them appear uncertain and places them in an inferior position. The effect of this on the listeners is illustrated by the many case studies she cites. For example, in a typical conversation between a man and a woman, the man makes more than 75% of the interruptions. When a man introduces a topic, it's developed further 96% of the time. But, when a woman introduces a topic, it's developed only 36% of the time.

Sarnoff describes women's speech characteristics which convey insecurity and a subordinate status. Among these are a tentative, sing-song voice; talking too much or too little; a questioning rise in pitch at the end of a sentence; and the use of indefinite modifiers such as "Don't you think?" and "sort of." Men speak more directly, which gives the impression of mastery. Her books give valuable suggestions and exercises which show you how to rid yourself of self defeating mannerisms and develop a way of speaking which advertises SUCCESS.

Slang and poor grammar should be avoided in a job interview. Ask the friend who rehearses the interview with you to be on the lookout for such boo-boos as "AIN'T" and double negatives ("I DON'T have NO dependents"). Save the slang for the club house gang. Put on your best business manner and speech when you go for an interview.

A LARGE VOCABULARY IS ASSOCIATED WITH CAREER SUC-CESS, studies show. It's never too late to enlarge your vocabulary. I know an 82-year old woman who reads with a dictionary on hand so that she can look up words she doesn't know. Although she had only three years of schooling in her native Ital-ian village, her English vocabulary is as good as, and probably better than, many recent high school graduates.

What does it mean to have a "large" vocabulary? It means to possess the basic word "tools" with which to express your thoughts clearly, concisely, and accurately. It does not mean bowling over the interviewer with 4-or-5 syllable words. Not only will you fail to impress him, you'll come across as a pompous egghead.

You'll also make a better impression if you answer questions with complete sentences rather than with a "Yes" or a "No," a shrug and a grunt, or phrases. For example, in response to the question, "What did you do from 1956 to 1965?," you might say, "Odd jobs." A better answer would be to describe the jobs you held, the specific responsibilities involved, your special achievements, and your reasons for leaving. This should be stated in complete, grammatical sentences.

The hands tell you more about what Eddie's going through than the words he has to speak. He might be saying one thing, but the body may be saying something else. - actor Tony Lo Bianco, speaking of his starring role in the Broadway hit, "A View From The Bridge."[1]

THE SILENT LANGUAGE

Body language exerts a powerful influence, writes anthropologist Edward Hall.[2] He is referring to the messages we transmit by the way we sit, stand, cross our legs, fold our arms, by our gestures and facial expressions. Its power lies in the fact that we are not conscious of what we're doing. A good part of the training of actors and actresses is learning how to control (make themselves conscious of) their body language.

Ronald Reagan is a master of communicating through body language. Notice how he crinkles up his eyes and smiles broadly at a gathering, how he ever so slightly leans forward in a warm, accepting manner, with arms outstretched, palms up, and head cocked in the manner of a lover gazing at a beloved. An experienced interviewer also understands the importance of body language. He or she can sense when the messages conveyed by your gestures and expressions conflict with your spoken words.

If you could meet Winnie, you'd think she is bizarre. She can think and do a job. She has a bachelor's degree in sociology and is now 50. But she doesn't smile. She holds the upper part of her body very rigid. Who wants to work with her? We have videotaped her. We have told her simple things like, when she looks at someone, to look away every now and then, to smile, to move her body. - Janet Roberts, executive director of the Women's Survival Center in Tampa, Florida.

Here are some tips on how to use body language in order to create a positive impression on an employer. Try them out first on friends and relatives and ask for their critical suggestions. Then practice, practice, and practice until they become like second nature to you.

- Avoid pointing with your finger in order to emphasize a point. It might be interpreted as rudeness or bossiness.

- Greet the interviewer by name. (Everyone loves the sound of his or her name.)

- Establish eye contact, smile, and offer a firm handshake.

- Look directly at the interviewer when you answer questions. If you look at the floor, ceiling, or even glance briefly at your watch, it might be interpreted as rudeness, shyness or, worse yet, as lying.

- Hold your head high and you will appear more self-confident. If you allow it to sink into your shoulders, you'll look like a frightened ostrich sticking its head into the sand.

- Sit in a relaxed manner and lean, ever so slightly, toward the interviewer. This conveys self-confidence, approval, and acceptance.

- Hold your hands gently cupped in your lap with palms facing upward, and you'll convey an inviting, friendly message; or, rest them lightly on the arms of the chair. If you clench your hands into a fist, grip the arms of the chair tightly, or fold your arms across your chest, you will create an aura of tension and hostility which will make the interviewer uncomfortable. Drumming or fidgeting with your fingers adds to the tension.

- Never take notes during an interview unless it's to jot down names, addresses and other facts which are easily forgotten. It can be misinterpreted as arrogance, lack of assurance, or forgetfulness. The latter, especially, is not what you want the interviewer to suspect of you.

-If you're a woman, sit with your legs crossed at the ankles. Placing your legs apart, even slightly, sends a subtle, sexual signal which is not appropriate to a job interview.

- Smile, but don't overdo it. Studies show that women smile significantly more than men. This is appropriate when tending a baby or gazing at a lover, but it's woefully out of place in a job interview. It may be viewed as a sign of submissiveness and dependency. Women managers who smile a lot are viewed by their male colleagues as less efficient and less likely to succeed, one study found. Many women need to learn that the business and professional world can be a jungle. It's not like the home and community where emotional bonding plays an important role in social interactions.

LEARN HOW TO REDUCE STRESS

Excessive stress can seriously lower your energy level and harm your health. Job hunting, career changing, and retiring, like any other major life change, are stressful events. Even joyous events, like getting married, earning a promotion or winning the lottery, create stress because they disrupt our established patterns of living.

Picture an actor trying to convey stress without uttering a word - body tense, lips tight, teeth clenched, brows knitted, and shoulders hunched. An alert interviewer picks up such signals. To improve your image, learn how to camouflage the signs of stress. To safeguard your health, learn to minimize or prevent excessive stress.

"Every pink slip should carry a Surgeon General's warning that it may be hazardous to your health," says Louis A. Ferman of the University of Michigan's Institute of Labor and Industrial Relations. Following a rise in the unemployment rate there is an increase in the rate of suicides, homicides, high blood pressure, and admissions to mental hospitals. Some mental health specialists say that getting another job can improve a person's mental health more than psychotherapy and medication.

If you have any of these symptoms, you may be suffering from undue stress: a continual feeling

102

of fatigue, increased irritability, vague aches and pains, insomnia, and difficulty in concentrating. Even making simple decisions, such as what to cook for dinner, becomes difficult. Stress is also an underlying cause of depression. The way you deal with the stressful periods of your life can make the difference between becoming ill or staying healthy, between getting a job or a bundle of rejections.

There are ways to reduce stress. One way is to reduce the number of major changes you need to make within a certain period of time. The way to do this is to establish priorities. First, make those changes which absolutely, definitely cannot be put off. The rest can wait. Spread them out in time so that they don't all hit you at once. For example, instead of getting married, changing your job, selling your house, and moving out of town all at the same time, do one or two at a time so that you can adjust better to each change.

Why blame yourself because you've lost your job and can't find another as easily as you thought it would be? Most workers are dismissed for reasons beyond their control - plant closings, mergers, company relocations, job obsolescence, age discrimination, a difficult boss - not because of incompetence. Just being aware of this can lighten your burden of guilt and reduce stress.

Displacing your anger onto those you love is not only unfair, it doesn't improve your situation, and it reinforces your feelings of unworthiness and misery. Take positive, rational steps to improve your situation instead - first, by analyzing the errors in your thinking which are self defeating; second, by correcting them; and third, by making plans for your next job or career.

This is called cognitive therapy, the latest psychotherapeutic technique for helping people who are suffering from depression and lack of self confidence. Basically, it focuses on our habits of thinking about ourselves. However, some psychoanalysts still believe that "The way you feel is the way you think."

Cognitive therapy has a different focus - "You feel the way you think. Change your habits of thinking and you'll feel much better." Studies suggest that cognitive therapy results in as much improvement as anti-depressant drugs. The beauty part of it is that it's faster and you can apply it to yourself, although some persons may need professional counseling as well.

Depression and lack of self-confidence are caused by distortions in the way we think, in our basic view of life. So, instead of concentrating on what you lack, concentrate on what you have to offer, your ASSETS.

Older women, especially, need positive cognitive therapy since they've been brought up to believe that females are by nature dependent, unassertive, shy, passive, subjective and emotional, all the traits that are deadly during a job interview.

First, write down all your negative, self defeating thoughts. Don't leave anything out, no matter how trivial it seems to you. Here are a few which especially afflict older job seekers.

.I'm too old to change.

.Nobody wants to hire me.

.I lost the job because I don't have what it takes.

.All these younger people applying for the same job are much better qualified than I am.

.I don't have enough education, and it's too late to do anything about it.

.I've been just a mother and housewife all these years. I don't have much to offer.

.All this new computer technology is beyond me. I'll never be able to learn it.

.I'll probably end my days waiting on soup kitchen lines.

When we're depressed, we tend to exaggerate the negative aspects of a situation and overlook its positive aspects. It sounds corny to say, "Every cloud has a silver lining," but it's true. Rarely are things as hopeless as they seem to us when we are unemployed. Losing a job may be one of the best things that's ever happened to you. It forces you to review your priorities, and you have the time to do something about improving your life.

Now, next to each negative thought you have written down, write all the positive facts and events which disprove it. If you can't think of something from your life experience, use your imagination. If you must force yourself to get ideas, it's because you have gotten into the wrong habits of thinking about yourself.

Every day there are many older persons who get hired. Many people have changed careers successfully in their later years, and some of them have had stunning success. Even persons in their eighties find jobs. One 79-year old woman applied for a job as part time bookkeeper in a local pharmacy. She managed to keep her age a secret during the interview, and was hired. Four years later, her boss still doesn't realize how old she is.

Finally, make a list of things you can do to improve your situation. Here are some suggestions to get you started.

- Go on a diet and slim down.

- Buy a good quality suit for job hunting.

- Get a more stylish, attractive hairdo or haircut.

- Throw out your old fashioned eyeglasses and get a modern pair.

- Join a local association and become an active volunteer.

- Enroll in an adult education course to upgrade your job skills or learn new ones.

- Get a medical check up, even though you feel good, so that any incipient problem can be cured before it gets worse.

- Read some of the references that are listed in the Appendix.

- Get a part-time job.

In Why Survive? Being Old in America, Dr. Robert Butler recommends this as a constructive way to deal with the "retirement syndrome" which afflicts even healthy persons. Its symptoms include headaches, gastrointestinal problems, sleeping too much or too little, irritability, nervousness and lethargy. People who haven't planned for their retirement are more likely to develop these symptoms, he writes. (People who aren't prepared for unemployment are in the same boat.) In order to restore a sense of purpose in life, he recommends doing volunteer or paid, part time work, or making a hobby or special interest a part-time or full time business venture.

Relaxation techniques, such as Yoga and transcendental meditation, also reduce stress. The biofeedback resulting from just 10 minutes of intense relaxation a day slows down the heart rate, lowers blood pressure, and sharpens mental alertness. You can find books on relaxation techniques in the library or bookstore. Low cost courses are offered at the Y's and other adult education centers.

Sit down in a quiet place and make a list of your assets (Your personal assets, not the material things you own.) These include your past achievements, skills, and the things you do best. You've probably forgotten how much you have going for you.

Make another list of all the persons you know who might be able to give you good job leads. This exercise will give you a sense of moving ahead. It's also a good start to polishing up your resume and preparing for job interviews.

IT'S BETTER TO WEAR OUT THAN TO RUST OUT

Keep up with your normal social activities as much as you can. Studies find that older persons who are socially active, who take care of their health and appearance, live longer on the average than those who do not. They also have more opportunities to obtain the support and advice of other people. Since unemployment cuts you off from many social activities, you should force yourself to go out more. One way to do this is to plan a weekly schedule of interesting things to do and people to meet.

Time can be a friend or it can be an enemy. The time we spend at work gives meaning to our lives and sanity to our thoughts. It's a vital component of the "cognitive map" we carry around in our heads to guide us through the network of relationships and events in our lives. Making a daily and monthly schedule of things to do, no matter how trivial, gives structure to your day and a sense of direction and control over your life until you find another job.

There are many things to do close by that are free or cost little. Plan barbecues on your lawn or a picnic in the park with friends. Visit the botanical gardens. Go to the library and read about job opportunities. Volunteer your services at the community association. Who knows, it might lead to your next job. Help others who are in need and your own problems will seem more manageable.

Every community has low cost or free recreational activities, such as concerts, block parties, walking tours, outdoor arts and crafts shows, bazaars, and community theater. You can find out what's going on from the local newspaper, the Y, library, and church.

If you're lucky enough to live in or near a college town, there are unending things to do on campus, such as enrolling in courses and attending concerts, playing on the tennis courts and swimming in the pool. Many colleges offer free or reduced tuition to unemployed and/or older residents of the community.

"MIDDLE AGE IS WHEN YOUR CLOTHES NO LONGER FIT AND IT'S YOU WHO NEED THE ALTERATIONS."   - Bob Hope

Some people get so depressed when they're out of work that they neglect themselves. They skip meals and grab anything from the refrigerator. They try to forget their problems by overeating or undereating. And they don't get enough exercise. Such practices are health risks which increase their susceptibility to high blood pressure, arteriosclerosis, cancer and heart attacks. They can also make a person look and feel as much as 15 years older.

"USE IT OR LOSE IT," advises Dr. James Fries of the Stanford Arthritis Clinic. Regular exercise is the closest thing there is to the legendary fountain of youth. It keeps your brain cells active and your body young by lowering your blood pressure, weight and cholesterol level. It also builds up your reserves of energy, and some experts claim it forestalls diabetes, depression and the flu.

Studies show that people who are physically active are three times less likely to have a heart attack than people who are sedentary, and they have a better chance of survival if they do have one. Dr. Josef R. Patsch, of the Baylor College of Medicine in Houston, reports that regular exercise increases the level of a high density lipoprotein which removes cholesterol from the arteries, a major culprit in heart attacks.

A 55-year old person who exercises regularly and eats well balanced meals is likely to have a younger medical age than a 35-year old who lives carelessly. Joggers in their fifties are often in better condition (and shape) than inactive persons half their age. Medical examinations of the astronauts found that even a brief period of inactivity caused stiffening of the joints, a loss of calcium from the bones, and the formation of blood clots and deposits in the urinary tract.

You're never too old to start a program of moderate exercise. But first consult with your doctor to learn what's suitable for your present state of health. Even persons who have recovered from a heart attack are advised to do mild, regular exercise under a doctor's guidance.

Gordon Wallace began racewalking to strengthen himself after recovering from triple bypass heart surgery at age 66. (Racewalking doesn't cause sprains and torn ligaments as strenuous jogging does.) By age 71, he had been crowned World Champion Racewalker in his age group and U.S. Outstanding Male Walker Over Forty. At the age of 73, he held 25 American records in distances up to 25 kilometers and had written a book to help others regain their health, The Valiant Heart: From Cardiac Cripple to World Champion.

If you've been inactive for some time or suffer from a chronic ailment, it's not wise to start out with a program of vigorous exercise. Strenuous exercise that is carried on without listening to your body's warning signals of pain, exhaustion and nausea can be dangerous. The body needs rest in order to eliminate the waste products of strenuous exercise. And the older we get, the longer and more frequent periods of rest our bodies need to perform this function.

There are many exercises and sports which are suitable for older persons. Ronald Reagan's program of horseback riding, canoe paddling and swimming are just right for keeping him looking decades younger than he is. Hiking, walking, weight lifting, and bike riding are also appropriate.

The American Youth Hostels operates low cost, 50-Plus Tours that are fun, educational and healthful. For information, contact AYH, National Travel Box G, Delaplane, Virginia 22025 or phone toll-free, (800) 336-6019.

Save gas and improve your health by keeping your car in the garage and doing your errands on foot, by bicycle or roller skates. Walking tours of local sites, galleries and museums combine physical exercise with mental stimulation. Dancing, bowling and golf are other suitable activities.

"Running Around Retirement," a New York Times article by Judy Klemesrud, describes several women runners who range in age from 64 to 81. Many had never put on running shoes until they were past 60. One woman who began running to combat a severe case of arthritis had completed 90 races and 7 marathons, a feat which earned her the title of "Senior Woman of the Year" by the New York Road Runners Club. The oldest woman known to have completed a marathon at the time was 81-year old Ruth Rothfarb of Miami Beach.

On the average, the women run 80 miles a week. All were described as looking at least 15 years younger. If you've been considering having a $7,000 face lift, first try the absolutely free and painless face lift provided by exercise.

HOW TO LIVE LONG - advice from Satchel Paige, who became a major league player at the age of 42.

1. Avoid fried meats, which angry up the blood.

2. If your stomach disputes you, lie down and pacify it with cool thoughts.

3. Keep the juices flowing by jangling around gently as you move.

4. Go very light on the vices, such as carrying on in society. The social rumble ain't restful.

5. Avoid running at all times.

6. Don't look back. Something might be gaining on you.

YOU CAN NEVER BE TOO THIN OR TOO RICH, said Wally Simpson. Obesity kills more Americans than any other health problem, say some experts. It also handicaps a person in the race for jobs and promotions.

Employment recruiters say obese persons are rarely promoted from lower management ranks, and among equally qualified job candidates, the one who is nice and trim is more likely to be hired. Women who are obese have an even greater problem because physical appearance counts much more for them. In general, overweight job seekers are viewed as health risks and less productive workers. They are even barred from some professional or trade training programs such as nursing or police work.

I can take my clothes off and loko better than any man in this gym, regardless of age. - Vince Gironda, runner up in the Mr. Universe contest at the age of 46.

Reduce your intake of foods that are high in saturated fats, salt and refined sugar, and you'll not only keep your weight down, you'll protect yourself from strokes, arteriosclerosis, hypertension and heart attacks. Increase your intake of high fiber foods such as raw fruits and vegetables, bran, wheat and other cereals, and you'll prevent gastrointestinal tract problems such as diverticulosis, constipation and bowel cancer.

OUR BODIES NEED MORE VITAMIN RICH FOODS as we get older, because the capacity to store these nutrients diminishes. Brittle bones (osteoporosis), for example, is caused by a deficiency of calcium and vitamin D. Some health gurus believe that a daily glass of raw fruit or vegetable juice mixed with brewers yeast keeps the wrinkles away. An experiment in which mice were fed large doses of vitamin B-5 showed a significant increase in their lifespan and gives a hopeful indication for humans.

Brewers yeast, nuts, liver and whole grain cereals are some of the foods that are rich in vitamin B and protein. Nobel Prize winner, Dr. Linus Pauling, claims that 8 to 10 grams of vitamin C daily prevents colds and may add up to 24 years to your lifespan. Some experts, however, say there isn't sufficient evidence to support this claim.

Foods rich in vitamin E increase the reproductive capacity of domestic animals, but it's not yet certain whether the same youth-giving effects occur in humans. A few experts believe a high intake of this vitamin has the Shangri-La effect of making a 50-year old person seem more like a 35-year old. Most medical experts, however, claim that an excess intake of any single vitamin can upset the body's total balance of vitamins.

Among the foods you are advised to cut down or eliminate are salt, sugar, alcohol and caffeine containing products such as coffee, tea, chocolate and cola drinks. One interesting experiment showed that large, daily doses of caffeine turned the hair of mice prematurely gray. Too much sleep, as well as too little (less than 5 hours daily), are also believed to speed up the aging process.

What all such research findings boil down to is that we should heed the ancient Greek principle, FOLLOW THE GOLDEN MEAN, which is a fancy way of saying, avoid excess of any kind.

A University of California study found that persons who were healthiest regularly followed these seven basic practices:

- REGULAR PHYSICAL EXERCISE
- REDUCED INTAKE OF ALCOHOLIC BEVERAGES
- NO SMOKING
- SEVEN TO EIGHT HOURS SLEEP DAILY
- MAINTAINING PROPER WEIGHT
- EATING BREAKFAST
- AVOIDING BETWEEN MEAL SNACKS

Seven years after the study began, they found a significantly lower death rate among persons who had followed these practices regularly. The life expectancy of a 45-year old man who had followed all 7 practices, for example, was 11 years longer than persons who had followed 3 or less.

.At 90, Albert Szent-Gyorgy, Nobel Prize winner, continues to work on cancer research.

.At 90, Sophocles is summoned into court to prove he is not senile. He reads to the jury his latest play, "Oedipus at Colonus," which he wrote at the age of 89.

.At 92, Justice Oliver Wendell Holmes begins to study Greek because, "When else would I have had the time?"

INTELLIGENCE REMAINS UNIMPAIRED AMONG HEALTHY, ACTIVE OLDER PERSONS

The old stereotype that aging is associated with an inevitable decline in memory, learning capacity and problem solving ability has bitten the dust. According to researchers, more often these problems are symptoms of emotional stress, depression, poor health and poor nutrition. Recent studies reveal that many older persons actually show gains in scores on tests which measure creative intelligence and the ability to solve problems.

There is evidence that older persons who exercise regularly have a lower incidence of senility. This is supported by studies of animals which show the brain shrinks with inactivity and understimulation, just as the muscles do.

A.H. Ismail, of Purdue University, reports the results of a 4-month study of middle aged men who were instructed to do one and one half hours of physical exercise three times a week. At the end of the period, they were retested on tasks involving logical reasoning and information processing. They showed a significant increase in scores. Ismail believes the improvement may be due to an increase in the brain's assimilation of oxygen and glucose brought on by exercise.

An active sex life can also boost the I.Q. scores of older persons, according to Dr. Edward Bussel of Duke University. His studies of persons ranging in age from their seventies to nineties suggest that maintaining regular sexual relations helps to keep them mentally alert and physically fit. Conversely, people who abstain from sex may drop as much as 25 points in one year. The question here, of course, is "Does sex activity increase the I.Q. score, or do persons with a high I.Q. have a stronger sex drive?"

Contrary to the popular stereotype, senility affects less than 10% of persons over 65 years of age. In at least half these cases, there is a physical cause such as anemia, infection, an uncorrected hearing problem, metabolic disorder, alcoholism, hardening of the arteries, and strokes. Even common drugs can cause symptoms of senility: sedatives, anti-inflammatory drugs, diuretics, digitalis, oral diabetes drugs and neuroleptic agents.

Most of these problems can now be treated with new drugs, by surgery, or a simple change in diet. Even computer games are being used successfully to stimulate brain dormant and brain damaged functions in patients. Alertness, memory, judgment, attention span and eye-brain-hand coordination show a dramatic improvement.

Over 90% of persons over the age of 65, and many who are well into their eighties, show no significant mental deterioration.

Our minds and bodies work together as partners. What's good for the body is good for the mind. There is evidence that the mental confusion found among a small percentage of the elderly is due to a deficiency of vitamin B and folic acid in the diet. Severe depression and senility can show the same symptoms.

Jane Brody[3] cites the case of a 63-year old man who misplaced things, suffered memory loss, and became so disorganized that he could no longer function well at his job. A doctor misdiagnosed him as prematurely senile, but later examinations showed he was severely depressed. Psychological counseling and antidepressant drugs resulted in a dramatic improvement.

It is often said that we use less than 10% of our mental capacity. Dip into the 90% that you are holding in reserve by keeping alive your curiosity and learning ability. Enroll in an adult education course to learn a new skill or knowledge which will increase your value on the job market. Get involved in social activities that keep your brain cells alive through stimulating conversations.

At the age of 80, B. F. Skinner, the famous psychologist, still professionally active, shared his secrets of maintaining his enormous intellectual powers.

   .Make a deliberate effort to create a stimulating environment. Eliminate monotony and boredom in your home. Keep a supply of intellectual games such as chess and crossword puzzles, and read mystery novels.

   .Participate in discussion groups and enroll in adult education courses.

.If your memory for recent events isn't as keen as it used to be, devise memory tricks to help you recall. (One trick is to simply concentrate harder.)

.Engage in shorter periods of intensive intellectual activity, interspersed with relaxing breaks which make few or no demands on the mind, such as watching the television soaps. Leisure activities which are too demanding, such as complicated puzzles and chess, should be reserved for other times.

Psychologist Donald Kausler, of the University of Missouri, believes a major cause of memory problems in older persons are simply inattention and lack of concentration.

Scientists have already learned to synthesize a brain hormone, vasopressin, which significantly improves learning and memory. Recently, researchers identified a human substance that acts like a cement which makes memories permanent. An enzyme called Calpain has also been identified as a key component in the biochemistry of human intelligence.

They are also investigating the connection between calcium deficiency and the learning difficulties that may occur in some elderly persons. Nutrients such as vitamin B, folic acid, the cholines found in dairy products, grains, legumes, egg yolks, and the lecithin in soybeans are also known to improve memory.

If you are interested in learning more about how to improve your mental and physical health, there are plenty of good books on the market. See the appendix for some suggestions.

1. Kinzer, Stephen. "How ethnic childhoods shaped 'Bridge' actors." @1983 by the New York Times Company. Reprinted by permission.

2. Hall, Edward. The Silent Language (Greenwood, 1980)

3. Brody, Jane. The New York Times Guide to Personal Health, (Times Books, 1982)

- 6 -

AGE & SEX DISCRIMINATION

All Secretaries of Labor are mandated by law to foster, promote and develop the welfare of the wage earners of the United States, to improve their working conditions and to advance their opportunities for profitable employment.

IT'S AGAINST THE LAW TO BE DENIED A JOB, A PROMO-
TION, OR A SALARY INCREASE BECAUSE OF YOUR AGE.

There are Federal, state and city laws which protect you from age and sex discrimination. In most
states which have anti-discrimination statutes,
age is included along with sex, race, national
origin and religion as reasons for which a person
cannot be denied the right to a job.

In the Federal government's Age Discrimination in
Employment Act (ADEA) the "older" worker is defined as anyone between 40 and 70 years of age.
One of its purposes is to promote the employment
of persons on the basis of ability rather than
age. Another is to help employers and employees
find ways to resolve problems resulting from the
impact of age on employment.

The ADEA protects you from discrimination in hiring, in holding on to your job, in wages and
salaries, and in the "terms, conditions and privileges of employment." This means that as an older
and/or female worker, you have the same rights to
fringe benefits, parking privileges, coffee breaks
and other perks as young, male employees.

It prohibits employment agencies from advertising
in a manner which excludes women and older persons. For example, a help-wanted ad cannot say,
"Only applicants under the age of 50 will be
considered" or "Only males may apply."

It protects you from being denied union membership
and from having your rights as a union member
limited in any way on account of age.

The law does not protect you if your job performance is poor.

Nor does it protect you if you have reached the
age limit in occupations where age is a bona fide

115

condition for employment. Such occupations generally involve the safety of the public, such as firefighters, police work, air traffic controllers, and airline pilots.

The law cannot prevent an employer from offering incentives which encourage you to retire early or leave voluntarily. It does, however, prohibit forcing you to retire against your will.

It is not unlawful for your employer to observe the terms of a bona fide seniority system or employee benefit plan, such as a retirement pension or insurance plan, as long as these are not used to evade the purposes of the Act. For example, the existence of such benefit plans cannot be used as an excuse to refuse to hire you if you are qualified for the job. Your employer is not required to include the years you were employed after the age of 65 in calculating your final pension benefits. Although employers are required to contribute to life and disability insurance for workers over 65, they are not prohibited from reducing their group life insurance or using Medicare payments to lower company benefits. Not all employers do so, however.

If you are disabled, an employer cannot force you to retire as long as you are able to do the work, nor can disability pay be withheld until you reach 70 years of age.

Mandatory retirement has been abolished for most Federal employees except prison guards, foreign service officers and other special groups.

It applies to establishments and labor organizations which have a minimum of 20 workers.

It permits the compulsory retirement of executives and high policy makers at age 65 and allows colleges and universities to retire tenured faculty members at age 65. Also, a high salaried executive or professor can be dismissed if the employer can prove it is necessary for cutting costs.

There is a need for such a law. Older workers are still being denied jobs, promotions, pay increases, education benefits and retraining opportunities. Many are being forced into early retirement or termination against their will. During a recession, many employers offer incentives to encourage workers to retire early as a way of reducing their payroll. And, once out of work, older persons have more difficulty than younger persons finding another job at the same pay and level of responsibility.

Age discrimination exists in private industry and government, in blue collar trade unions and in the professions. Many apprenticeship programs in the skilled trades, for example, have arbitrary age limits for recruits which have little or nothing to do with the ability to do the job - 24 for union electricians, 30 for truck mechanics, 35 for plasterers, and so on.

The reasons underlying most cases of age discrimination are irrational. A lawsuit was filed by over 500 applicants who were denied jobs at a tire and rubber plant because of its policy of not hiring persons over 40 on the grounds that they wouldn't be able to meet the physical demands of the job. Yet, a similar plant in a neighboring state gave preference to applicants over 40 because it had found the work performance of its older workers was superior to that of its younger workers.

A lawsuit was filed against Greyhound Bus Lines because of its policy of not hiring drivers over 35 on the grounds that some of the driving assignments constitute arduous and hazardous conditions. Yet, company officials admitted that its older drivers had better safety records than their younger colleagues.

In 1977, the U.S. Commission on Civil Rights reported there was age discrimination in at least 10 Federal programs designed to aid the disadvantaged. Among these programs were vocational rehabilitation services, training and public service employment, and vocational and adult education.

In 1982, 7 out of every 10 workers between the ages of 40 and 70 were protected against age discrimination in employment. A report to the House Select Committee on Aging concluded these protections were inadequate because of the following reasons.

- 51% of all workers still face an employer imposed mandatory retirement age.

- 42% of all workers covered by pensions would receive minimal or no pension benefit increases for work performed after age 65.

117

- All workers who forfeit Social Security benefits in order to keep their jobs will never regain those lost benefits because of a gap in the ADEA which allows employers to freeze pension benefits for workers who remain employed after age 65. Any discontinuance of these benefit accruals is equivalent to a reduction in total pay. (This encourages older workers to retire.)

- About 15% of persons looking for jobs in 1981 were 45 and older, yet only 4% of Federal employment and planning funds were allotted to this age group. A 1982 report prepared for Congress predicts that about 30 million workers will be displaced by robots, computers and foreign competition, yet the Federal job retraining programs being proposed focus on disadvantaged youth.

- This violates another Federal law, the Age Discrimination Act of 1975, which prohibits discrimination in the distribution of benefits from Federal programs, some of which are aimed to help persons find unsubsidized jobs.

Some improvements have been made in the way workers' complaints are handled by the Equal Employment Opportunity agencies. These include the following.

- If you file a complaint, it must be opened within a reasonable period of time, but no later than 90 days.

- If you live in a state which enforces age discrimination laws, you and your employer must be notified that the agency has received your complaint notice. If you lodge the complaint with the state agency, the Equal Employment Opportunity Commission (EEOC) will withhold the processing of the complaint until it obtains the results of the state's action.

- Your identity must be kept confidential in order to protect you from harassment by an indignant employer.

- The agency will first try to resolve the matter through conciliation with your employer. If that is unsuccessful, you must be notified promptly so that you can take private action.

- If your complaint is considered unsuitable for litigation, you must be notified of your legal

rights and responsibilities.
     - If you live far from an ADEA office, you can
take your case to the nearest Department of Labor
office, or phone the ADEA collect, or write to
them.

Passage of the law has already produced these
results.

     - Thousands of workers have been able to post-
pone retirement.

     - There is evidence that more employers are
using job performance criteria rather than age as
a basis for hiring and firing.

     - There has been a sharp increase in the number
of age discrimination lawsuits filed with Federal
and state agencies - from 5,734 in the fiscal year
1979 to 15,311 in fiscal 1981. One of these was
filed by a 62-year old sales manager of General
Motors who was fired so that a younger, lower
salaried executive could replace him. At last he
was suing for $69 million!

"Discrimination on account of age is as bad as
discrimination on account of sex or race or anything else."   - Claude Pepper

Recent court rulings have been in favor of the
older worker. For example, a 47-year old administrator for a financially troubled transportation
agency was fired, despite his outstanding work
record, so that a younger man could be hired at
lower pay. The older man sued, and was awarded
over $200,000 in back pay and damages. A part-time
order writer for a prominent mail order house was
fired after five months on the job when her employer discovered she was 70, the firm's mandatory
retirement age. She filed a discrimination suit
and won back pay and additional money for "humiliation and embarrassment."

Another case involved a school board which was
sued for refusing to hire an experienced, 55-year
old teacher on the grounds that the community
could not afford his higher salary. The court
ruled in favor of the teacher, claiming that cost
saving is an inadequate defense to a charge of age
discrimination.

Within a period of 10 years, a New Jersey corporation replaced 24 executives who were in their

fifties with younger, less experienced persons so that it could beat them out of their pensions. Two of the dismissed executives won their lawsuit.

In 1982, a California appeals court granted a complainant the right to sue the company he had loyally served for 32 years on the grounds of wrongful discharge. The court decreed that 32 years of continuous service constitutes an implicit contract between two parties which is governed by a "covenant of good faith and fair dealing," and which should not be breached without good cause.

Another landmark case occurred in Michigan where the court ruled in favor of an employee who was dismissed without prior warning or hearing as was specified in the company's employee handbook.

In March 1983, the Supreme Court ruled that Congress had acted within its constitutional authority when it overturned a ruling by a Wyoming Federal District Court which upheld the forced retirement of a 55-year old game warden by the State's Game and Fish Department. The decision is a landmark because it contradicts a 1976 Supreme Court decision which held that state governments had a certain immunity from the ADEA.

"Fighting age discrimination probably seems a peculiar cause to urge upon the young. But unless they join the battle, they will one day face the same cruelties now being practiced upon workers over 50 who are routinely wrinkled up and thrown away."   - Patricia O'Toole[1]

HOW CAN YOU TELL IF YOU HAVE SUFFICIENT GROUNDS?

Age discrimination can be so blatant that there's no problem in being able to supply the required evidence. There's the case of the sales manager who was told on July 30 that he would be replaced on August 1, because "It's time for the younger generation to take over." Even in this case the EEOC was reluctant to proceed, because the younger replacement was the boss' son.

Most discrimination is subtle. No employer wants to invite the penalties of the ADEA. For example, employers have used subtle forms of harassment in order to induce a worker to quit. These include being ignored, having your office or desk moved to a poor location, or creating a work situation which makes it almost impossible to do your job. For example, a sociologist was hired to work on a special college research project and, when the promised state funds failed to come through, she was harassed into quitting. The harassments included sharing with two other persons a small desk in an office not much larger than a broom closet, excessive delays in the delivery of essential supplies, and a deafening drilling in the office above.

After you are hired, you're asked to submit proof of age. (This is a legal request.) Soon after, you are fired and you're certain it had to do with your age.

Someone less experience is hired or promoted over you, despite concrete evidence of your good or excellent work record.

You are dismissed without good cause after serving your employer for many years. Evidence of "no good cause" would include having received regular pay raises, promotions and/or commendations through the years, with little or no criticism of your work.

You are dismissed in retaliation for doing what is just and necessary as a good citizen and employee. For example, "whistle blowers" have been dismissed for reporting to the authorities illegal or dangerous practices committed by their supervisors or employers.

You complain to the personnel department about age or sex discrimination regarding a pay increase and/or promotion. Shortly thereafter, you are fired.

You are fired just before you become eligible to retire early on a company pension, or before your employer is due to pay you a fat commission, or because you refuse to "play ball" with a lecherous boss. Such practices violate the test of good faith and fair dealing.

There is evidence that your employer systematically practices discrimination against workers age 40 to 70 by "limiting, segregating or classifying them in a way which deprives them of opportunities for promotion and raises."

A verbal guarantee of certain benefits, such as medical insurance, paid vacation and long term job security, made during the job interview fails to materialize. The sociologist referred to above had not been told that the funds for the project she was hired to direct were not guaranteed and that her job was in jeopardy if they failed to come through. Courts now hold that a verbal promise made at the time of hiring takes on the binding force of a written contract.

HOW CAN YOU PROVE IT?

A lesson to anyone who is eager to rush off to a lawyer or the EEOC is provided in the case of Gill v. Union Carbide, Inc. in which the court upheld the employer on the grounds that it had a reasonable set of performance evaluation criteria which were applied fairly to employees at all occupational levels, which had been clearly communicated to all of them, and had informed them of their performance rating.

One way is to get a sworn affidavit from reliable witnesses. Another is to tactfully ask the employer to put any promises made at the time you are hired in writing. If you sign a contract, make sure that it clearly specifies the job benefits, your responsibilities, the scope of your authority, and the person to whom you should report. If any of these conditions are changed without notice to you, the employer has failed to live up to the terms of the contract.

Find out if your state has a ruling that every employment agreement involves an implied guarantee of fair dealing. Some states, like Massachusetts and New Hampshire, have recently introduced such regulations. Less than 30% of workers in 1982 were not protected by an employment contract or a union's collective bargaining agreement. The courts are now taking steps to rectify this situation through the use of the implicit contract or fair dealing guarantee, even when there is no written document.

Take careful note of the "fringe benefits" clause before signing an employment contract. Unless these have been clearly spelled out, you may wake up one day to learn that you're not going to get the promised holiday pay, the tuition refund, and the medical insurance. The sociologist mentioned earlier learned several months after she was hired that she was not going to get the medical insurance and holiday pay promised at the interview. Since the contract was vague on the terms of these benefits, there was no way she could get satisfaction at the time.

Also, make sure the criteria of "satisfactory performance" are clearly defined if the contract says, "continued employment, promotions, and salary increases depend on satisfactory performance." Employers have used the "substandard performance" argument as an excuse to fire, refuse promotion, or downgrade older workers. Without clearly defining a set of criteria, the employer can use any excuse to get rid of you.

Even if your work has been below standard, the employer should have given you sufficient warning in the form of written performance evaluations before any legal dismissal action can be taken.

After years of getting satisfactory to excellent performance ratings, you suddenly get a poor rating. Shortly thereafter, you are dismissed, transferred, demoted, or denied the expected promotion or pay raise. There is the case of a 52-year old woman who, after 18 years as buyer for a well known retail chain, was dismissed for "insubordination." She had never been fired before in her life. A discrimination suit revealed later that several other long term employees in their fifties had also been summarily cut off.

You are dismissed after you refuse to support a breach of public policy or an illegal act which is requested by your supervisor or employer. A recent California Supreme Court decreed that a salesman had the right to sue his employer for firing him because of his refusal to take part in a price fixing scheme.

WHAT CAN YOU DO ABOUT AGE DISCRIMINATION?

If you can prove it, the employer must pay you the earnings you should have received, including back pay, pension plan contributions plus interest, and vacation pay. All seniority rights must be restored.

Avoid taking action until you are certain you have a good case, because it may cost plenty if you lose. Even though the law protects you from dismissal on the grounds of retaliation, your employer can find subtle ways to make your life so miserable on the job that you will want to quit. On the other hand, if you stick to your guns, the cumulative effect of these insults on your morale can affect your work performance and your relations with co-workers, thereby giving the employer cause for dismissing you.

Before you file a complaint, speak to someone at the nearest ADEA office and/or get the advice of a nonprofit advocacy organization.

THE COMPANY MANUAL (OR HANDBOOK) is your ally. It describes the responsibilities of each job, the criteria used to evaluate a worker's performance, and the procedures for filing grievances. It should be made available to every new employee. If you think you are the victim of discrimination, ask to see the handbook. If it's unavailable, without reasonable explanation, your suspicions should be aroused.

The handbook might reveal that the reason for your dismissal or failure to get a promotion or pay increase is justified. On the other hand, it might show that your employer has failed to uphold the job termination rules or that he has broken an implicit contract with his employees.

Success or failure depends solely on one's attitude. All things are conquerable. It's simply a matter of beliefs and accompanying attempts.
David V.A. Ambrose

In 1982, New York State's highest court ruled in favor of a 57-year old copywriter for a major publisher who was dismissed without prior warning. The decision was based on a breach of implicit contract as revealed in a statement in the company manual that workers would be dismissed "for just and sufficient cause only...after all practical steps toward rehabilitation had been taken and failed."

According to some labor lawyers, any statement in the manual or handbook which refers to permanent employment after the worker passes a probationary period could be interpreted as an implicit contract. In several states, the courts have already found legal protection against dismissal in such statements. Even an application form which contains such a statement can create an implied contract.

JOB DESCRIPTIONS for each occupation in a well-run organization should be fully described in the company manual and/or employee handbook. A job description specifies all the duties and responsibilities of a worker, the skills, education and experience required for the job, and the criteria used for evaluating work performance. A job description is used by supervisors to train new employees and evaluate a worker's performance. It is also useful to an employee as a standard for judging his or her own performance.

Make sure you have met all the stated responsibilities to the best of your ability. Do this each time you are promoted or transferred to another job within the company. Make sure you are kept informed of all changes in the job description.

Use the stated criteria to assess your own job performance. Has your attendance record been good? Has your work performance been at least up to standard? Have your relations with co-workers and supervisors been good? Better yet, have you been told so by a supervisor?

Your file should contain periodic job performance ratings in writing. These should have been made available to you.

KEEP A RECORD OF ALL COMMENDATIONS YOU RECEIVE for good work. Note also your exceptional achievements which have helped the company. However, don't get so compulsive about it that you jot down every insignificant event. You may end up losing your spontaneity and, in the long run, damaging your performance record. Take note of the times you are absent and late, also. These are precautionary measures in case there is a conflict later on between what a supervisor says about you and what you know to be the actual facts.

DISCUSS THE MATTER WITH YOUR EMPLOYER before you go rushing off to the nearest ADEA office to file a complaint. In the nicest manner you can muster, remind him or her of your accomplishments. It's possible that your exceptional qualities and contributions have been taken for granted, and you might even get a raise.

Small and medium-sized firms (with up to 1,000 employees) are more likely to be poorly informed about age discrimination laws than are major corporations. Even in large companies, lower level and young supervisors are generally less informed. This is where age discrimination usually takes place. Also, an employer may be so busy that he fails to keep up with the laws.

One clever employee sa d his job by pointing out that the cost of paying his retirement pension over the years would amount to more than the savings the company would gain by replacing him with a younger, lower paid worker who is more likely to quit as soon as a better opportunity knocks. There's the case of a 62-year old employee whose much younger supervisor frequently brought up the subject of retirement. Instead of getting angry, the employee calmly explained the law to him, and the matter was never brought up again.

EMPLOYERS MAY USE DELAYING TACTICS, such as offering a nice, fat severance check to an employee who is about to be dismissed. This is done not out of altruism, but to protect the company's hide. Although most companies do this out of fairness, it has been used a lure to keep the employee from filing an age discrimination claim or to delay the filing of a claim until the deadline has passed. Experts also say that hiring an outplacement firm to help dismissed workers find a new job can also be a delaying tactic.

"It seems strange that it takes a lawsuit to bring about an extensive age analysis of a company's workforce....Early detection of problems facing older workers can be rectified by retraining, job reassignment, counseling or combinations of these. Positive human resource management for older workers should be employer policy."
Michael D. Batten, Center for Studies on Social Policy, University of Southern California

HOW CAN TELL YOU DIDN'T GET THE JOB BECAUSE OF AGE OR SEX DISCRIMINATION?

This is more difficult to do than if you are already employed. Nevertheless, job seekers have won suits based on this charge. It depends on the evidence. For example, any one of the following should arouse your suspicion.

    - You pass the required qualifying tests and

are still refused a job.

- You are denied the opportunity of taking such tests.

- You take the test, and you are positive that you did very well. However, you are informed that the reason why you cannot be hired is that you failed. You ask for verification, and it is denied.

(This happened to a 52-year old college graduate who had been a Phi Beta Kappa student in mathematics years earlier. She recently completed a computer science program of study, again at the head of her class, and applied for a job in a well known company. The entrance examination was, in her words, "a breeze." Yet, she was informed later that she was not hired because she had failed the test.)

- Your credentials for the job are more than adequate, but you are not hired on the grounds that you "lack the formal education."

- You learn, from observation or through the grapevine, that the company has not been hiring any (or few) workers age 40 and older in the past few years. A report to the U.S. Senate's Special Committee on Aging, April 1980, states "if comparatively few older workers are hired, this could spell trouble..."

- You are asked to take a physical examination or some other test that is not relevant to the demands of the job.

- At the interview, you are asked to state your age or to submit proof of age, and you naively agree. You have good reason to believe that you were not hired because of your age. It is illegal for an employer to request such information before hiring you. (But it is legal to request this after you are hired.)

- The employer describes the requirements of the job, and then asks if you have any physical or mental handicap which prevents you from doing the job or if there are any other duties you cannot perform. You blurt out the fact that you have a minor handicap, but it does not interfere with your ability to do good work. You are certain you weren't hired because of this revelation.

Federal, and some state, laws prohibit U.S. government agencies and contractors from discrimination based on physical or mental handicaps which do not affect job performance.

- At the interview, you're asked if you belong to any association or organization. You blurt out the fact that you are a member of a political action group, such as the Gray Panthers or the ERA. You believe this is the only factor, in your otherwise outstanding qualifications for the job, which disqualified you.

The law prohibits employers from inquiring about membership in any organization other than one which is related to the occupation you are applying for (such as a trade union or professional association).

- In order to discourage you from accepting the job, the employer falsely tells you that you are not entitled to your own benefits as an employee because your working spouse is covered by health and insurance benefits.

- You receive a rejection notice, and you suspect discrimination. You then phone the interviewer and ask, tactfully, in what way you failed to meet the company's requirements. You are told that someone with better qualifications was hired. You ask what those qualifications are. (It's very likely that the person hired is better qualified than you are.) If you learn the person has less experience and was hired at a lower salary level, there is cause for suspicion.

Show me a woman garbage collector and I'll show you a woman who makes $30,000 a year. Show me some women electricians, roofers, tree trimmers, carpenters and mechanics, and I'll show you some well paid women. Only when women destroy forever the myth that cleanliness is next to godliness and truck driving ain't ladylike will we see women's salaries equal to men's. Merideth A.Tarney[3]

OLDER WOMEN FACE THE DOUBLE WHAMMY OF AGE AND SEX DISCRIMINATION

And, more often than for a man, getting a job depends more on good looks and youth than ability. Studies show that women and members of minority groups are most likely to be the victims of job discrimination. Even a Ph.D. is no protection against discrimination. A microbiologist with 20 years of research experience was fired so that a more attractive, but less qualified, younger woman could be hired.

A 1982 report to the U.S. Department of Labor showed that women's average weekly earnings are significantly lower than those of men in the same occupations. The National Research Council reports women are paid less than sixty cents for every dollar paid to men. In bookkeeping jobs, for example, women earn an average of $98 a week less than men.

Even in traditional "female" occupations, women earn less than their male colleagues and are less often promoted to managerial positions. Female elementary school teachers, for example, earn an average of $68 a week less than males; female hospital technicians earn $51 less.

In high technology and scientific jobs, where ability and education would appear to be the sole criteria for hiring and promoting, women still get the short end of the stick. A 1982 survey showed male computer systems analysts earned an average weekly salary of $546 compared to $420 earned by females. Female scientists and engineers earned 80% of the average man's salary and were promoted to managerial ranks only half as much.

A 1978 Study by Stanford University found that five years after graduation with a Master's Degree in Business Administration, males earned an average of $8,000 a year more than females. Another study reports that women, who comprise half the Federal labor force, hold only 6.25% of the top level positions.

Part of the problem lies in the fact that women workers are not included in the "old boy" networks which provide valuable contacts. Nor are they given the responsibilities which groom them for executive level positions.

Women also have to take some of the blame because many still train for the low status, low paying "pink collar" occupations (teaching, nursing, librarianship, clerical work, etc.) despite increased opportunities to enter better paying fields such as computer science and business administration. Also, women in general are not active members of labor organizations, which carry political clout.

Nevertheless, being a woman has its advantages. One of these is the plethora of groups and legal protections dedicated to shielding her from employment abuses and helping her to get ahead in the business and professional world. In the appendix you will see that the list of groups whose function is to help women workers is much longer than the list for older persons of both sexes. This disparity is not due to the author's bias. There simply aren't as many groups working for the welfare of the older job seeker at present.

Working women are protected by the following Federal laws.

- Age Discrimination in Employment Act (ADEA) which prohibits discrimination against persons age 40 to 70 regardless of sex.

- Title VII of the Civil Rights Act of 1967 which prohibits employment discrimination based on sex, race, religion and national origin.

- The Equal Pay Act which requires an employer to pay equal wages to women and men doing essentially equal work.

Title VII of the civil Rights Act of 1964 covers hiring, wages and salaries, job benefits, job advertisements, and job interviews. If a woman is hired at the same job title as a man, she must get equal pay. If a job is offered on condition that she accepts lower pay, that is against the law.

In 1980, a Federal district judge awarded over $16 million to 324 women employees of the Government Printing Office. They had sued on the grounds that the Office had been using a different job classification for men and women despite the fact that each did essentially the same work. The job classification for men paid an average of $25,000 a year, whereas the women were paid an average of $15, 000.

The Equal Pay Act of 1963 states that women and men should get the same pay for doing the same work. But the idea that they should receive equal pay for doing work requiring comparable (although not equal) skills and having comparable worth to the employer is relatively recent. It's based on the fact that jobs traditionally held by women, such as teaching, nursing and clerical work, pay poorly because these are "pink collar jobs." If the Supreme court supports this concept, nurses' salaries, for example, will rise to the level of salaries in "male" occupations which require a comparable level of skills and training and make an equivalent contribution.

A test case is the suit brought in 1981 by jail matrons whose job is to guard female prisoners at a Washington County jail in Hillsboro, Oregon. They received about $200 a month less pay than male prison guards. The women sued under Title VII of the Civil Rights Act of 1964 which prohibits discrimination on the basis of sex or race with regard to the "compensation, terms, conditions or privileges of employment."

To be successful, a woman has to be much better at her job than a man.   - Golda Meir

According to the law:

   - A woman cannot be forced to retire earlier than her male colleagues.

   - Company "perks" such as time for lunch, special parking, use of company cars and similar benefits must be assigned equally to men and women employees.

   - A help-wanted advertisement must not state, "Men only are considered."

   - If an employer specifies to a placement agency that he does not want women to be referred for a certain vacancy, such as selling mainframe computers, the agency cannot refuse to arrange an job interview for a qualified woman on those grounds. However, in jobs where sex is a bona fide qualification, such as modeling and acting, an employer can legally refuse to hire a women, and an employment agency can refuse to refer a woman for such a vacancy.

NOTE: Although you are not required by law to give your age on a job application form, it is legal to ask you to state your sex.

Nice guys finish last.   - Leo Durocher

WHERE TO GO FOR HELP IF YOU THINK YOU ARE THE VICTIM OF DISCRIMINATION

Before you spend a fortune filing a private lawsuit, discuss your situation with an advocacy group which helps disadvantaged persons. (Older workers are considered to be disadvantaged along with females and minority group members.) These often serve as ombudsmen in cases involving citizens and a public agency. Consider the resources given below and in the appendix.

The Suffolk County Family Service League, Inc., of New York, is an example of such a group. In 1981, this nonprofit agency helped over 2,000 persons over the age of 60 with advocacy and counseling through a program called Project SAFE (Service and Advocacy for the Elderly).

It is one of the many public and private agencies across the nation that serve as advocates for older persons. They help clients understand their rights, negotiate with larger organizations on their behalf, and often accompany the older person to a public agency. Some of them accept clients under the age of sixty.

If you have sufficient evidence, file a written complaint with the nearest office of the U.S. Department of Labor or with your state's Fair Employment Practices Agency. These are listed in the White Pages of your phone book.

The U.S. Equal Employment Opportunity Commission (EEOC) is the chief agency dispensing advice and information on how to file a charge of discrimination. Look in the phone book for the nearest local office (under "U.S. Government") or write to the Commission's main office which is located at 2401 E Street, NW, Washington, D.C. 20506.

A complaint must be filed within 180 days of the discrimination event. The law now requires your identity to be kept confidential until action is taken. If the employer is stupid enough to take any obvious retaliatory actions, you have additional legal grounds.

The EEOC will make an appointment for you to come in and discuss your case with the compliance officer. Be sure to bring a written list of your evidence so that you don't omit anything.

The first thing the agency will do is to investigate your charges and try to resolve the matter with the employer out of court. If this fails, the agency will start court action. There is such a backlog of cases brought before government agencies, it will probably take a long time before yours comes up.

The law requires that you file a claim with the Equal Employment Opportunity Commission AND with your state agency if it has an anti-discrimination law. This must be done within 60 days before you take private legal action or within 180 days of the alleged violation if you do not intend to take private action.

WORKING WOMEN helps women in white and blue collar jobs below the top management level. It advocates equal treatment in overtime pay and grievance procedures, job descriptions for clerical and blue collar occupations regardless of level, regular salary reviews, the right to refuse to do personal favors for the boss such as getting coffee or doing his Christmas shopping, and other matters which have weighed against women. It offers women legal advice on such matters as how to get raises and promotions and whether there is clear evidence of discrimination.

THE CIVIL LIBERTIES UNION has chapters all over the country. Look in the White Pages or contact the Civil Liberties Union headquarters at 132 West 43rd Street, New York, N.Y. 10036 (or phone 212/944-9800) for the address of the nearest chapter. If your request for counsel is accepted, the Union may check the employer's files to learn the reasons for not hiring or dismissing you. Any evidence of illegality is turned over to the state's Human Rights Commission, or to the EEOC if your state doesn't have one.

THE NATIONAL LEGAL AID AND DEFENDER ASSOCIATION has over 2,800 offices across the nation which deal with civil and criminal matters. It can refer you to attorneys who specialize in this area of the law. Fees are often based on ability to pay. It also publishes a directory of offices and members. The directory (which cost $6.00 in 1982) and other information can be obtained by writing to the association at 1625 K Street, NW, Washington, D.C. 20006, or you can phone (202) 452-0620.

THE NATIONAL EMPLOYMENT LAW PROJECT is another place where you can obtain an attorney referral list. The New York office phone number is (212) 870-2121). It, too, helps persons who believe they are the victims of age discrimination.

Some private lawyers specialize in discrimination suits, but their fees are high (from $100 to $200 an hour in 1983.) However, it's possible to find more reasonably priced legal services.

GREY LAW, INC. of Los Angeles is a nonprofit law firm that serves persons who are 60-plus.

THE LAW SCHOOL OF A LOCAL UNIVERSITY may be able to give you advice and/or referrals. Hunter College of the City University of New York, for example, has a special Institute on Law and Rights of Older Adults.

THE AMERICAN BAR ASSOCIATION sponsors the National Bar Activation Project for the Elderly which recently began helping local bar associations initiate legal services for older persons with modest incomes. There may be reduced fees or free legal work by volunteer attorneys. Contact your local bar association for current information or write to the national headquarters at 1155 East 50th Street, Chicago, Ill. 60637.

THE AMERICAN ASSOCIATION OF RETIRED PERSONS has a project, called Legal Counsel for the Elderly, which involves volunteer lawyers helping low income persons age 60-plus with their problems at no charge. In 1982 there was more than 340 practitioners and 43 law firms involved in the program. Its address is 1909 K Street, NW, Washington, D.C. 20049 and the phone number is (202) 331-4215.

EQUAL RIGHTS ADVOCATES (ERA) deals with sex discrimination suits. It brings class action suits on behalf of its plaintiffs who are victims of discrimination in employment, and gives legal advice to victims of discrimination. Its headquarters are located at 1370 Mission Street, San Francisco, CA 94103 and the phone number is (415) 621-0505.

LEGAL SERVICES FOR THE ELDERLY helps persons living in the New York metropolitan area who meet the general poverty guidelines. It is funded by the Legal Services Corporation. A case may be handled by its own lawyers or referred to another agency.

The address is 132 West 43rd Street, New York, NY
and the phone number is (212) 391-0120.

SUGGESTED READINGS ON THE SUBJECT

The American Bar Association will send you the
following publications if you send one dollar for
each to: Order Billing, American Bar Association,
1155 East 60th Street, Chicago, Ill. 60637.

.The American Lawyer: How to Choose One
and Use One

.Your Rights Over Age 50

The Rights of Older Persons by the American Civil
Liberties Union. Send $2.50 plus postage to Avon
Books, Mail Order Dept., 250 West 55th Street, New
York, N.Y. 10019.

Termination Handbook, by Robert Coulson, president
of the American Arbitration Association. (Free
Press, New Jersey 08370, $15.95)

All the Justice I Could Afford, by Eugene V.
Goodman. (Harper, Brace & Yokanovich, 1983)

*The real costs of age discrimination involve more
than monetary value. They involve the misuse or
incomplete use of thousands of older workers and
untold amounts of lost productivity. The loss to
the labor force and the economy, and the burden to
the retirement income system, are too complex to
quantify....The costs can be reduced and, hopeful-
ly, eliminated only through a vigorous civil
rights strategy and an educational awareness program.* - Toward a National Older Worker Policy,
Special Committee on Aging, United States Senate,
September 1981.

1.® 1981 by The New York Times Company. Reprinted
by permission.

2. As quoted in "Toward a national older worker
policy: An information paper for the use by the
Special Committee on Aging, U.S. Senate," September 1981.

3. As quoted in a letter to the editor of The New
York Times, March 9, 1981.

8

SELF-ASSESSMENT TIPS

You are undergoing a dramatic life change at present. Either you've lost your job, or your present job is driving you nuts, or you find that retirement isn't a bed of roses. Now is the time to explore new opportunities and chart a fresh course in life.

First, you must throw all modesty to the winds and take stock of yourself - your aptitudes (talents) and the skills and knowledge you have acquired in your lifetime. Next, learn which occupations and work environments match these assets. Then, determine whether your knowledge and/or skills need some updating and, if they do, enroll in an adult education course. Only after you have done all these things will you be ready to tackle the resume and job interview.

Some people need the advice of an experienced career counselor to do a self-assessment. Some can do it themselves with the help of a good guidebook on the subject. Others know what they want, but need a little hand holding from books such as this one.

IDENTIFY WHAT YOU CAN DO AND ENJOY DOING.

No matter how much education you've had, or how long ago you held a paid job, you have accumulated a valuable storehouse of skills, knowledge and experiences which can be applied to several occupations, not just one. Whether you are a homemaker looking for a job after years of raising a family, or a man whose job has been mowed down by technological change, you possess a unique set of assets which can be put to use in more ways than you think. And, in lean times, the job seeker who keeps as many options open as possible is better off than the narrow specialist.

Life can only be understood backward, but it must be lived forward. - Kierkegaard.

Doing a self-assessment is like drawing up a balance sheet of your assets and liabilities. ASSETS refers to your special skills, interests, aptitudes and your work related achievements and experiences. A set of skills and aptitudes is something you can do as well as, or better than, most people. LIABILITIES, in this case, refers to any need for further training or education, and any restrictions on your occupational choices caused by health or family reasons.

You can identify your assets by scrutinizing, one by one, your favorite leisure activities, your education and training, and your paid and non-paid work experience. To begin your self assessment, take several sheets of paper, and across the top of each page write one of the following headings.

A. MY PAID WORK EXPERIENCE
       1. JOB RESPONSIBILITIES
       2. SKILLS AND APTITUDES REQUIRED
       3. WHAT I LIKED MOST ABOUT IT
       4. WHAT I DISLIKED ABOUT IT

B. MY VOLUNTARY WORK EXPERIENCE
       1. JOB RESPONSIBILITIES
       2. SKILLS AND APTITUDES REQUIRED
       3. WHAT I LIKED MOST ABOUT IT
       4. WHAT I DISLIKED ABOUT IT

C. MY EDUCATION AND TRAINING
D. MY FAVORITE LEISURE ACTIVITIES
E. THE JOBS I WOULD LIKE TO HAVE
F. PERSONAL FACTORS

YOUR JOB RESPONSIBILITIES On the first sheet of paper, list the paid jobs you've held, including part-time and freelance work. List them in reverse order, starting with the most recent job and going back in time. Leave ample space under each one to include the following.

    1. Name and address of employer
    2. Your supervisor's name
    3. Your job title
    4. Your major responsibilities
    5. Your major achievements and contributions
    6. The dates you began and left each job
    7. Starting and final salary or wage

SKILLS AND APTITUDES REQUIRED Look over your list of responsibilities and achievements, and ask yourself, "What assets do I possess which make me good at certain kinds of work?" Look also beyond the obvious ones, such typing, filing, bookkeeping, selling or woodworking. For example, are your strong points any of the following?

initiative	detail work
creativity	leadership
writing	fast worker
quick to learn	lots of energy
dealing with people	problem solving
carrying out orders	well organized

Write down every single asset that your work experience supports. Read the following list to get ideas and see if there are any you have overlooked. Notice that action words predominate. Action words carry more of a wallop than passive words, and you should liberally use those which describe your qualifications on your resume or informational letter. Check those words which express what you can do. Then go through the list a second time and check those that you do particularly well. Finally, check the ones which you enjoy most. If you use different colors it will be easier to distinguish the different categories.

According to Josephine Lerro, director of human resources at TempsAmerica, you should be able to market the skills you enjoy doing in the business world. The nice thing about this simple exercise is that you can identify such skills and experiences yourself and add them to your resume, whether they are skills acquired in your life experiences or through business experiences. Use a dictionary to find other action words which are more relevant to your situation.

public speaking	interviewing
designing	acting
inventing	delegating
directing	purchasing
analyzing	recruiting
appraising	lobbying
repairing	team building
driving	mapping
revising	supervising
cataloging	mediating
scheduling	motivating
screening	catering
negotiating	selling
classifying	fund raising
consulting	hosting
training	organizing

Next, ask yourself, "What else did I do and learn on the job that I can use in another position?" For example:

DID YOU LEARN TO OPERATE A MACHINE?
sewing, industrial, robot, automobile, drill
press, X-ray, centrifuge, etc.

DID YOU LEARN TO OPERATE OFFICE EQUIPMENT?
paper copier, overhead projector, calculator,
telephone switchboard, word processor, mainframe
computer, etc.

DID YOU LEARN A SPECIAL SKILL?
reading blueprints and maps, drawing charts and
graphs, programming a computer, etc.

Make a list of everything, no matter how trivial
it seems to you. You'd be surprised at the number
of people who don't know how to use, for example,
a paper copier or an electric typewriter. Employers value such expertise because it saves them
the time and money needed to train a new worker.

Let's suppose you are a real estate salesperson
who is planning to change careers. First, you
would identify every single task and responsibility you had in this occupation. Next, you would
analyze each in detail. Each one you identify
involves exercising one or more skills and areas
of knowledge. The following is a list of some of
the skills that are required in selling real estate.

ESTIMATING the market value of houses

SALESMANSHIP, or influencing people to buy houses.

OFFICE SKILLS: organizing and maintaining accurate
records, typing, answering telephone inquiries,
etc.

MATHEMATICAL SKILLS: estimating mortgage payments, interest rates, etc.

WRITING SKILLS: writing newspaper ads, sales
notices and articles for the real estate newsletter; composing letters to clients and members of
your real estate association

INTERVIEWING SKILLS: getting information from and
about prospective tenants and landlords.

MAP READING SKILLS: studying district maps, reading blueprints and road maps.

RESEARCH SKILLS: studying documents, census reports and survey data; making on-site observations of a neighborhood

OPERATING EQUIPMENT: operating a computer and reading computer printouts; using computer software; duplicating machine; driving a car, etc.

As you can see, these and other skills not mentioned can be applied to other occupations as well.

WHAT YOU LIKED/DISLIKED MOST ABOUT THE JOB
Take two sheets of paper and write one of the above headings on each. Then, for each job you've had, write down the aspects you particularly liked and disliked. Put them under the following categories.

1. JOB RESPONSIBILITIES

2. WORK SCHEDULE: night shift, overtime, deadlines, part-time

3. PHYSICAL DEMANDS OF THE JOB: standing, sitting, lifting heavy objects, peering into a microscope or computer screen, detailed eye-work, involves traveling a lot, etc.

4. "PERSONALITY" OF THE COMPANY - conservative, competitive, relaxed, fast paced, hierarchical, large, small, family business, etc.

5. WORK SETTING - indoors, outdoors, in the city, in the suburbs, cramped, spacious, modern, own office, sharing office with others, cultural attractions nearby, etc.

On a new page, transfer those characteristics you would like to have in your next job or career, in order of priority, under this title: WHAT I WOULD LIKE IN MY NEXT JOB OR CAREER

Repeat this exercise on a new page entitled, WHAT I WANT TO AVOID IN MY NEXT JOB OR CAREER

Finally, study all your lists, searching for characteristics which occur throughout all the jobs and work settings you've held. Here is a list to get you started.
    writing
    planning
    researching
    detail work

entertaining
helping people
public speaking
keeping records
solving problems
working with plants
working with animals
working under pressure
working indoors/outdoors
working alone with ideas
working alone/with others
creating, inventing, designing
carrying out other people's ideas
applying mathematical/arithmetic skills
exchanging ideas, information with others

NEXT, PICTURE YOURSELF IN THE IDEAL JOB. Imagine
the following:
- YOUR WORK RESPONSIBILITIES
- THE PEOPLE YOU WOULD BE WORKING WITH
- WORK CONDITIONS
- WORK SETTING

NEXT, PICTURE YOURSELF IN THE WORST POSSIBLE JOB
and do the same analysis.

The purpose of these exercises is to help you
identify occupations which utilize your abilities
and interests, and which you'll enjoy most. Those
mentioned in the following examples are in no
danger of being replaced by computers. All it
takes to prepare for them are a few adult education courses.

For example, if you are good at arts and crafts
and enjoy helping people, you can work as an art
therapist in a nursing home, a psychiatric hospital, or with emotionally or physically handicapped
children. If you are good at analytic reasoning
and solving numerical problems, and you enjoy
working with people, you can teach computer programming in an adult education class or computer
literacy to office workers.

*All of you have untapped resources and skills
which you don't recognize. I ran an ad in the
newspaper recently for a telephone receptionist. I
wanted a mature person, not someone who is inex-
perienced, who might be abrasive. Thee were about
thirty inquiries, and very few were women returning to the workforce or retirees. You apparently
lack confidence. You don't know that we need you.
Believe me, we do.* - Josephine Lerro addressing

older job seekers at the "Ability is Ageless" Job
Fair in New York City.

VOLUNTARY AND OTHER NON-PAID WORK On a separate
page, list all the non-paid work you've done.
Include homemaking and child rearing responsibilities. Then do the same analysis as you did for
PAID WORK EXPERIENCE, using the same guides.
You'll discover there are many words on the skills
lists which apply to the work women do as homemakers and community volunteers. For example, here
are some skills women develop as homemakers which
are directly transferable to paid jobs.

MANAGING: Setting production goals (family plans);
supervising; maintaining family teamwork.

COUNSELING: Children, spouse, children's pals,
neighbors.

CLERICAL: Setting up files; keeping records; typing correspondence; editing homework.

NURSING: sick members of family, family pets.

FINANCIAL PLANNING, BOOKKEEPING: Budgeting the
family income; keeping a balance sheet on income
and expenditures; income tax preparation; keeping
track of debts, loan payments, real estate mort-
gages and investments, etc.

MANUAL DEXTERITY/ARTS AND CRAFTS: Sewing; uphol-
stering; repair of small engines; carpentry (and
any other work requiring precise eye-brain-hand
coordination).

Ann Slater, director of the Northampton County
Area Agency on Aging in Pennsylvania recommends
that a homemaker with little or no paid work
experience is qualified to be an activity aide in
senior centers or an outreach worker. Gladys
Sprinkle, director of the Over-60 Counseling and
Employment Service in Chevy Chase, Maryland, says
such women are excellent for helping older people
in home care and in child care. She cites one
widow, who has been supporting herself for about
10 years this way, who was remembered in three
wills.

Women who are looking for their first paid job in
years should consider non-paid work as a source of
job related skills and experiences. Many women,

for example, have developed skills in volunteer
work which they later use to get paid jobs. Displaced homemakers who get entry level or part-time
jobs as a result of their volunteer work are often
able to move up to better paying, full-time jobs.
Women's associations, such as Displaced Homemakers
and Catalyst, have had much success in helping
women identify the skills acquired through non-
paid work, and then negotiate these into paid
jobs. If you need advice, contact one or more of
the associations listed in chapter 6 and the appendix.

The following list shows some of the skills involved in volunteer activities. The purpose of
this partial analysis is to show you how it's
done. If you need help, a good guidebook or a
professional career counselor will help you identify additional skills.

Bear in mind that of all the responsibilities a
woman has in volunteer work, committee appoint-
ments and leadership positions are especially
valued by employers, so put these at the top of
your list.

1. FUND RAISING
        - Salesmanship
        - Planning/organizing fund drives
        - Public speaking
        - Knowledge of community resources

2. TREASURER
        - Bookkeeping
        - Purchasing for large events
        - Budgeting

3. CLERICAL
        - Keeping accurate, detailed records
        - Typing documents
        - Writing letters and other documents
        - Organizing and filing documents

4. PUBLIC RELATIONS
        - Public speaking
        - Planning, promoting, carrying out events
        - Writing copy for the media
        - Interviewing community leaders

5. PRESIDENT/COMMITTEE CHAIRPERSON
        - Organizing events
        - Managing others
        - Building teamwork

6. POLITICAL WORKER
   - Lobbying (influencing others)
   - Doing research

7. EDITOR/WRITER OF NEWSLETTER
   - Writing
   - Editing
   - Doing layout, art and graphics work

8. HOSPITAL WORK
   - Counseling
   - Teaching arts and crafts
   - Nurses aide

Fifty is nifty.
- Josephine Piscitelli, at her fiftieth birthday party held in New York City.

YOUR TRAINING AND EDUCATION - Education refers to the knowledge and skills you have acquired by attending a formal institution, such as a high school, technical or vocational school, college or university. It is validated by a diploma, certificate, degree and by C.E.U.s (Continuing Education Units).

Training is what you've learned in non-formal settings such as workshops, lectures, seminars and on-the-job. It is generally measured by actual performance. Even a one day seminar or workshop should be included in your resume, if the topic is relevant to the job you want.

First, list all your relevant education and training. Then, ask yourself:

1. Which courses or training did I like best? Why?

2. Which courses or training did I dislike, or like the least? Why?

Next, list all the relevant extracurricular activities you were involved in. Do this only if you were recently a student. For example,

   - Served as discussion group leader.
   - Planned and organized class outings
   - Edited alumni newsletter
   - Class president

Include, also, those special events in your past which served as creative learning experiences, even those ugly experiences which have resulted in personal growth and increased knowledge.

A case reported to the U.S. House Select Committee on Aging involved a woman who had suffered through a particularly bitter divorce. Naively, she agreed to hire the lawyer recommended by a family friend. Later, she learned that he was also her husband's lawyer and an incompetent, too busy or unwilling to be of any help to her. This forced her to learn a few law facts on her own.

First, she had to learn how to use the law library. Then, step-by-step, she acquired the skills which eventually led to her becoming a self-taught expert in domestic law. Then, with the help of a Displaced Homemaker Center, she was able to get on-the-job training which led to a paid job as a legal para-professional. This provided an opportunity to establish a divorce clinic to help other women in similar circumstances.

YOUR INTERESTS AND LEISURE ACTIVITIES - List the skills and talents involved in your favorite leisure activities. Here are a few.

- Repairing cars
- Learning foreign languages
- Sketching/painting
- Playing a musical instrument
- Writing short stories or poetry
- Creating computer programs in FORTRAN

Next, list your special interests. They may be photography, baking, art, music, astronomy, theater, medicine, politics, the stock market, sewing, etc.

These exercises will also help you to identify the occupations and work settings you are most likely to enjoy. Generally, people do best what they enjoy the most.

The exercises will also prepare you for the job interview and job application form, where you'll be asked to state your interests and hobbies. Employers want to know this because they've learned that workers who enjoy their job and work environment are more productive. They also want to avoid hiring a square peg for a round hole of a job slot.

A review of your interests, talents, training and education should show a pattern of characteristics which, ideally, will match the jobs you've had. If not, now is the time to choose an occupation that will be a joy instead of just a job.

PERSONAL FACTORS should also be considered in narrowing down your list of choices.

- YOUR ENERGY LEVEL should match the demands of the job and the pace of the company. Some companies, such as those in the publishing and media industries, are fast paced and operate under frequent deadlines. Will you be able to handle it?

- YOUR PHYSICAL LIMITATIONS should also be taken into account. Does the job involve more walking, reading, standing, sitting, writing or talking than you can take? Suppose you spend a lot of time and money studying computer programming only to discover, after you are hired, that your eyes can't take staring into a lighted screen six hours daily? Possessing the right skills and aptitudes won't do you much good in this case.

- YOUR BIORHYTHMS: Are you in peak form in the morning, afternoon, early evening, or after midnight? If your peak hours do not fall within the traditional, 9-to-5 work schedule, consider companies which operate on flexitime schedules. Or, look into the growing demand for "cottage industry" workers - people who are paid to work at home through the use of high technology equipment. If you have real, weird hours, consider starting a small, home business.

- IS YOUR PERSONALITY COMPATIBLE WITH THE ORGANIZATION? Are you happiest in a relatively tight or loose structured organization? Companies vary in their decision making structure and the values which they reward. Conservative industries, such as oil, banking and insurance, tend to follow a top-down management style in which orders issued from above are expected to be carried out unquestioningly. Some experts believe the older worker, brought up to respect authority, is more adapted to this style. But, not everyone fits the same mold.

The new, high technology firms, on the other hand, tend to follow a pattern of decision making in which employees at all levels work together to improve productivity. No matter what the job status, everyone is expected to play a creative role. If you favor this type of structure, consider whether you would also like what usually accompanies it - a fast paced, highly charged atmosphere. According to Allan A. Kennedy and Terrence E. Deal, co-authors of Corporate Cultures, there are other types, such as the "macho" companies which reward aggressive go-getters and super-competitors. The entertainment industry, for example, falls in this category.

A review of all the lists you have made should give you a general picture of which occupations best suit you.

SKILLS YOU CAN TRANSFER TO OTHER OCCUPATIONS Now comes the fun part. Write down the jobs you think you are best qualified to do. For example, a woman who had worked as a staff aide with an overseas United Nations mission was hired as an administrative assistant in a large corporation. The same skills and experience - planning, arranging and scheduling conferences, trips and business luncheons - were applicable.

Despite the celebrated shortage of engineers, many who are 40-plus can't find jobs because their training has been made obsolete by new technologies. Still, they possess valuable, marketable assets which can be transferred to other careers. These include analytic and quantitative aptitudes and technical skills.

For example, engineers have found jobs as managers in high technology firms, as mathematics teachers in high schools, as salespersons in computer firms, and in financial departments of companies. With a few adult education courses, they can become safety inspectors, computer repairers, or computer programmers.

Persons with liberal arts degrees also have plenty of opportunities, despite the recent, sharp decline in jobs which traditionally require a Bachelor's Degree. Among the abilities they possess are written and oral communication, creative thinking, and problem solving of a high order. Such skills are valued in a variety of occupations: advertising, training and human resource development, management, and writing for scientific and high technology publications.

If you're wondering how the skills you acquired as homemaker/mother and volunteer are transferable to the business world, here are some suggestions from Ms. Lerro.

SOLICITED DONATIONS FOR HOSPITAL

1. SKILLS AND APTITUDES INVOLVED: verbal skills, ability to sell an idea, fund raising, public speaking, doing research.

2. JOBS WHICH UTILIZE THESE ASSETS: telephone soliciting, marketing surveys, receptionist, sales representative, retail sales.

ARRANGED GARAGE SALES/ARTS & CRAFTS EXHIBITS AND BUFFET DINNERS FOR LARGE GROUPS

1. SKILLS AND OTHER ASSETS INVOLVED: organizing, planning, ordering, calculating, coordinating, hosting, purchasing.

2. JOBS WHICH UTILIZE THESE ASSETS: administrative assistant, executive secretary, purchasing agent, owning your own catering business, manager in a restaurant.

COMMITTEE CHAIRPERSON

1. SKILLS AND OTHER ASSETS INVOLVED: administration, training, communication skills, team building, researching.

2. JOBS WHICH UTILIZE THESE ASSETS: training representative in a retail organization, administrative assistant in a sales promotion department, restaurant hostess.

THE 1982/83 OCCUPATIONAL OUTLOOK HANDBOOK which is published by the U.S. Department of Labor, should be at your side as you do this exercise. It classifies about 250 occupations into 20 different clusters of related "job families."

For example, if you are good at, and enjoy, helping people, you would look at these job families. (1) Teachers, librarians and counselors and (2) Registered nurses, pharmacists, dietitians, therapists and physician's aides.

If you want a job which utilizes your creative abilities, the job family which includes writers, artists and entertainers might interest you.

Let's suppose you're thinking of going into the field of marketing and sales. There are many different occupations in this job family, among which are retail sales, cashier, wholesale trade sales, store manager, manufacturer's sales, insurance sales, securities sales, wholesaler, travel agent, real estate appraiser, etc.

The administrative and managerial family is even larger. Among the occupations it encompasses are restaurant, cafe and bar manager, sales manager, purchasing agent and buyer for the retail trade, inspector, public administration, underwriter, assessor, tax preparer; credit analyst, claim examiner, safety inspector, tax examiner, and revenue agent.

To learn more about a particular occupation in a cluster, you then would turn to the section in the Handbook which describes each according to the following characteristics.

- Earnings
- Job prospects
- Working conditions
- Related occupations
- Job responsibilities
- Tools and equipment used.
- What workers do and how they do it.
- Education and training requirements.

It also tells whether the job involves overtime, evening or night shifts, whether much of the work is conducted outdoors or indoors, the physical demands of the job, such as crouching or heavy lifting, opportunities for part-time work, and more.

It even describes the personality characteristics needed by workers in a particular occupation; for example, whether it requires someone who likes making decisions, working in a highly competitive atmosphere, working with people as opposed to inanimate objects, etc.

The local Jobs Service office can also give you information and advice. Ask for an appointment to have aptitudes and interests tests administered, and to help you with your self-assessment. You can also go to one of the career counseling services listed below.

APTITUDES AND INTERESTS TESTS

These, also, cannot measure precisely your potential to succeed in an occupation. They help to
increase your self awareness so that you'll be
able to make a more appropriate career choice. Too
many persons assume these have magical powers
which can lead them to fame, fortune and happiness
in a new career. Some tests must be administered
by a psychologist. Others can be self administered.

APTITUDE TESTS help you to estimate what you can
do best or learn to do best. Aptitudes cover a
wide range of abilities: musical; clerical; analytical and inductive reasoning, verbal and mathematical reasoning; mechanical; creative thinking;
artistic, etc.

Different occupations require a different combination of aptitudes. Teaching, for example, requires
verbal communication skills, inductive and analytical reasoning, creative thinking and a host of
other skills in addition to the subject taught.

In order to assess your suitability for a particular occupation, your score is compared with those
of persons who are already working successfully in
that occupation. Aptitude tests can uncover abilities you never realized you had, abilities which
are needed in more than one kind of occupation.

INTEREST INVENTORIES help to clarify your job
related experiences and activities which interest
you most. They are based on the premise that
people do best what interests them most. You may
have a high aptitude for mechanical work, for
example, but if you also enjoy working with people
it would be best to select an occupation which
combines your aptitude and interest, such teaching
in a technical college or high school.

Your responses on an interest inventory are compared with the norms established by persons who
are successful and happily employed in various
occupations. Psychologists have discovered that
people in the same occupations generally have
interests which differ from people in other occupations. For example, several hundred successful
lawyers who indicated they enjoyed their work were
administered a 325 item inventory and it was found
that the pattern of interests for 90% of them
differed from those of real estate salespersons,

engineers, social workers and people in other occupations.

Some interest inventories can be self administered and interpreted. Among these are the following.

- THE SELF-DIRECTED SEARCH INVENTORY by J. L. Holland identifies six basic personality types which conform to different patterns of interests, and suggests occupations which are compatible with these. Many people display a mixture of the following "pure" types.

1.Enterprising: Tendency to be ambitious, self-confident, domineering, energetic, impulsive. Often possess leadership ability but lack scientific ability. Related jobs include sales, manager/executive, buyer, and media producer.

2.Conventional: Often described as conformers who tend to be cautious, orderly, persistent, self-controlled, and unimaginative. Possess strong clerical and numerical skills. Related occupations include bookkeeping, tax analyst, and banking.

3.Realistic: Possess mechanical abilities, but may lack social skills; Practical; Stable; Conforming. Related jobs include mechanic, surveyor, farmer, electrician, military, etc.

4.Investigative: Possess mathematical and scientific aptitudes and interests but often lack leadership ability. Tend to be introverted, analytical, curious, and rational. Includes biologists, anthropologists, chemists.

5.Artistic: Possess artistic skills but often lack clerical skills. Tend to be imaginative, impulsive, non-conforming. Prefer occupations such as composer, musician, stage director, interior decorator, actor/actress, novelist, etc.

6.Social: Possess strong interpersonal skills, but may lack scientific or mechanical abilities. Described as idealistic, persuasive, understanding, etc. Jobs include teaching, clergy, social worker, counseling, and speech therapy.

- THE QUICK JOB HUNTING MAP by Richard Bolles is designed to help you answer these questions: What skills do I possess? Which do I enjoy using most? In what settings would I like to apply these skills? You can order it from Ten Speed Press in

Berkeley, California.

- THE BEHAVIORDYNE INTEREST INVENTORY was created by Harrison Gough of the University of California in Berkeley, and Jo Ida Hansen of the University of Minnesota. After completing the test at home, you mail it to Behaviordyne where it is processed by a computer. The cost of scoring and interpreting the test is $25. The address is 599 College Avenue, Suite One, Palo Alto, CAL 94306.

- THE WISCONSIN CAREER INFORMATION SYSTEM (WCIS) is a computer processed inventory in which you indicate on a list of job characteristics those which apply to the jobs you have held, and those you would like in your new career. Your responses are fed into a computer which sorts out all the compatible occupations. There may be as many as 27 occupations which share these characteristics. These are added to a list of occupations which you have already identified on a written inventory. Finally, you narrow the list down to the occupations which interest you most. For more information, write to: Wisconsin Career Information System, Vocational Studies Center, University of Wisconsin, 1025 West Johnson Street, Madison, WI 59709.

- THE CAREER COMPATIBILITY PROFILE can be obtained from the Women's Center for Executive Development, 111 East Wacker, suite 2210, Chicago, Ill 60601.

- THE STRONG-CAMPBELL INTEREST INVENTORY is a well known inventory which must be administered and interpreted by a professional counselor or psychologist. It saved the author a bundle of money and time which would have been spent on the medical education she thought she wanted. The test revealed a pattern of interests which were inconsistent with those expressed by the majority of successful physicians. Years later, she realized that her interest in becoming a doctor was due more to a desire to keep up with a best friend who was attending medical school than to a deep interest in the field.

Another person learned to his surprise that his aptitudes and interests were in the field of writing rather than bookkeeping which he had done for many years. A few adult education courses led to a career in copywriting for an advertising agency which he enjoyed much more.

CAREER COUNSELING SERVICES

They can help you do an assessment of your job related skills, aptitudes and interests. They will then match these assets with occupations in which you are more likely to be successful and happy. They do this through personal counseling and psychological testing. They can also show you how to improve your job finding techniques, such as resume writing and interviewing. Some also provide counseling to help resolve personal and family problems resulting from unemployment. Referrals to on-the-job training programs may also be available.

Some, like the Forty Plus Clubs and the Federal Job Service offices, provide job placement as well. The Employment Security Department of the State of Washington, for example, has a career change program which offers aptitudes and interests testing, career and psychological counseling, and vocational training. It also finds temporary jobs for people who need some income while preparing for a new career.

WHAT THEY CANNOT DO FOR YOU - They cannot choose the right occupation for you. Only you can make that decision. The wisest counselor and the best psychological tests can only suggest options for you to consider. An illustration of this is the case of the registered representative who, on the basis of some expensive career counseling, quit his job to study for the law. Eventually, he discovered that the satisfactions of his new career could not compensate for the six figure income he earned in his previous career.

A counseling service is generally not an employment agency. Its main function is to help you to determine your job related assets and interests, and teach you how to find a job on your own. Many persons can do this for themselves with the help of a good guidebook.

WHERE TO FIND GOOD CAREER COUNSELING SERVICES. There are independent, for-profit counseling agencies which may charge a hefty fee, and there are non-profit services which operate through one or more of the following organizations in your community and which charge little or nothing at all.

- Colleges and Universities
- Public Libraries

- Federal Job Service Office
- Young Men's/Women's Christian Association and Young Men's/Women's Hebrew Association
- Religious associations
- Adult education centers
- Special interest groups: women's centers, senior citizen agencies, ethnic associations, etc.

In New York State, for example, a variety of services exist to help the general public and persons who are considered disadvantaged find satisfying work. The latter include the undereducated, unemployed, underemployed, handicapped, and minority group members, women, senior citizens, and low income persons. The services are available at the the State's vocational rehabilitation offices, the Veteran's Affairs Offices, adult education divisions of public high schools, and various community organizations such as ethnic groups, adult centers, and public libraries.

The services provided include job and career exploration, information on education, job referrals, career counseling, testing and assessment and, where necessary, advocacy on behalf of a person who needs it. The services may be offered in group sessions, by mail and correspondence, by telephone, via closed circuit or cable television, as well as through individual counseling. Generally, the services are free, but fees may be charged according to the services requested and the use of equipment and materials.

THE DIRECTORY OF EDUCATIONAL AND CAREER INFORMATION SERVICES FOR ADULTS lists more than 465 centers which are recognized by the National Center for Educational Brokering. Their services are free or low cost. If the book isn't in your public library, write to the Center at 1211 Connecticut Avenue, Suite 301, Washington, D.C. 20036 for the names and addresses of those in or near your community.

THE DIRECTORY OF COUNSELING SERVICES is an annual publication which lists accredited members of the International Association of Counseling Services, an affiliate of the American Personnel and Guidance Service at Two Skyline Place, 5203 Leesburg Pike, Falls Church, VA 22041.

CATALYST, a national, non-profit organization which helps working women, also issues a directory of career centers nationwide. Write to Catalyst, 14 East 60th Street, New York, N.Y. 10022 for a free copy.

PROJECT ACCESS is a program designed to help home-makers who are returning to the labor force. Its services include the administration and interpretation of self-assessment inventories and workshops on resume writing and interviewing techniques. The main office is located at the Educational Testing Service, Princeton, New Jersey and there are branches in Los Angeles, Chicago, Dallas, and Bergen County in New Jersey.

YOUR LOCAL COLLEGE OR UNIVERSITY has a career guidance and placement office which may offer its services to local residents. It can also refer you to other accredited counseling centers in your community.

Under the Older American Program, many two year (community) colleges established workshops, special courses, as well as counseling and/or placement services for this age group. Some offer their services to registered students only. Others open their doors to all older residents of the community.

The Adult Career and Education Counseling Center of Duchess Community College in New York, for example, offers its services to workers age 40-plus who are changing careers and to housewives planning to re-enter the job market. There are workshops and seminars to help them explore career options, select appropriate educational opportunities, and start their own business.

HOW TO CHOOSE A CAREER COUNSELING SERVICE

First, locate all the private and nonprofit services in your community and compare what they have to offer. Ask for their brochures and fee schedules and compare the services and cost. Make an appointment to speak with the counselors in those which seem to offer what you want.

Don't be put off by a high fee, if you can afford it. It may be a wise investment if you receive expert counseling which leads to a good career choice. Some of these agencies follow up on the progress of their clients during the early stages of a new job in order to ensure that it will be a successful placement.

Private agencies generally require that you sign a contract before offering their services. Before doing so, ask for a copy of the contract to take home to study. If there is anything in it that is ambiguously worded or not fully described, ask for clarification, IN WRITING! Only after you have the complete information on all the services you are entitled to receive and the length of time such services are provided, should you sign it. Insist on a detailed, written list of all the costs involved or you may discover, too late, that several hundred dollars were added to your bill when you asked for the counselor's opinion of your resume.

Fees can vary widely, and the price and quality of service do not always correspond. In 1982, the cost of a 50-hour course on career changing was as high as $650, and a one day workshop cost from $40 to $60. (You see what a bargain this book is?)

Consumer complaints were filed against several New York agencies which charged as high as $8,000! One of them simply helped clients prepare a resume and cover letter, and gave them a list of employers to contact which the clients could have obtained themselves from the directories listed in this book.

Some agencies require advance payment, but if you find a job through your own efforts before the service is completed, you will be paying for services you didn't get.

The reason why some counseling agencies get away with charging exorbitant fees is that in some states they are not covered by the same licensing regulations as employment agencies. The law limits the fees employment agencies can charge to a fixed percentage of your first, monthly salary. It also prohibits the agency from charging a fee before it finds you a job. In 1982 only seven states required licenses for career counseling firms. Contact the Better Business Bureau or the Consumer Protection Agency if your state does not require this.

Ask for the names of former clients and call them up to find out if they have any complaints about the agency. Better yet, check to see if any consumer complaints have been filed against it. Contact the Better Business Bureau, the Consumer Affairs Department of your city or county, or the State Attorney General's office.

Ask about the training and experience of its career counselors and whether they are members of any professional association. A counselor who is a member is more likely to be up-to-date in the profession.

A good counseling service should have trained and experienced counselors administer and interpret the results of certain aptitudes and interests inventories.

They should also explore your work background and job related personal history before advising you on various career choices. It is unprofessional to recommend an occupation simply on the basis of test scores. And only an accredited psychologist should counsel you for emotional or family problems resulting from unemployment.

A reputable agency should not promise, or even imply, to find you a job. In 1982, two nationally prominent agencies were under investigation in New York for falsely implying they could find jobs for their clients. Because they were not licensed as employment agencies, they were in violation of the state's law.

One firm led its clients to believe that it regularly found jobs paying $25,000 or more which they would be able to find within three months of registering with the agency. Be especially wary of counseling agencies which promise "results guaranteed to find you a job, or refund."

If you plan to enroll in a career change course or workshop, find out if the instructor is a trained, experienced counselor. It does happen that persons with degrees in related fields, such as teaching, have substituted as career counselors because of the short supply of qualified counselors. Also, inquire about the size of the class or workshop. If it's overcrowded, you will not get the individualized guidance members of small groups generally receive.

For more information, go to your library. The following is a sample of organizations and guidebooks which can help you. See the appendix for other sources of help

- _Focus on Choice: A Program Guide,_ is written to help women with little education improve their self-confidence and develop life planning skills. Write to Fort Wayne Women's Bureau, P.O. Box 554, Fort Wayne, IN 46801

- _Matching Personal and Job Characteristics,_ published by the U.S. Department of Labor. Discusses how to select the right career; includes a chart for comparing your work background, training and personality with the requirements of over 200 occupations. Send $1.75 to the Superintendent of Documents, U.S. Government Printing Office, Washington, DC 20402.

- _Matching Yourself With the World of Work_ is the Winter 1982 issue of _Occupational Outlook Quarterly,_ also published by the Department of Labor. Send $4.50 to the Superintendent of Documents, at the above address.

- _Discover What You're Best At: The National Career Aptitude System and Career Directory,_ by Barry and Linda Gale. (Simon & Schuster, New York, 1982.) It includes a series of self-administered, self-scored tests which help you identify your career strengths. The aptitude tests includes business, clerical, logic, mechanical, numerical, social and other areas. The book also shows you how to match these with over 1,000 different occupations so that you can set a realistic career goal.

- CATALYST has a list of publications for women (but also helpful to men) on such topics as career opportunities, job hunting tips, career advancement and skills development. The address is 14 East 60th Street, New York, N.Y. 10022.

- _What Color is Your Parachute?_ by Richard N. Bolles.(Ten Speed Press, berkeley, CAL.) This best seller includes _The Quick Job Hunting Map_ and discusses other topics such as how to deal with rejection, where to get help, who has the power to hire you, how to sell your abilities to an employer, and much more.

- _Group Career Dynamics Participant Workbook_ by Andrew A. Helwig. (Group Career Dynamics of Logan, Utah) It includes exercises to help you do a self-assessment, develop a career plan, and practice and learn job search skills. It can be used by individuals and groups. Also has a trainer's manual which includes exercises and instructions needed to cover a 3-or-4 day workshop which covers areas such as self-assessment, resume preparation, communication skills, telephone canvassing of employers, role play job interviews, and more.

- Guerrilla Tactics in the Job Market by Tom Jackson. (Bantam Books, 1981.) It includes exercises which help you to analyze your skills and create new job targets.

Exercise is the only thing that really keeps your mind clear when you get older. Tennis is only good if you play five sets or more, and retiring is for the birds.
Benjamin V. Buttenwieser who, at age 81, walks 5 miles every morning to his office on Wall Street.

9

THE RESUME

WHY BOTHER WRITING A RESUME?

The purpose of a resume is to advertise your qualifications for a job, to "market" yourself. It should be so convincing that the employer will want to discuss your credentials in greater detail at an interview.

The most effective resume is one that is uniquely yours. It should be molded to your measurements like a custom made suit. A good resume takes weeks, even months, to prepare. If you're invited to a job interview before your resume is ready, select one from a guidebook which suits your needs, and adapt it. This is an emergency procedure, however. Most experienced personnel recruiters can spot a "canned" resume, and most are turned off by it.

The secret to effective resume writing is not to be satisfied with your weeks of effort. Put it away for a week or two and then study it with a fresh, critical eye. You are bound to see room for improvement. Then ask a friend or guidance counselor to edit and evaluate it for you. He or she will probably see omissions and flaws which you have overlooked.

A resume should advertise to the world that you are concise, articulate, logical, literate and creative. One that is prepared by a resume writing service may look as if it came off the assembly line. It shouts, "I'm not creative." No professional resume writer knows you as well as you know yourself.

Another reason for doing it yourself is that, if you are doing a targeted resume, it should be tailored to each job title you are qualified to do. This isn't as onerous a job as it seems. The difference lies in the way you organize, emphasize, and express your credentials.

By the way, a resume isn't necessary for an entry level job. In fact, it's likely not to be read at all. An informational letter (see below) or a walk-in are more suitable.

FIRST, DO A SELF-ASSESSMENT

- Decide which occupations best match your interests, aptitudes and personality.

- Know your qualifications: education and training, skills and aptitudes, and work related experiences.

- Identify the industries in which you hope to be employed. Then select the companies or organizations that will be your targets for job hunting. Learn as much as possible about them. Instead of asking yourself, "What can these companies do for me?" ask, "In what ways will my qualifications be useful to them?"

NEXT, USE THIS INVENTORY TO WRITE YOUR RESUME

THE TARGETED RESUME

This is tailored to a single, specific, job title, rather than to a "family," or cluster, of related occupations. It takes longer to prepare but it gives more information about your qualifications for each job title.

Prepare a resume for each job title which you are qualified to do. A job title differs from an occupational category in that it refers to the major, specific responsibilities involved. Some examples of job titles are:

TILESETTER
FIGURES CLERK
PHOTOENGRAVER
HOTEL HOUSEKEEPER
SHEET METAL WORKER
BOAT/YACHT SALESPERSON
COMPUTER TECHNICAL WRITER
PHARMACEUTICAL MARKET RESEARCH
DIRECTOR OF CONVENTIONS AND MEETINGS

- Select the data from your inventory that is relevant to each job title. Include all the pertinent details. If you are writing a functional resume (see below), omit all unrelated job information. If you are doing a chronological resume, list the jobs you have held that are not relevant to your job objective without going into the details of each.

162

The job title should be an accurate and precise designation of what you are qualified to do. This is important, because some job titles, such as supervisor, office manager, or product manager, encompass a wide variety of responsibilities, and different persons holding the same title may actually do different things. In business, especially, it's not always easy to categorize jobs.

Another reason for doing so is that often a person is hired under a prestigious title which bears little resemblance to the kind of work actually done. For example, "sanitation engineer" might be used as a title for garbage collector, but it has little to do with the technology of engineering. If you need help in defining your job title, look in the OCCUPATIONAL OUTLOOK HANDBOOK or the DICTIONARY OF OCCUPATIONAL TITLES.

You'll be asked to describe the exact nature of your job responsibilities at the interview, anyway, so you'll save yourself and the interviewer time by stating precisely the title of the job you want on the resume.

The New York Times reports the case of a job seeker who had no luck using the title of his previous job, "Advertising Account Executive." A career counselor noticed that he had actually been in charge of marketing, and advised him to prepare a new resume which reflected his responsibilities and achievements more accurately. Within a week he had seven job offers.

Decide the best way to arrange your information so as to capture the reader's interest immediately. The way to do this is to put the qualifications that are most relevant to the job title first.

For example, if you have a Bachelor's Degree in anthropology, your job titles might be: "Social Studies Teacher," "Publisher's Representative," or "Editorial Assistant". For each of these you would prepare a different version of the same resume.

If you were to apply for a job with a school system, you would place first those qualifications that are most relevant to this position, such as your academic background and experience with young people. The resume for the job in a publisher's clearing house would first list evidence of your sales ability, specifically your ability to persuade people and your experience with books. For

the editorial assistant job, you would emphasize
the writing courses you've taken, articles you
have published, and any experience as a writer or
editor for the school newspaper, community newsletter, or other publication.

AN ALL-PURPOSE RESUME

This type of resume lists the several jobs you are
qualified to do, in order of preference, and then
describes the relevant information for each one.
It is faster to prepare than a targeted resume,
and it can be used for job openings which call for
a generalist background. (Employers who have such
vacancies may reject the targeted resume on the
grounds that you are too specialized.)

Instead of stating job titles or occupations as
your objectives, you may decide to state a more
general objective, such as "An opportunity to use
my skills in (list your relevant skills)."

It isn't necessary to state your job objective in
the resume. Some persons prefer to do it in the
cover letter instead. The advantage of doing this
is that you can use the same, all purpose resume
for different, but related, job vacancies.

TIPS ON HOW TO WRITE YOUR RESUME

The important thing to keep in mind is the employer's needs. Try to picture his recruiter in danger
of drowning under a deluge of resumes from anxious
job seekers. For a single job opening there might
be hundreds, even thousands, of applicants. Will
there be time to read each resume carefully? How
do you suppose the recruiter will react to a 3-or-
4 page resume? Or to a sloppily prepared one? Here
are some tips to ensure that your resume will be
placed in the "follow up" pile.

USE ACTION WORDS. Place them at, or near, the
beginning of each paragraph or phrase which introduces a new qualification. Here is a list of
action words which have been used effectively in
resumes. Use a dictionary or thesaurus to find
others that are more relevant to your situation.

Organized	Marketed	Trained
Designed	Created	Implemented
Initiated	Sold	Simplified

Presided	Planned	Participated
Improved	Modernized	Directed
Brainstormed	Authored	cataloged

Here are some more action words that homemakers who are returning to the job market have used.

PRESIDENT, P.T.A.
TREASURER, Briarwood Community Association
COMMITTEE CHAIRPERSON, Jamaica Senior Center.
FUNDRAISER, Volunteer Ambulance Corps.

AVOID INDECISIVE WORDS like "somewhat," "perhaps," "rather." They take up valuable space and make you appear wishy-washy.

AVOID STUFFY, PEDANTIC WORDS unless they are buzz-words used in your occupation. Stick to simple, everyday words. For example, use "job" or "occupa-tion" rather than "appointment," "salary" rather than "remuneration."

AVOID VAGUE, ABSTRACT WORDS such as "well quali-fied," "extensive experience," "versatile," "ex-pert," "outstanding." These sound good, but they give little factual information. A resume is not an advertisement, although they are both sales instruments. It is not meant to bedazzle and hyp-notize the recruiter.

Be specific. For example, saying you were an "out-standing student" is not as specific as saying "I was in the top 2% of my graduating class." Des-cribing yourself as an "expert" salesperson gives less information than saying you sold three times as many vacuum cleaners as the average door-to-door salesperson in the company. Other examples of being specific are: "I supervised 15 typists," or "In 10 years I wrote (n) number of copies for BEST BEER which increased my company's sales by 25%."

BE CONCISE.The rule of thumb is that a resume should never exceed two pages. How then, do you cram 25 or more years of valuable experience into such a small amount of space? This is a problem, especially if you've had quite a few job or career changes. Most counselors advise you to include only the last 10 years or so if you are preparing a chronological resume, or to select only those jobs which highlight your qualifications for your job objective.

The experts also warn against giving in to the temptation to cram all your relevant experiences so tightly together on a page that it looks terrible and is difficult to read. Do some selective editing, even though it breaks your heart to leave out some things.

Most people find it difficult to condense a lengthy, first draft. If you attempt to do it in one sitting, it can be exasperating. The way to tackle this without losing your mind is to cut it down by one page or a half page the first time. Put it away for a while and then cut it down some more the second time around. Do this for as many sittings as is necessary to cut it down to one or one and a half pages.

Here are some ways to eliminate superfluous details.

- Keep in mind that the employer is not interested in the story of your life. Only your job related aptitudes, skills and experiences count, so dump everything else.

- Use one or two words, or a brief phrase, instead of a complete sentence. If you must write sentences, keep them short. Better yet, use phrases such as "Supervised 20 clerks," or "Composed and edited vice-president's correspondence." For example, instead of writing, "I was responsible for writing copy for the Best Beer account," you can say, "Wrote copy for Best Beer account." No one expects elegant prose in a resume.

- Eliminate all adjectives and personal pronouns (I, You, He, etc.)

THE WAY YOUR RESUME IS ORGANIZED MAKES A DIFFERENCE. Generally, the recruiter's decision to reject a resume or read it through is made on the basis of what's on the first half of the first page. So, put the most important items, such as your name, address and phone number at the top of the page, followed by your job objective, if you decide to include it. Then begin with your most important credentials.

Keep the facts for each category of experience, skill and aptitude together, just as you would arrange them in a logical filing system. Don't scatter them higgeldy-piggeldy across several categories. Use paragraphs liberally, one for each category of skills and aptitudes, education and training, and work experience. The last thing you want to do is give the impression that you are scatterbrained.

MAKE IT ATTRACTIVE AND EASY TO READ. Don't send a handwritten resume even though your calligraphy is superb. Type it with a fresh, good quality ribbon and with clean typewriter keys. If you can't type well, ask a friend or relative to do it for you. Or, have it done professionally for a few dollars.

Highlight the important facts by using captions, or headings, underlining, centering, spacing or indentation, whichever is most appropriate and space-saving.

Separate logical sections with paragraphs and/or ample spacing.

Use margins of no less than one inch.

Use good quality paper. Avoid erasible paper that smudges easily.

Make sure there are no mis-spellings or typograph- ical errors. Use a dictionary and have someone edit it for you just to be sure.

Don't send faded photocopies.

There should be absolutely no cross-outs, no ob- vious typewriter correction fluid marks, no hand- written notations.

MAKE IT STAND OUT FROM THE CROWD. If you follow the above tips, it will already stand out. Incred- ible as it seems, some people send resumes that are sloppy and difficult to read.

Some job seekers use additional aids to make their resumes stand out. Whether these will work for you depends on the type of job you want and the "per- sonality" of the company. An offbeat, flashy re- sume may appear "cool" to a young electronics or cable TV executive, but it will definitely be out of place in a staid, conservative bank or school system.

Some persons use a conservatively tinted paper instead of white for their resume. A subtle blue, gray or beige tint on high quality paper, with matching envelope, looks attractive and doesn't cost much more. It is also less likely to get lost in the pile of resumes.

Some have their resume typeset or written on a word processor which has proportional spacing, justified (even) right margins, italics, and different type sizes for highlighting important facts.

Some of the flashier gimmicks that have been used include attaching a photograph of yourself on the resume. This works if you are applying for a job as actor or actress for TV commercials. But for other jobs it's risky, unless you're absolutely gorgeous and/or look at least 15 years younger. And, suppose your face reminds the reader of someone he or she dislikes?

Others have tried resumes printed on a balloon or a T-shirt, or painted on a sandwich board and paraded back and forth in front of the company's office building. One young graduate who wanted a marketing job in the recording industry covered a 40x30 foot area on the rooftop parking lot that faced the RCA building with his resume stenciled on a bedsheet. Another prepared his resume in the style of a balance sheet, listing his "Assets" and "Liabilities."

After months of getting nothing but rejection notices, a young M.B.A. graduate put on her best business suit, and handed her resumes to executives coming into Grand Central Station. She had a flier attached which said, "M.B.A. For Hire. Help Fight White Collar Unemployment. Write Today!" It worked!

There is no doubt that such gimmicks will make your resume stand out from the crowd. But, unless your field is in advertising, marketing or communications, it's best to avoid flashy gimmicks. You always run the risk of offending a conservative employer.

Try to think of a more dignified way of attracting attention. For example, if you are in an occupation that shows visible results of your abilities and achievements, send photographs, charts, drawings, videotapes, and other concrete evidence. These should accompany the resume, never substitute for it. Teaching, art, training, television, advertising, theater, marketing and sales are some of the occupations where audiovisual evidence can be used effectively.

MAINTAIN A POSITIVE TONE. One way to do this is to avoid long gaps between jobs on a chronological resume. The employer may wonder if you've been in prison or incapacitated in some other way. You must have done something constructive during that time, such as freelance carpentry, typing, computer programming or writing. Did you work part-time, attend adult education classes, start a home based business? If so, state it. If you can't think of anything, you can always say, "Attended to personal matters."

If you were fired, or laid off for health reasons, don't mention it. If you've changed jobs a lot, you risk being viewed as a job hopper who isn't likely to stay long. Use a functional resume instead of a chronological one, and include only the most important and/or recent jobs held.

AVOID REFERRING TO YOUR SEX IF YOU ARE A WOMAN. Men don't call attention to their sex, so why should you. Say, "chairperson" instead of "chair-woman," or "I am a 48 year old accountant" instead of "I am a 48 year old woman with a degree in accounting." It sounds more business-like and you'll avoid losing an invitation to an interview on account of sex bias. The time to deal with that hurdle is when you get there.

IT'S OKAY; IN FACT, IT'S EXPECTED THAT YOU EMBEL-LISH YOUR ASSETS the way high powered ads sell good wine. Everyone does it, and if you state the facts unimaginatively, the worth of your creden-tials may fail to come across.

This is not the same as stating falsehoods. That is a No-No! It means every relevant facet of your credentials should be exhibited and clothed in appropriate action words. Use action words liber-ally to highlight the skills and knowledge you have acquired as a student, at work, in your leisure pursuits and through volunteer work.

DON'T INCLUDE ANYTHING THAT ISN'T TRUE. These days more employers are investigating a prospective employee's record. Most investigating agencies are hired by employers to check the resumes of appli-cants for jobs paying $20,000 or more yearly. Smaller firms are likely to contact previous em-ployers themselves. Persons given as references may also be contacted.

Many companies will ask you to declare, in writing, that what you have stated on a job application form is true. If any lies are uncovered, it's considered justifiable cause for dismissal. Some companies may ask you to bring proof of your training and education.

This state of affairs has come about because of a recent increase in cheating and falsification. Social scientists attribute this to the severe competition for good jobs and to a changed code of ethics. A sensational example of this is the case of the journalist, Janet Cooke, who was hired on the basis of unverified credentials. She won the Pulitzer Prize for her articles on childhood drug addiction which turned out to be pure fiction, as was her presumed educational background.

Some job seekers reassure a prospective employer by paying a fee of about $20 to an investigating agency, such as The National Credential Verification Service, 4010 West 65th Street, Minneapolis (phone number: 612/920-2578.) It verifies the job seeker's credentials and issues a card which can be presented to an employer. The card lists the phone number of the agency which the employer calls in order to verify that what is in the resume is true.

The items most frequently investigated are education and dates of jobs held. Some employers check for credit history, court and arrest records, and a few even interview neighbors for evidence of alcohol or drug abuse!

HOW TO DEAL WITH YOUR AGE ON A RESUME.

You are not required to state your age, race, sex, religion or marital status on a resume.

On a functional resume, you don't even have to indicate the dates of employment and schooling, which would be a dead give-away. Omit your birthdate. List your schooling and training in reverse chronological order; that is, start with the most recent and go back in time. You can omit dates entirely or list only the dates of your most recent education. There is no need to include your high school education if you have had more recent, work related training and education. State, "high school graduate" and leave it at that.

List your paid and volunteer work experience in reverse chronological order. If it's too long and varied, list only your most recent and/or most relevant activities. Leave out the jobs you held in the early days of your working career. Instead of giving dates of employment, state the length of time you held each job.

Another tactic is to give only the dates of your most recent jobs. Or, you can trust the wisdom and intelligence of the employer by putting the dates at the end of the description of your achievements and responsibilities for each job in the hope that he or she will be so impressed with your background that your age won't matter.

A functional resume is probably the best way to deal with a long and varied work history. It categorizes your qualifications according to abilities, achievements, job responsibilities and on-the-job training instead of jobs held and, therefore, no dates are required.

IF YOU ARE A PROFESSIONAL WHO IS MAKING A CAREER CHANGE

You probably have been advised to underplay or omit all reference to advanced degrees and professional work experience. Yet, you might well ask, why should you apologize for your many years of university teaching, research, or any other professional activity? There must be a better way. Few career experts have dealt adequately with this problem.

Others, like the Career Opportunities Institute of the University of Virginia, advise you to translate the knowledge, skills and other assets involved in your profession into terms the business community understands and values.

An earned Ph.D., LL.D., or other higher degree is evidence of superior analytic reasoning and problem solving abilities. It's also proof of above average communications skills and a passion to see a piece of work well done. These qualities are sorely needed nowadays. You can apply the same self-assessment techniques that housewives are advised to use in order to translate unconventional work activities into job relevant terms.

A SUGGESTED OUTLINE FOR YOUR RESUME

The following outline is recommended by the Employment and Training Administration of the U.S. Department of Labor.

1. NAME, ADDRESS, TELEPHONE NUMBER

2. JOB GOAL/JOB TITLE
   On an all purpose resume which you will use for more than one job title, list them in order of preference.

3. WORK HISTORY
   CHRONOLOGICAL RESUME
   List each job separately, starting with the most recent and going backward. Give dates of employment, name and address of employer, your position. Then state your duties, responsibilities, and achievements.

   FUNCTIONAL RESUME
   List types of work (engineering, market research, sales promotion, secretary, etc.) you performed that are relevant to your job goal. Then, briefly describe your responsibilities and accomplishments in each of these fields without breaking them down according to jobs held.

4. EDUCATION AND TRAINING
   Your formal education; degrees or certificates received; courses, workshops, on-the-job training, and seminars that are relevant to your job objective.

   Scholarships, honors, other awards. Extra-curricular activities that are pertinent to your job objective. Include these only if they are recent.

5. PERSONAL DATA
   See below

YOUR NAME, ADDRESS AND PHONE NUMBER should go at the top of the resume. Don't forget your address zip code, and be sure to include your telephone area code for the convenience of employers who live out of town.

JOB TITLE - If you include a job title, it should be centered several spaces below the above data.

It should be concise and preferably in the buzz-words (jargon) of the occupation or industry. It sounds more up-to-date if you write "Human Resource Manager" rather than "Personnel Manager."

For an all-purpose resume which you intend to use for more than one job title, list your relevant abilities ("I am qualified to do ..., and ....") Omit the job title altogether and rely on the cover letter to describe the job you want.

WORK EXPERIENCE - This should also include all relevant non-paid work experience. The skills, responsibilities and achievements involved should be included in the same categories as for paid work, not placed separately. You can organize the data in two ways - by the jobs held (chronological resume) or by your work responsibilities and skills (functional resume).

EDUCATION - Include all your relevant formal and non-formal schooling and training. Also mention specific courses you have taken which are relevant to the job. (i.e., If you're applying for a job which involves dealing with statistical data, mention the mathematics courses you've taken.)

If you did not graduate from high school, don't mention it. Include instead any on-the-job training, home study, and/or adult education courses you've completed.

If you have a Ph.D. or any other higher degree, and you are applying for a job in a different field, indicate the abilities and knowledge which are transferable. Employers in the business world aren't interested in academic degrees unless the specialty is relevant to their industry, such as biochemistry or computer science. There is no need to hide your abilities and achievements if you can clearly show that these are relevant to the job at hand.

For example, it would seem that a Ph.D. in literature, history or anthropology has no relevance to a job in the computer industry. Yet, all industries and most employers need workers who have analytic reasoning ability, who are literate and articulate, who have proven skills of concentration and hard work, who are crackerjacks at creative problem solving. All these qualities and more distinguish persons with earned higher degrees.

YOUR INFORMAL EDUCATION includes all knowledge and skills acquired through volunteer work, on-the-job training, workshops, seminars, home correspondence courses and travel. If you did not finish high school or have no college courses to your credit, make the most of this section. List these activities under the same heading, "Education and Training," not under a separate heading.

PERSONAL INFORMATION is generally placed at the end of the resume. It should include only the facts which highlight your qualifications for the job.

-Academic Awards: scholarships, fellowships, prizes or other honors.

-Health: The older you are, the more important it is to say you are in "excellent" or "good" health, and give your height and weight as proof. If you're excessively overweight in relation to your height, omit it. If you have a chronic health problem which does not affect your ability to do the job, don't mention it. If, on the other hand, you have a disqualifying disability, ask yourself if that particular job is suitable for you.

-Leisure Activities: Another way to show you're fit for the job is to include sports activities under this category. There is no better way to convince an employer than to mention that you regularly go hiking, play several sets of tennis or engage in some other physical activity.

Hobbies and other leisure pursuits are also indicators of your aptitudes and interests which are compatible with the job. For example, bookkeeping would be compatible with collecting coins or stamps; salesmanship with activities, such as Little League Baseball, which involve the ability to persuade others. A job which involves repetitious work, such as keypunch operator, is compatible with such pastimes as knitting and crocheting. Computer programming and accounting are suited to persons whose hobbies indicate an analytic, problem solving mind, such as reading mystery novels, solving puzzles and math problems.

-If you are willing to travel, relocate, work evenings or weekends, this is the place to say so.

-Omit irrelevant personal matters such as your sex, marital status, number of children.

-Include only positive things about yourself which will serve as a door opener to further information about yourself.

REFERENCES take up valuable space, so just state "References available on request," or leave it out of the resume and put it in the cover letter. Most employers want this information only after they've had an opportunity to interview you.

THE CHRONOLOGICAL RESUME

This lists each job separately, in reverse chronological order, starting with the most recent one and going back in time. Include your job title, name and address of employer, the dates you started and left the job. Then describe the job, briefly, including the following.

-SPECIFIC JOB DUTIES:Include also any equipment and machinery you used, such as cash register, calculator, duplicating machine, overhead projector, word processor or use of company car.

-SCOPE OF RESPONSIBILITY: Include also the number of workers you supervised, if any; title of persons reporting to you; title of persons you reported to, or your supervisor

-ACHIEVEMENTS: Anything you did which helped your employer increase productivity and profits, improve worker morale, reduce costs and bring in new business should be mentioned. For example, instead of simply stating that you were a "File Clerk," you might add: "Improved method of organizing personnel records which saved (n) hours of time for my employer." Also describe any promotions and salary increases.

A chronological resume is effective if your recent jobs were in the same field as the one you are applying for. It's also much easier to prepare than a functional resume.

The disadvantage to this type of resume is that it gives away your age. There is another type which highlights your experience and abilities in a way which may interest the employer enough to hire you, regardless of how old you are. This is the functional resume.

THE FUNCTIONAL RESUME

This highlights your work responsibilities and credentials into distinct categories (sales, word processing, interviewing, supervising, sewing machine operator, copy writing, training and development, etc.) without listing the jobs you've held. Include only those credentials that are relevant to your present job objective. Dates can be omitted and credentials listed according to their importance rather than chronologically.

Within each category, describe the abilities and knowledge involved, your responsibilities and achievements in one paragraph or section.

Each section begins with an action word which identifies your major responsibilities and abilities.

The trick is to place those credentials that are most important to the job you're applying for at the beginning.

For mature job seekers who have a rich and varied work history, this type of resume is ideal. Instead of bringing attention to your age, it puts the spotlight on what you can do.

It's also ideal if you are a returning housewife, because it allows you to describe volunteer and other non-paid work experience without bringing attention to the paucity of paid work experience.

If you are changing careers, it enables you to emphasize the abilities and experiences which are transferable to the new job.

A functional resume is not difficult to prepare if you have done a thorough self-assessment. It takes much longer, but it's more effective than a chronological resume.

You can list employers' names, addresses and the length of time you were employed at the end of each section which describes a particular skill or aptitude. Or, you can include a separate page which lists this information in reverse chronological order. This is a "two tiered resume."

Nowadays, there's a lot more flexibility in writing resumes. You don't have to follow a format. The sample resume at the end of this chapter should be used only as a guide to creating one that is more original and better suited to your background.

THE COVER LETTER

This always accompanies the resume. Its purpose is to give additional information about your qualifications for the job which is not mentioned in the resume, to express your interest in working for the organization, and to re-emphasize your most important assets and how they can benefit the employer.

Fewer than 10% of the resumes received by a major company had an accompanying cover letter, and many of these were hack jobs, written on word processors or photocopied. You'll be way ahead of your competitors if you send an original letter describing a specific job opening in a specific organization, and addressed to a named individual.

Some experts recommend that you send the cover letter and resume to the person in charge of the department or division which has the job vacancy rather than to the personnel director. This is because the personnel (or human resource) department generally handles lower level jobs. If you do send a cover letter to the personnel director, it should suggest other departments where your abilities can be valuable. The letter to a department head, on the other hand, should have a more specific job goal.

The president, division head, or supervisor is said to be more flexible regarding the qualifications needed for a specific vacancy. Since he or she knows the job better than the personnel staff, substitute qualifications are more likely to be considered. For example, "must be a college graduate" is often listed among the "required" qualifications for a job which does not require a college degree. On the other hand, the personnel manager may know of other openings in the organization and where you fit in.

Furthermore, if you are rejected for the job, you can ask the personnel manager to hold your resume until a more suitable vacancy comes up. Since it's impossible to hire every qualified applicant for an opening, the resumes of top contenders may be kept on file for as long as a year.

This piece of intelligence leads to another tip. If your resume is filed for future reference, write an occasional letter to remind them of your continued interest in working for the company.

Even though you lack one or more of the "required" credentials, the tone of your letter, the interest you express in working for that firm above all others, the degree of literacy and good sense it conveys, can result in an interview.

THE INFORMATIONAL LETTER

This describes your qualifications for a job in narrative form. More people are finding jobs these days by sending an informational letter instead of a resume. An increasing number of employers favor a well written letter which is addressed to them and describes the applicant's abilities and experience in an interesting manner. It's somewhat like the direct mail letters which use a personal, narrative approach in order to persuade you to purchase something.

HOW TO WRITE AN INFORMATIONAL OR COVER LETTER.

More so than a resume, the letter should make you come across as a real person, not as a formula. Compose it yourself. Make it stand out from the crowd. Don't follow the model letters in the guide books too slavishly. One job seeker opened his letter this way: "You may not know me, but I know a great deal about your company..."

The focus of the letter should be on what the employer needs, not what you want. Use it to display what you have learned about the organization, and to convince the employer that your qualifications are perfect for the job. Remember, they're in business for profit, not for charity. All too often, the tone of a letter is "me-me-me."

Your letter goes a long way toward obtaining a coveted interview if it shows that you have gone to the trouble to learn about the company and how your assets will help to increase its productivity and profits. That's why pleading for a job is wrong. Offer your services, instead, in a business -like tone.

Never force yourself on an employer by saying you will arrive for an interview at a certain date. End the letter by thanking him and saying you are available for an interview at his convenience.

The letter should be:

- Short and punchy, like a sales letter.

- Directed to the employer's needs.

- Written in simple, not pedantic, language.

- Edited to correct mis-spellings and grammatical errors.

- Natural sounding. You can achieve this effect by writing as if you were speaking to the employer. Try tape recording the letter before typing it.

- Typed on good quality paper, with no cross-outs or obvious ink eradicator marks.

- Addressed to a specific person, name spelled correctly.

- Opened with a strong sentence which captures the reader's interest.

A week or so after you have mailed the resume and/or letter, telephone to ask if it was received. Use this opportunity to express your interest in working for the organization and why you are qualified for the job. The mere act of following up with a phone call is known to have a positive effect.

JOB HUNTING IS A FULL-TIME JOB IN ITSELF

Don't expect to get an offer after mailing a few resumes or informational letters.

In addition to answering help wanted ads, some people send mass mailings to a large number of firms in a particular industry or geographical area. Obviously, they cannot send a hand typed letter with each resume. In this case, an all purpose resume and cover letter will do. Some persons make a point of mailing several each evening or weekend.

The French are true romantics. They feel the only difference between a man of forty and one of seventy is thirty years of experience.
                                    - Maurice Chevalier

Mass mailings are said to be ineffective and not worth the cost in time and postage involved. This only works if a person has outstanding or unique qualifications, or if there is a shortage of skilled workers in a field. It is definitely not recommended for entry level jobs. Even a resume is not recommended for such openings. An informational letter or simply walking in and filling out a job application form is more effective.

If you don't hear from the employer after a reasonable length of time, or if you receive a rejection notice, send a second resume or letter. It happens occasionally that a resume is lost in the flood of applications. Others are rejected after a careless reading. The same resume or letter may be read by two different screeners and get contradictory responses. The same screener will accept a resume on a day he or she is feeling good and reject it on a bad day.

A college professor who was changing careers applied for a job with a publishing firm. A few days after receiving a rejection, she resubmitted the same resume and cover letter, and this time she was asked to come in for an interview. A business executive applied directly to a company and was turned down. He then registered with two recruiting firms. Each submitted his qualifications to the very same employer, with no results. Finally, he answered a blind newspaper ad and was invited to an interview. It turned out to be the same company!

See the appendix for suggested guidebooks on this topic.

A SAMPLE OF A FUNCTIONAL RESUME

The following sample is adapted from one that is recommended by the Employment and Training Administration, U.S. Department of Labor. This is just one of many varieties that have been used successfully. See one or more of the guidebooks listed in the appendix for more ideas.

Name   Address
Phone number
JOB OBJECTIVE

MAINFRAME COMPUTER SALES EXECUTIVE

Devised and supervised sales promotion projects for business
firms and manufacturers in the electronics field. Originated
newspaper, radio, and television advertising and coordinated
sales promotion with public relations and sales management. Ana-
lyzed market potentials and developed new techniques to increase
sales effectiveness and reduce sales costs. Developed sales
training manuals.

As sales executive and promotion consultant, handled a great
variety of accounts. Sales potentials in these firms varied from
$100,000 to $5 million per year. Was successful in raising volume
of sales in many of these firms 25% within the first year.

SALES MANAGEMENT
Hired and supervised sales staff on a local, area and national
basis. Established branch offices throughout the nation and
developed uniform systems of processing orders and sales records.
Promoted new products as well as improved sales of old ones.
Developed sales training program. Developed a catalog system
involving inventory control to facilitate movement of scarce
stock bewtween branches.

MARKET RESEARCH
Devised and supervised market research projects to determine
sales potentials as well as need for advertising. Wrote detailed
reports and recommendations describing each step in distribution,
areas for development, and plans for sales improvement.

SALES
Retail and wholesale. Direct sales to consumer, jobber and manufacturer. Business software, home computers, and electronic ac-
cessories.

ORDER CLERK
Received, processed and expedited orders. Trouble shooter. Set up
order control system which was adopted for all branches.

EMPLOYERS

date began/left   name/address   job title
                (start with most recent employer)

EDUCATION AND TRAINING

PERSONAL DATA

181

10

THE JOB INTERVIEW

WHY IT'S IMPORTANT TO PREPARE FOR THE INTERVIEW WEEKS BEFORE MAILING YOUR RESUME

- You'll make a better impression.

- You'll know in advance the kinds of questions you may be asked and how to answer them.

- You'll be prepared with questions of your own to ask so that you can learn more about the job and if it's what you really want.

- So you'll know what employers look for in a new employee.

- You'll be less nervous and better able to focus on the important issues.

- So you won't waste the interviewer's time.

- You'll be able to fill out a job application form properly.

WHAT'S THE PURPOSE OF THE JOB INTERVIEW?

From the employer's point of view, it's to learn more about you than the resume or informational letter reveals; to find out whether your abilities, interests, personality and appearance match the requirements of the job and the needs of the organization. The employer wants assurance that you'll be a happy, productive worker who won't quit at the earliest opportunity.

From your point of view, it's an opportunity to get more information about the job and organization which will help you to decide if it's what you really want.

I'm constantly amazed when I ask, "Describe yourself," and they begin to describe their physical characteristics. Then they ask, "Is that what you want?" and I'll say, "No, I want to know who is Joe Blow." You know what? They can't describe themselves. They apparently don't know themselves. They don't know whether they are outgoing, aggressive, etc. They've never stopped to assess themselves.
                              - Josephine Lerro, Human Resources

Director, TempsAmerica.

PUT YOUR ASSETS ON DISPLAY

After you've done a self-assessment, memorize all your strengths and assets. Are you especially good in dealing with people? Are you a teamworker? During a crisis do you keep a cool head while everyone else is losing theirs? If you're a cheerful person, let that quality shine through. If the interviewer asks you to describe yourself, show that you have a thorough knowledge of yourself.

Know your weaknesses, too, and admit to a minor flaw or more, because nobody's perfect. If you try to come across as a demi-God, the interviewer will wonder about your truthfulness or whether you know yourself well enough to have chosen the right career path.

SHOW THAT YOU'RE A WINNER You can do this by telling the interviewer about your job related achievements and successes. A job interview is no time to be modest. Older women, especially, must put aside their traditional female modesty and submissiveness. This is such a widespread problem that the YWCA and other women's centers include assertiveness training in their job programs.

BELIEVE IN YOURSELF! Practice auto suggestion, now called "cognitive therapy." This has a powerful influence on changing aspects of your behavior that you want to improve or change. It will also increase your self-confidence. Memorize your strong points and repeat them to yourself aloud while you're doing chores. This will condition your mind to accept a new image of yourself. Soon, you'll be believing in yourself again.

If you think no one is going to hire you because of your age, if you lack faith in your abilities, you're creating a self-fulfilling prophecy. If you don't exhibit faith in yourself, the interviewer is not going to have faith in you. - Ms. Lerro

LEARN HOW TO PROJECT A POSITIVE IMAGE. According to Ms. Lerro, *Most interviewers are trained to learn as much as they can about an individual, and this includes personality. Sometimes, because of bitter experiences, an older person becomes disillusioned and somewhat embittered. That comes through during the interview. The person's inter-*

personal skills don't shine as they should, and so the interviewer may label him or her as "inflexible" or "cantankerous." These terms are used far too frequently with regard to the mature worker.

The older job candidate should ask himself, "What kind of an image am I projecting? Is it bitterness? An air of skepticism? Am I going to the interview with preconceived notions that I'm not going to get the job?"

Look at yourself in the mirror. Take a good look at your facial expression. Many older people walk around with a dour, set expression much of the time. Practice a new and brighter one.

Practice smiling more so that it will come naturally during the interview. How many times during the day do you smile? Can you make yourself appear relaxed during the interview? Or, will you reveal your nervousness? Will your body language say, "What am I doing here? This person knows I'm in my fifties, and he's not going to hire me." That's projecting a defeatist attitude.

REHEARSE THE INTERVIEW

Ask a friend to help you or, better yet, a counselor, former employer or co-worker. Prepare ahead for the questions you may be asked. See the list below for suggestions. Ask your critics to take notes on how your speech, voice tone and body language can be improved.

Tape record the rehearsal for later study. Then practice before a mirror to perfect your technique. The use of videotapes for interview rehearsals is growing among career counselors and outplacement firms. If you can't afford their fees, borrow the equipment from someone you know. A sound film helps you to be more objective in admitting your mistakes.

Whenever possible, accept interviews for jobs you're not keen about. It's better to make your blunders where it won't matter at first. The more practice you get in live situations, the more focused your answers and the less nervous you'll be during the really important interview. After the interview is over ask, "I would be grateful if you give me some advice on how I can improve my interview techniques." Be careful not to let the interviewer know that you aren't serious about the job.

If you need more help, there are plenty of workshops, seminars and adult education courses on how to improve your job interview skills. There are also many books on the subject. But nothing can take the place of live interview rehearsals.

WHAT DO EMPLOYERS WANT?

Employers use two levels of criteria in deciding which, among many qualified job candidates, to hire.

- Does the person have the skills, aptitudes and work experience I want?

- Will that person contribute to my organization over and beyond these qualifications? Will he or she help to make my workforce a happier, more harmonious and productive team? Is there anything in that person's life experience which suggests initiative, drive and achievement? Does he or she project the image I want for my organization?

Personality is the key. If you project enthusiasm - about the job, the company, about life in general - employers will overlook lots of other things. Age becomes irrelevant because you have a positive, youthful attitude. A few wrinkles, a few pounds extra, and whatever else connotes age, don't matter.

An inability to get along in the workplace has been the undoing of more employees than an inability to master a skill. Some people fail to recognize that there is a place for everyone in a particular area of work. They may feel put upon; they gossip and don't mean well, or they feel the supervisor has it in for them. Whatever their problem is, if they let it affect their relations with their coworkers, there isn't going to be a harmonious workflow.

In my years as director of human resources, I have found that poor interpersonal skills account for about 65% to 75% of job terminations. Sometimes it's not the employee's fault. Sometimes the problem lies with a supervisor who is difficult to get along with. Nevertheless, the employee must find ways to get along, otherwise that's not the place for him. - Josephine Lerro

Many studies support Ms. Lerro's observation that a major reason for dismissal is not poor job performance, but an inability to get along with coworkers, habitual lateness, a sour attitude which casts a demoralizing spell, emotional instability and disloyalty to the organization. Even a case of bad blood between the worker and the boss or supervisor is a frequent cause for dismissal.

The ideal, mature job candidate is easy to get along with, adaptable, open-minded and has a cooperative attitude toward younger supervisors. These qualities counteract the prevailing, negative age stereotypes. An Over-60 Employment Service office reports that the most frequent excuse employers give for not hiring older persons is that they might be inflexible, cantankerous or difficult to work with.

WHAT ELSE DOES THE EMPLOYER WANT TO KNOW?

-How loyal will you be to the company?

-Do your beliefs and manner reflect positively on the firm's public image? For example, do you have political, racist or sexist views that might embarrass the company?

-Will you be a clock watcher or, conversely, a workaholic who is likely to pressure valued subordinates into quitting?

-Are you so ambitious that you are likely to mow down others and subvert the company's long range goals in your aggressive attempts to climb the ladder of success?

-Is your personality compatible with that of the company? Previous chapters have made you aware of different organizational styles and which you are more likely to be comfortable with. How would you feel if the vice-president eats in the cafeteria alongside the typists and janitor? (You might even be asked this question during the interview.) Older candidates must contend with the stereotype that they are better suited to a centralized, top-down organization in which lower level workers are expected to carry out orders without question. Do you have initiative? Employers want workers who don't wait to be told what to do and how to do the job better. This is another reason for doing a thorough self-assessment. You'll be able to tell the interviewer about your past efforts to contribute something beyond the ordinary requirements of the job. This is also where your voluntary work experience, the home correspondence course you completed or night school classes you attended will make you shine.

-If you are changing careers, don't assume the interviewer will be able to infer from your resume how the abilities and responsibilities demanded by your previous occupation relate to the new one. Another way of showing initiative is to point this out.

TELL THE INTERVIEWER ABOUT YOUR LEISURE ACTIVITIES AND VOLUNTEER WORK WHICH DEMONSTRATE THE DESIRED QUALITIES FOR THE JOB. This is why job application forms ask about such aspects of your personal life. They are indicators of your ability to get along well with others, your creativity, initiative and drive, and your interests which lie beyond the narrow orbit of SELF. Ms. Ierro especially looks at a candidate's voluntary work experience."It shows you're involved, caring, energetic."

WHAT TURNS OFF EMPLOYERS THE MOST?

He who slings mud, loses ground. - Adlai Stevenson

The interviewer doesn't know by your appearance alone that you are a peach. Nor, for obvious reasons, can you be asked, "Do you get along well with people?" The interviewer can only rely on cues. So, in order to avoid sending the wrong cues, do the following.

NEVER SAY ANYTHING NEGATIVE ABOUT YOUR FORMER EMPLOYERS AND COWORKERS, no matter how awful they are, or were. It will make you appear crotchety. Don't complain about the working conditions, either, unless they were truly intolerable. In that case, begin by saying something nice about the company so that you project an attitude of fairness. One job seeker who had legitimate reasons for complaining, later learned that the interviewer and the employer he had bad-mouthed were brothers-in-law.

There are more subtle ways of explaining why you quit or were dismissed which won't make you appear to be a difficult person. The interviewer will get the message, and you'll be respected for your diplomacy if you say something to this effect. "I quit in order to find a job where I can develop further in my career," or "I quit because the conditions for doing the work to the best of my ability were not available."

AVOID DISCUSSING YOUR PERSONAL, FINANCIAL OR FAMILY PROBLEMS so you won't be viewed as a whiner. Trying to win sympathy won't get you the job either. It will only make the interviewer uncomfortable in your presence and want to terminate the interview prematurely.

LONG GAPS IN YOUR WORK RECORD SHOULD BE EXPLAINED. Tell the interviewer about the many constructive activities in which you were involved: study, volunteer work, raising a family, part-time or freelance work, travel, caring for someone who needed your help, etc. Never leave these gaps unexplained or the interviewer may wonder if you were ill, in prison or just plain, lazy.

KEEP YOUR FAILURES TO YOURSELF. Never reveal that you've been fired or rejected for a job. However, if these matters are brought up by the interviewer, don't lie. Heed the old saying, "There's a silver lining behind every cloud" and point out the positive aspects of a negative situation. You might say, for example, "I quit my job because it didn't offer the opportunity to do my best work," or "Yes, my work was affected by a family problem. But that's over now, and I've learned a lot from the experience."

DON'T BE APOLOGETIC ABOUT YOUR AGE OR LACK OF FORMAL EDUCATION. Refer instead to your "hands on" experience and life achievements. The interviewer probably doesn't know about the many studies which reveal the superior qualities of older workers, so inform him or her. If your skills are rusty, say you are taking, or planning to take, adult education courses in order to upgrade them.

LOW ENERGY LEVEL - Watch how you walk into the room and sit down. See the section on body language. Try to match the tempo of your response to that of the interviewer.

YOUR OWN NEEDS COME FIRST - Instead of focussing on what YOU want, pitch your sales talk to the needs of the organization. Describe the ways in which you'll be a valuable addition to the workforce.

LACK OF SELF-CONFIDENCE - Practice the right body language. Eliminate all negativisms from your speech. Practice auto-suggestion in order to psyche yourself up just before you go to an interview.

DIDN'T DO HOMEWORK - Be prepared to discuss your assets. Learn all you can about the company and how you fit in. Learn about the job responsibilities; the skills, education and training requirements; and how work performance is evaluated. This is known as the Job Description. Note especially those aspects of the job that you can do particularly well.

This information will help you to avoid the worst sin of the job interview - appearing fuzzy minded about what you want to do and are qualified to do. Saying "I'll take anything," or "I like to work with people" can be forgiven in a 20-year old, but not in a 50-year old.

Some experts say the first 30 seconds are the most crucial for capturing the interviewer's attention. You'll be better able to do this if you know enough about the organization so that you can describe how you can meet its needs.

If you aren't offered the job, you will be better able to convince the interviewer that you are qualified for other jobs in the organization. If there are no other appropriate vacancies at the time, say that you would like to be considered when they do occur. Many employers keep the applications of promising applicants for as long as a year.

In the competition between two equally qualified candidates, the one who knows the most about the firm will be hired. However, employers are wary of hard-sell tactics. The best approach is to show a sincere interest in the job and the organization, and the way to do this is to show that you've made an effort to learn more than the run-of-the-mill job seeker knows.

YOUR ATTITUDE TOWARD THE INTERVIEW CAN INFLUENCE ITS OUTCOME

If you view it as a situation in which you are on trial, your nerves will be tied up in knots. But, if you view it as an exchange between equals, you'll make a more favorable impression and get more out of it.

TRY TO CONVEY A CONFIDENT, POSITIVE ATTITUDE, especially if you're a woman returning to work after many years of raising a family. "Far too many bring a hang-dog attitude in with them," says a job counselor.

On your way to the interview, picture yourself as a competent employee rather than "just a house-wife." This should be easy if you've done a self-assessment. Take a course on assertiveness train-ing if you need help in achieving an attitude of success. Contact women's organizations such as the YWCA, Catalyst and Displaced Homemakers. Or go to the local college or university for information.

Before going in, say to yourself, "The person sitting across the desk from me is trying to do his job and means me no harm. I'm going in with an open attitude which says, 'Your company is going to be proud to have me on board.'"

LEARN TO OVERCOME THE INTERVIEW JITTERS

If the interviewer appears cold or hostile, it may be an attempt to cover up his nervousness or it may be a pose to test your poise. "Once I was interviewed by a younger woman executive whose every pore seemed to exude hostility or dislike for me - so I imagined," said a professional woman who was changing careers. "Later, I learned she was new on the job and trying hard not to show her nervousness. Although I wasn't hired, the inter-view was a valuable learning experience. When I called later to thank her and ask for advice on how to improve my interview techniques, she was very helpful. She also gave me some valuable job leads."

Some interviewers appear unusually tough because they first screen out the traits they don't want in a candidate. Once this is accomplished, they relax and focus on the candidate's positive quali-ties.

During the interview, you may be so preoccupied with your own jittery feelings that you overlook the interviewer's situation whose competence is being measured by his or her ability to select the best person for the job. If you remind yourself that the two of you are in this pressure cooker together, your tensions will ease, and the interviewer will feel more comfortable in your presence

PRACTICE THE BODY LANGUAGE WHICH PROJECTS AN ATTITUDE OF SELF-CONFIDENCE, even though you are quaking inside. Rehearse the following actions until they become natural to you.

- SMILE AND ESTABLISH EYE CONTACT with the interviewer as soon as you walk in. This is even more necessary if the interviewer is much younger than you are. Greet the interviewer by name and offer a firm handshake. Look directly at the interviewer when you answer questions. Looking at the desk, wall or anyplace else may be interpreted as evasiveness.

- IT IN A RELAXED (NOT SLOUCHED) POSTURE, with your hands loosely cupped, palms facing upward in your lap or with your arms resting lightly on the chair. Avoid clenching your hands or folding your arms tightly across your chest. Such gestures transmit a belligerent signal.

- SPEAK SO YOU CAN BE HEARD, clearly and in a firm voice, but not so loud that you give the impression of being hard of hearing.

- THE MOST BEAUTIFUL SOUND IN THE WORLD IS THE SOUND OF A PERSON'S OWN NAME. Mention the interviewer's name at appropriate times during the interview.

- SHAKE HANDS BEFORE AND AT THE CLOSE OF THE INTERVIEW. Don't wait for the interviewer to initiate this.

- KEEP YOUR BRIEFCASE, NEWSPAPER, PURSE, OR WHATEVER ELSE YOU'RE CARRYING ON THE FLOOR, next to you, never on your lap.

- DON'T SMOKE UNLESS YOU ARE INVITED TO DO SO, AND ABSOLUTELY NO GUM CHEWING IS ALLOWED. If you are offered a cigarette, it may be to see if you are a smoker. More employers these days are refusing to hire smokers. Don't accept it unless you know the interviewer is going to smoke also.

KNOW IN ADVANCE THAT YOUR ABILITY TO HANDLE STRESS
MAY BE ASSESSED AT THE INTERVIEW.

This will happen if the job involves a lot of stress, such as many deadlines to meet or dealing with the public.

No sane interviewer is going to ask you outright, "Are you calm when under stress?" The only way to find out is to ask indirect questions. These, generally, have no wrong or right answers and may even seem far fetched. Another tactic is to arrange mildly stressful events to happen during the interview in order to see how you will react. There may be frequent, annoying interruptions such as doors slamming and phones ringing. The way to deal with this is to know in advance that such situations might occur so that you won't be taken by surprise. This matter was put before Josephine Lerro, and here is her advice.

Before going to the interview, they should say to themselves, "This is just a job interview. If I can't handle the stress involved, I should honestly ask myself whether I can handle the day to day pressures of the job." The interviewer will be asked to bombard the candidate in order to test his or her poise. So, in all honesty, maybe the candidate who worries about it shouldn't be there to begin with.

Don't take what appear to be hostile questions personally.

Remind yourself that the interviewer is trying to do his or her job and holds no personal grudge against you.

Don't be too shy to ask, "Will you please tell me why this information is important to you?"

See comments on how to relax before going in to the interview.

HOW TO DISPEL NEGATIVE AGE STEREOTYPES

BODY LANGUAGE SPEAKS A LOT. There's a certain level of enthusiasm which should come through. Enthusiasm and energy go hand-in-hand. If older applicants project these qualities, it suggests the opposite of inflexibility and all those other negative stereotypes.

DEMONSTRATE A WILLINGNESS AND ABILITY TO DO ANY-
THING THE JOB REQUIRES within reason of course.

MAKE IT CLEAR, EVEN IF IT'S NOT ASKED, THAT WHILE
YOU HAVE HAD MANY LIFE EXPERIENCES, YOU'RE WILLING
TO LEARN SOMETHING NEW. Back this up by citing
things you have done in the recent past, such as
taking adult education courses, completing creative projects, doing volunteer work.

MENTION RECENT ACTIVITIES WHICH INDICATE YOUR
OPENNESS TO CHANGE AND YOUR ABILITY TO ADAPT, such
as travel, volunteer work, adult education courses, preparations for a career change, etc.

REASSURE THE INTERVIEWER THAT YOUR ENERGY LEVEL IS
UP TO THE DEMANDS OF THE JOB. If you had an excellent attendance record in your previous job, if
you are in reasonably good health, if you engage
in sports activities regularly, say so. If you
walk a mile each day to buy the newspaper, let the
interviewer know this.

Cite recent medical reports which show older Americans today have more more stamina and energy than
those of a generation ago.

Walk into the room briskly and offer a firm handshake. Notice the way Ronald Reagan enters a room-
ful of television cameras with a purposefully
brisk and bouncy step. He literally leaps onto a
platform.

Try to match the pace of your responses to that of
the interviewer. If the interviewer's pace is
brisk, and you reply in the rocking chair tempo of
a lazy summer afternoon, you may give the wrong
impression.

AVOID GIVING THE IMPRESSION OF "TALKING DOWN," of
being condescending or overbearing, so as to allay
any discomfort a much younger interviewer may have
about your seniority. Tone down the assertiveness
that all job applicants are advised to demonstrate, but without giving the appearance of pas-
sivity. Inform the interviewer of the many studies
which show that older workers have a better attitude toward the boss, that they're more willing to
carry out orders. You can also cite examples of
your own good teamwork skills.

Solly Wishnick, age 64, of the Bronx, has been a waiter in a garment district coffee shop for the past 19 years. Solly holds the world's record for repeating 4,287 times, "Sorry, this ain't my table," despite the fact that Solly is the only waiter and there is only one table in the restaurant.- Stan Burns & Mel Weinstein, The Book of Jewish World Records (Pinnacle Books, N.Y. 1978)

SHOW ENTHUSIASM ABOUT THE JOB AND THE FIRM. A candidate who is looking for any job, and shows it, raises the suspicion that nobody else wants to hire him or her.

IF THE INTERVIEWER DOESN'T BRING UP THE SUBJECT OF AGE, THERE'S NO REASON WHY YOU SHOULD, especially if the interviewer is young enough to be your son or daughter. If the subject comes up, don't apologize for your age. Instead, convey a sense of pride in your years of achievement and learning. (It's illegal for the interviewer to ask questions regarding your age.)

IF YOU DON'T UNDERSTAND OR HEAR A QUESTION CLEARLY, the way to avoid giving the impression of being hard of hearing is to ask for clarification rather than mumbling or saying something inappropriate in reply. Say something to this effect, "The way I define your question is.....Is that how you define it?" That's much better than saying, "I didn't hear you. Will you please repeat the question?"

THE INFORMATION YOU GIVE SHOULD BE RELEVANT TO THE QUESTIONS ASKED AND THE PURPOSE OF THE INTERVIEW. Omit personal matters and other irrelevancies, such as the trouble you had getting there. The interviewer is not interested in your problems or the story of your life, no matter how fascinating these are to you.

BE CONCISE. Don't lead up to the punch line in the drawn-out manner of Dingbat, of All In The Family. Give the important facts first, followed with examples if more clarification is needed. Then, stop and ask if the interviewer would like more information.

DON'T MENTION ANY HEALTH PROBLEM which doesn't interfere with your ability to do the job. On the other hand, if you have a chronic problem which will affect your performance, you shouldn't be applying for that job. There are other opportunities and work situations where you will be more comfortable and happy.

MORE TIPS ON HOW TO HANDLE AN INTERVIEW

DON'T ANSWER QUESTIONS WHICH REQUIRE A MORE COMPLETE ANSWER WITH A BLUNT "YES" OR "NO." For example, if you are asked, "Does computerized office equipment scare you?" don't just say "No." Give examples of your interest in and/or knowledge about this new technology. It's a daily topic in the media these days.

NOW IS THE TIME TO BRING UP INFORMATION WHICH ISN'T INCLUDED IN THE RESUME, but don't waste the interviewer's time by repeating what's in the resume.

OMIT JARGON AND JAWBREAKER VOCABULARY UNLESS IT'S USED IN THE INDUSTRY. Professionals who are changing careers should be especially careful to avoid being viewed as ivory tower types who don't belong in the business world. Also, leave the slang and bar room language for more appropriate settings.

IF YOU'RE OFFERED A JOB THAT IS LESS THAN WHAT YOU HOPED FOR, but is a stepping stone toward your goal, you can say you're interested in proving your ability and hope to increase your responsibilities in the near future. Then, see what the interviewer says.

Don't expect to be viewed as management material just because you were president of the P.T.A. or have a Ph.D. People in the business world are more impressed by "hands on" experience which shows concrete results in the form of increased profit. They first want to test your competence before promoting you to a position that is more commensurate with your abilities.

BE SURE TO SMILE AT THE RECEPTIONIST AND SECRETARY. It's polite and it's also in your best interest. The interviewer may later ask them, "Well, what was your impression of....?"

WHAT TO DO IF YOU WERE FIRED OR QUIT YOUR JOB

Getting fired or quitting a job doesn't mean you're finished. It's happening more often and to the best of us. Many persons have used it as an opportunity to go on to better things, to do the kind of work they've always dreamed of doing, but couldn't. I asked Josephine Lerro some questions about this matter. Here is her advice.

Q: DURING THE INTERVIEW, THE MATTER OF MY HAVING BEEN FIRED COMES UP. HOW SHALL I HANDLE THIS?

A: I suggest that you be as honest as possible. Begin by saying something favorable about the job and the company. "I enjoyed my coworkers and the supervisor was a nice guy," or something to that effect. If it was a matter of performance, and you were responsible for the termination, you can say something to this effect: "There were certain problems at the time which influenced my performance. I've learned from it and I know darned well that I won't let it happen again, because this job is valuable to me."

If it was due to a personality conflict with the supervisor, do not malign that person, because the interviewer will assume the same thing might occur in the new work setting.

Q: I SHOULD DO THIS EVEN IF MY SUPERVISOR WAS AT FAULT?

A: Yes, because you might be viewed as a person who bears grudges. Even if there is justification, it shows a lack of professionalism to denigrate previous supervisors or employers. It also shows an inability to forgive and forget something that happened in the past.

Q: THEN, HOW DO I EXPLAIN IT?

A: Say something to this effect: "My supervisor and I had a difference of opinion which could not be reconciled and so we agreed that it would be best if I leave." That's much better than saying, "The supervisor was an S.O.B. He made my life miserable," and so on. Anyone who knocks someone, especially to a person he or she doesn't know, is taking a chance.

Reassure the prospective employer that you are not a poor risk. Use your past achievements and good references to accomplish this. Say something like this, "Let me tell you what I achieved and what I learned on the job." The interviewer is bound to be impressed with your humility, honesty, desire to improve and the even-handed way you've answered the question.

If you quit your last job because your conscience wouldn't permit you to cheat your employer by searching for another job on company time, say so. Such qualities mean more to an employer than the fact that you were dismissed.

Some personnel experts advise that you state the reason for the misunderstanding, as long as you don't say it with a sour grapes attitude. Be sure to support your view with positive evidence. "My supervisor was new on the job and he didn't have time to arrange for the conditions which were necessary for me to do good work. Would you like to hear what I accomplished during that time?"

Bob C., a computer technician, was fired at a time his life was falling apart. His wife had left him and their two sons in order to "find herself." This affected his relations with his boss and co-workers, and eventually he was fired. Despite the high demand for his skills, he was turned down repeatedly, because each time he was being considered for a job, his former employer was contacted and the recommendation given was poor.

Bob's mistake was trying to hide a reality that eventually came to light. It make him appear untrustworthy. The situation took a brighter turn after he decided to be honest about the reasons for his dismissal. He assured the interviewer that the situation at home had improved since he was granted custody of the boys, and he pointed to his prior excellent work record. "Iron becomes steel when it has been tempered with fire," he said. He got the job and now he's more careful about letting his personal problems interfere with his work.

There are always positive aspects to a negative situation. Most people learn from them. Look for them.

If your parting involved some unpleasantness, there may be a way to salvage the situation so that your former employer will remember you more kindly when he is contacted for a reference. Time heals all wounds, so wait until things cool off. In the meantime, a review of your assets and past achievements will help to reestablish your self confidence.

Some experts advise that you swallow your pride and visit the employer after things have cooled down. Thank him for giving you the opportunity to work for him and ask for advice on how to improve your performance. You might learn something valuable, and your humility and desire to improve will make a positive impression. Then remind him of your achievements while you were his employee. He may have forgotten. Finally, ask for advice on how to clear the record so you won't have problems getting another job. Most employers are willing to help dismissed workers. They, too, must maintain a positive image.

This advice, like so many others, needs qualification. The degree of finesse required to follow it through depends on the personalities involved and the situation which led to the unpleasantness. For some people, it could backfire. You've got to play it by ear.

THE EVENING BEFORE THE INTERVIEW.

ASSEMBLE THE INFORMATION YOU'LL NEED
    - Social Security number, union card, driver's license, etc.

    - Names, addresses and phone numbers of persons you'll use as references.

    - Names, addresses and phone numbers of former employers; names of supervisors; job titles you held and your major responsibilities. (Bring your resume if it includes all this.)

    - Volunteer work experiences: names, addresses and phone numbers; dates you began and left; major responsibilities.

    - Education and Training - schools attended; dates of graduation or completion of courses; certificates, diplomas, degrees or   C. E. U.s earned; awards and honors which attest to your special competence for the job; extra-curricular activities, leadership positions held, assignments to special projects.

Include this information only if it's relevant and doesn't make you appear to be a Rip Van Winkle. Generally, a job application form doesn't have much space in which to list all your achievements, so include only the most relevant, most recent and most impressive ones.

- Transportation: Learn the best route to get there. Find out how long it takes, and leave at least a half hour earlier in order to avoid slow-downs and give yourself time to relax and get used to the surroundings.

ASSEMBLE THE THINGS YOU'LL NEED
- Samples of your skills and achievements: photocopies of commendations and awards; photographs; art or design work; published writings; graphs and charts which show your sales record, etc.

Any visible evidence of your accomplishments which can turn a decision in your favor should be brought to the interview. If you have a videotape or slides which make the point, phone ahead of time to see if arrangements can be made to show them.

- Pens or pencils; several copies of your resume, if you have one; a small pocket stapler to attach the resume to the job application form; a small notebook to jot down important information you might forget (tax deductible job hunting expenses, ideas that occur to you on how to improve your next interview, interviewer's name, etc.)

- Set the breakfast table. Have the coffee or tea pot ready.

- Lay out the clothes you'll wear. Check for rips, runs and spots. Make sure they fit. Make sure your shoes don't pinch so that you'll be comfortable during the interview.

- If you're driving, check to see that the car runs and has plenty of gas. Have sufficient coins ready for parking meters and toll collectors, If you're taking public transportation, have plenty of coins or tokens ready.

- Go to bed earlier than usual so that you'll feel refreshed and rested at the interview.

THE MORNING OF THE INTERVIEW

- Get up earlier than usual so you'll have time to prepare and leave early.

- Quickly review your qualifications for the job, the questions you plan to ask and how you'll answer some of the questions you may be asked.

- Calm down. One young man followed all the rules except this one and lost his opportunity. He arrived at the company before dawn, knowing there would be thousands of applicants for the job. (It was the height of the 1982 recession.) When the office opened three hours later, he was first in line. His grooming and attire were perfect, and he smiled at everyone. He was young, good looking, and had two years of college. But he tried too hard. He worried so much about being nervous that he appeared overly withdrawn to the interviewer. This was the small, fatal flaw which cost him the job.

It's natural to feel nervous. The interviewer expects it and is trained to make you feel at ease. If you still feel jittery, admit it openly, in a way which makes you look good. For example, you might say something to this effect, "I guess I'm a bit nervous. That's because this job means a lot to me."

Neither flatter wealth nor cringe before power.
- anonymous

Try to imagine the interview as a learning experience rather than a trial. Think of the interviewer as a friend rather than as an adversary or stern judge.

If you think of the interview as a two way exchange of ideas between equals (which it is), it helps to shift your focus from yourself to the real issue. This perspective also takes some of the pressure off the interviewer, since you'll be taking some initiative in bringing up matters he or she might overlook.

Take a brisk walk just before the interview so that you'll arrive smiling, calm and with good color in your cheeks. If the weather is bad, do some tension relieving exercises in the company lounge. Breathe deeply, stretch your muscles, raise and lower your shoulders, touch your toes, or put your head down between your knees. Arrive early so you'll have time to calm down, and get used to the surroundings.

THE JOB APPLICATION FORM

Before the interview begins, you will be asked to fill out a job application form. Much of the information it requests has already been included in the resume you may have sent. So, why bother?

It's for the company's records. Only standardized forms are used.

It's a legal statement that the information you give is true. Therefore, don't lie!

The care and accuracy with which you answer the questions is taken into account in assessing your eligibility for the job. So, be sure to do the following.

- Write legibly. If your handwriting is awful, ask to take the form home to type.

- Answer every question and follow every instruction. If it says, "PLEASE PRINT," don't write in cursive style. Answer all that's asked for: zip code, telephone area code, etc. If it asks "EXPECTED SALARY," don't write "ANYTHING" or something to that effect. Write "NEGOTIABLE" or "OPEN" and you'll appear more business like. If some of the questions do not pertain to you (i.e, military experience) write "NONE" or "DOES NOT APPLY."

If you leave some questions blank it might be construed as carelessness. Answer each question as completely as space permits. Use your resume to jog your memory.

Tomorrow is the 31st anniversary of my 39th birthday.   - Ronald Reagan
              on the eve of his 70th birthday.

SHOULD YOU LIE ABOUT YOUR AGE?

The law prohibits employers from asking you to state your race, religion, nationality and birthdate on a job application form. Some older forms which ask for this information may not have been discarded. Since this is an illegal question, you may leave it blank.

However, it is legal to ask for your approximate age such as, FILL IN THE BLANK NEXT TO YOUR AGE RANGE (of, say, 55 to 65). If you leave it blank,

it might be construed as carelessness. For DATES
OF GRADUATION (or SCHOOLING COMPLETED) some experts advise you to write only the most recent
dates and ignore the earlier ones (high school and
elementary attendance.) Others say you must include all dates since this is not an illegal
question.

Stating a falsehood on a legal document poses
other problems. Soon after you are hired, you'll
be asked to submit proof of age for Social Security and insurance purposes. A lie can cost you the
job. Nowadays, more employers are investigating
the background of prospective employees, and modern communications make it easier to detect falsehoods.

A 52-year old teacher subtracted ten years from
her age for an overseas job and was hired. But,
the white lie was discovered a few months later
when the university's insurance representative
asked for proof of age. Fortunately, her passport
contained the correct birthdate, or she would have
been liable for immediate deportation. The lie
itself was considered a serious matter, not her
real age, because she had been hired for her
ability and accomplishments.

Question:
         "How do you feel on your 100th birthday?"
Answer:
      "Much better than I did a hundred years ago."

One of the most important questions in the application is why you want to work for the company.
This is where you should stress your skills and
other qualities which will be assets to the firm.
Avoid focusing on your own needs.

A SAMPLE OF QUESTIONS INTERVIEWERS ASK

Knowing in advance the questions you may be asked
makes it less likely that you'll be taken by
surprise and blurt out something inappropriate. It
will also help to clarify your goals so that your
answers will be specific and to the point rather
than rambling and vague.

There are far more questions here than you will be
asked in a 15 to 20 minute interview. The reason
for including so many is to help you cover all
bases. Not every question is appropriate to your

203

situation. There are no "right" answers to the questions. Nevertheless, a few guidelines have been included.

There are two basic types of questions, the factual, or straightforward, and the probing, psychological question. Each is designed to elicit different kinds of information from you. Listen carefully to the questions and know exactly what is being asked before replying.

FACTUAL QUESTIONS

1. WHY DO YOU WANT TO WORK FOR OUR COMPANY?
Flattery will get you everywhere. One personnel recruiter put it this way: "People who say they want to work for us because it's such a great company score a lot of points; let's face it."

2. WHAT ABOUT THIS JOB INTERESTS YOU THE MOST? THE LEAST?

3. ARE YOU WILLING TO WORK OVERTIME?

4. WHY SHOULD WE HIRE YOU? ("Why do you think you're the best person for this job?" "What can you offer us that someone else cannot?")

Avoid giving the impression that you're interested only in your needs. Describe how your qualifications will benefit the firm. Cite studies which show that older workers are more reliable, have fewer accidents, a lower absenteeism rate, and need less supervision than younger workers. If the interviewer is much younger than you are, be careful not to give the impression you think the younger generation is hopeless.

5. HOW IS YOUR HEALTH?
If you have a health problem which will seriously affect your work, don't lie about it. If you are asked to come in for a second screening, you may have to lift 50-pound weights, or demonstrate other proof of your physical fitness.

6. HOW GOOD ARE YOU WHEN WORKING UNDER PRESSURE?
Simply answering, "Excellent" isn't enough. Cite situations in which your performance was top notch.

7. WHY DO YOU WANT TO CHANGE CAREERS AFTER SO MANY YEARS?

8. HOW WOULD YOU FEEL WORKING FOR A YOUNGER BOSS AND WITH MUCH YOUNGER CO-WORKERS?
If the question is phrased as, "Will you be uncomfortable working for a much younger supervisor?," don't just say "No" and leave it at that. Give concrete examples of how well you get along with younger co-workers, especially those in a supervisory position.

9. ARE YOU GOOD AT SUPERVISING WORKERS?
Again, "Yes" is an inadequate reply. Give examples. Avoid confirming negative stereotypes about older persons being "bossy" or "condescending."

10. WHAT DID YOU LIKE MOST ABOUT YOUR LAST JOB?
Avoid vague answers such as, "working with people" unless that is a key feature of the job you're applying for. Mention specific job responsibilities, your achievements, the work conditions, etc.

11. WHAT WERE YOUR MOST IMPORTANT ACCOMPLISHMENTS IN YOUR LAST JOB?

12. WHAT METHODS DO YOU USE TO SUPERVISE WORKERS?

13. WHAT ARE YOUR STRONGEST QUALITIES?
Describe only those qualities that are relevant to the purpose of the interview.

14. WHAT ARE YOUR WEAK POINTS?
If you say something like this, "I really can't think of any," you won't make the great impression you imagine you will. Nobody is perfect. The interviewer might think you're conceited, insincere or plain dumb. An applicant who admits to some weaknesses is viewed as being more honest. Slant your description of your "weak" points in such a way, however, that you come out smelling like a rose. You might say, for example, "Sometimes I neglect my own needs because I get so involved with my work."

15. WHICH OF YOUR WORK EXPERIENCES ARE PROFESSIONAL AND WHICH ARE VOLUNTARY?
Say, "All my work is professional" and go on to describe those abilities involved in your volunteer work which are transferable to the present job.

16. WHICH POSITION IN THIS COMPANY WOULD YOU CHOOSE IF YOU HAD THE OPPORTUNITY?
Don't fence yourself into one job. Apply what you have learned about job families to describe how

your skills and aptitudes fit into a variety of job niches. This is also a good opportunity to display your knowledge about the company.

17. ARE YOU CONSIDERING OTHER POSITIONS AT THIS TIME?

18. WHY HAVE YOU HELD SO MANY JOBS?
Some of the reasons for "creative" job hopping include these. "They weren't challenging enough," "My skills and training weren't utilized," "The opportunities for advancement were poor," or "There were things I wanted to learn from each job so that I would be ready for the present one, which is my real goal."

19. WHY HAVE YOU STAYED WITH ONE EMPLOYER SO LONG?
The interviewer is probably concerned about your ability to adjust to change.

20. WHAT ARE YOUR LONG RANGE GOALS?
The interviewer wants to know how ambitious you are, how long you expect to stay with the company.

21. WHAT WERE THE BIGGEST PROBLEMS YOU HAD TO FACE IN YOUR PREVIOUS JOB AND HOW DID YOU RESOLVE THEM?

22. WHAT WERE THE MOST SATISFYING ASPECTS OF YOUR LAST JOB? THE MOST UNSATISFYING ASPECTS?

23. WHAT WERE SOME OF THE BIGGEST MISTAKES YOU MADE IN YOUR PREVIOUS JOB?
Show that you've learned from the experience.

24. AREN'T YOU OVERQUALIFIED FOR THIS JOB?
This may be a sneaky way of asking, "Aren't you too old for the job?" The interviewer wants assurance that your energy level matches the demands of the job, that your experience and qualifications as a mature employee will be assets to the firm.

If you are making a radical career change, such as from teaching to a business career, the interviewer may be wondering if you'll quit at the earliest opportunity. You can allay such doubts by:

- Describing how the abilities required in your profession are transferable to the present job. Draw as many parallels as possible between the two occupations.

- Assuring the interviewer that you have no intention of going back to the old career by pointing out its negative aspects (low salary, poor advancement opportunities, etc.)

- Avoiding the use of fancy vocabulary and jargon from your old profession, and using the buzzwords of the new one in order to convince the interviewer that you have made a clean break.

Don't expect your M.A. or Ph.D. to get you the job. Some employers view it as a liability. Others might be intimidated by it.

25. WHAT KIND OF BOSS DO YOU PREFER?
The interviewer wants to know if you are a team-worker who doesn't have to be continually told what to do and how to do it.

26. TELL ME ABOUT YOURSELF.
Mention only those aspects which demonstrate your qualifications for the job.

- Hobbies which utilize the same skills and interests that are required by the job.

- Personality traits that match the job. ("I like working with people" if the job involves much contact with the public.)

- Volunteer work and membership in organizations where you have exercised some of the abilities required by the job.

CAUTION: This is an open-ended question which can lure you into telling your life story and other irrelevancies. That's not the purpose of the question. The interviewer may also want to see how focused your thoughts are. Get to the point fast.

27. WHY DID YOU LEAVE YOUR LAST JOB?
The way you answer this question can make or break you. It's important to show that you've learned from experience, that you harbor no ill will toward your previous employer.

28. HOW DID YOU GET ALONG WITH YOUR PREVIOUS EMPLOYER?

PROBING QUESTIONS are designed to elicit information about your personality, including interests, attitude toward work and authority, political views and energy level. The interviewer cannot ask you directly, "Do you go to pieces when under pressure?" One way to get such information is through indirect questions.

For example, the head of a Federal agency uses astrology as a point of discussion in job interviews. If an applicant is a Pisces, she mentions the tendency of this group to go in two different directions, and then asks if the applicant also has this problem. Then she casually mentions that Ralph Nader is a Pisces and watches to see if the applicant becomes very positive or very defensive.

Although it's important to convey sincerity, it's not dishonest to slant your answers in a manner which emphasizes your best qualities. Anything you say which reassures the interviewer that you are the right person for the job will be appreciated.

1. HOW DO YOU FEEL ABOUT YOUR PREVIOUS (OR PRESENT) EMPLOYER?
The interviewer wants to know if you are difficult to work with, disloyal, unstable or crotchety.

2. TELL ME ABOUT YOURSELF.
You'll probably ask, "What do you want to know?" and the answer will be even more confusing, "Anything you want to say." Your response shows whether you are easily put off balance by such a broad, unexpected question, and if you can focus on the essential facts without going into the rambling story of your life. The interviewer may also want to know if you know yourself well enough to be certain this is the right job for you.

3. PLEASE SUMMARIZE YOUR WORK EXPERIENCE FOR US.
This is a jawbreaker question for applicants who have many years of work experience, especially those who have had many jobs. The challenge is how to organize, select and summarize the essential facts, how to determine where to begin and end. If you ask, "Which job do you want to hear about?" the interviewer may throw you into further consternation by saying, "All of them."

The interviewer may want to know if you are able to focus on the relevant issues and relate them logically and concisely to the job you're applying for. He may want to know if you're articulate and if your thoughts wander easily. If you have done a thorough self-assessment, this question should be easy for you to answer.

4. TELL ME ABOUT AN EXPERIENCE YOU HAD BEFORE THE AGE OF 16 WHICH GAVE YOU THE GREATEST SENSE OF FULFILLMENT?
The interviewer wants to know if your basic personality and interests match the demands of the job and the company. If there is a mis-match, it's more likely that you will quit at the earliest opportunity or, worse yet, become a clock watcher.

Were you, for example, happiest in the company of others or alone? Did such events involve mechanical objects, solving crossword or mathematical puzzles, learning about nature, or caring for animals? These and similar questions are the basic ingredients of interest inventories which are administered by career counselors.

5. WHAT HAVE YOU LEARNED FROM YOUR PAST MISTAKES?
The interviewer wants to know if you are still growing as a person, and how well you deal with your mistakes.

6. WHAT DO YOU DO IN YOUR SPARE TIME?

7. AN EMPLOYEE UNDER YOUR SUPERVISION IS USUALLY OUT SICK ON FRIDAYS OR MONDAYS. HOW WOULD YOU DEAL WITH THE SITUATION?

8. WHAT DO YOU LIKE TO DO?

9. DO YOU FEEL YOU NEED ANY IMPROVEMENT?

10. WHERE WOULD YOU LIKE TO BE IN FIVE YEARS?

11. WHAT IS THE MOST DIFFICULT SITUATION YOU EVER EXPERIENCED AND WHAT DID YOU DO ABOUT IT?

12. WHAT IS THE MOST WONDERFUL SITUATION YOU EVER EXPERIENCED?

QUESTIONS THE INTERVIEWER SHOULD NOT ASK

A recent study by the Civil Liberties Union in New York found that of the 65 private employers and government agencies involved, 62 had asked discriminatory questions which, if not illegal, bordered on illegality. The worst offenders were the government agencies, because they had not upgraded their recruitment policies in years. Some of the questions regarded previous arrests, alcohol and drug abuse, medical history, relationships with neighbors and credit rating.

The law requires that employers consider only factors that are relevant to your PRESENT ability to do the job.

There is no clear cut answer on how to reply to such questions. If you refuse to answer, it could jeopardize your chances of getting the job. On the other hand, if you blurt out the naked truth, without adding the positive, qualifying aspects of the situation, you've done yourself in.

The Civil Liberties Union has published a handbook on how to deal with this situation. See the appendix for details.

In some states it is illegal for the interviewer to ask questions about the following.

1. Your age, or a request for proof of age (birth or baptismal certificates, driver's license, etc.) However, it is legal to ask this after you have been hired.

2. Your height, weight and past illnesses.

3. Whether you have a disability which does not affect your ability to do the job under discussion.

4. Your religion, race or national origin.

5. Child care arrangements; marital status.

6. Whether you have ever been arrested.

7. Whether you have ever taken addictive drugs.

YOU DO NOT HAVE TO ANSWER ILLEGAL QUESTIONS.
The law protects individuals in certain categories, and age is one of these. However, be careful not to reply bluntly, such as "That's none of your business" or "I won't tell you because it's illegal for you to ask such a question." Be tactful and say something to this effect:"I think my experience and qualifications are excellent for the company and I really don't see why my age has any bearing on the job." Smile as you say this.

If the interviewer starts probing into your personal life ask, in as tactful a manner as possible, "I'd like to be as helpful as I can, but I don't see what my personal life has to do with the requirements for the job." Better yet, assure the interviewer that there is nothing in your personal life which will interfere with your ability to do the work.

The interviewer may ask questions about your political beliefs and activities, such as "Are you active in the Gray Panthers?". Skirt the question gracefully, tactfully. Ask, "Will you please tell me why that information is important to the company?" or something to that effect. A sociology professor who was applying for a job during the heyday of campus radicalism was asked, "What is your opinion of legitimate murder?" The college president wanted to know her attitude toward the death penalty as a condition for being offered the job. This is clearly illegal.

QUESTIONS YOU MAY WANT TO ASK

If you ask questions at appropriate times or when the interviewer seems to be finished, you will make a better impression. Be careful not to give the impression that you're trying to take over the interview. Prepare a list of questions to ask. Here are some suggestions.

WHAT WILL A TYPICAL DAY ON THE JOB BE LIKE?

WHAT KIND OF PERSON DO YOU WANT FOR THIS JOB?

WHAT ARE SOME OF THE BIGGEST PROBLEMS THAT MUST BE RESOLVED ON THE JOB?

WHERE DOES THIS JOB LEAD? ("Are there opportunities for increased responsibilities?")

IS THE VACANCY DUE TO COMPANY EXPANSION OR DID SOMEONE LEAVE?

WHY DID THE PERSON WHO LAST HELD THIS JOB LEAVE?

WHICH JOBS WOULD BE AMONG THE FIRST TO BE AXED SHOULD THERE BE A NEED FOR COMPANY RETRENCHMENT?

WHAT KIND OF SUPPORT WILL THE PERSON HIRED FOR THIS JOB GET? FOR HOW LONG? WHO WILL GIVE THE SUPPORT?

HOW IS JOB PERFORMANCE EVALUATED? HOW OFTEN WILL THERE BE AN EVALUATION?

DOES THE COMPANY SUPPORT (pay for) CONTINUING EDUCATION FOR ITS WORKERS? IS EVERYONE ELIGIBLE? WILL AGE DISQUALIFY A PERSON?

ARE THERE ANY OTHER ADVANTAGES TO THIS JOB?

WHAT IS THE WORK SETTING LIKE? MAY I SEE IT?

HOW MUCH FLEXIBILITY DO YOUR EMPLOYEES HAVE RE-GARDING HOURS OF WORK, CLOTHING TO WEAR, VACATION SCHEDULES, LUNCH HOUR, ETC.?

ARE THERE ANY DISADVANTAGES?

DOES YOU PREFER TO PROMOTE FROM WITHIN OR OUTSIDE THE COMPANY?

WHEN CAN I EXPECT TO HEAR THE RESULTS OF THE INTERVIEW?

THE SUBJECT OF SALARY

When this comes up, be prepared to say how much you want. To find out what the going pay range is for the occupation, read the help wanted ads and contact the Job Service office.

The experts have conflicting suggestions on how applicants near retirement age should deal with this question. It depends on where you're starting from, how many years you have left to give to the company, and the degree of competition for the job. Whatever the situation, the employer is going to try to get you as cheaply as possible. According to one placement counselor, many older applicants price themselves out of a job because they fail to be realistic about the job market.

On the other hand, if you are highly skilled and the demand for your skills is greater than the supply, the experts advise you NOT to undersell yourself, otherwise the interviewer will think you're not as good as you really are. Get off your knees and ask what you think you're worth.

Be flexible and keep the door open for negotiation.

Don't be afraid to say, "I don't think the salary you're offering reflects my skills and experience," if you think it won't jeopardize your chances of being hired.

If the interviewer fails to budge, try to negotiate on specific fringe benefits such as vacation, tuition refund, office and secretarial facilities.

If you accept a lower salary than you think you're
worth, some experts advise you to ask for salary
reviews based on frequent (quarterly or semi-
annual) job performance evaluations.

Don't go in knowing little or nothing about the
pay range for the job.

SOME FINAL NOTES

If you are not offered the job at the time of the
interview, ask when you may call to learn the
decision.

Thank the interviewer before leaving. If you still
want the job, say so, and add that you are confident that you can do it well. If you don't express
your interest, the interviewer may think you are
lukewarm about it. You'll have a competitive edge
if you do, since most job applicants neglect to
say this.

WHAT ARE THE MOST COMMON MISTAKES MADE BY OLDER APPLICANTS DURING AN INTERVIEW?

I asked a placement counselor this question, and
here is his reply.

They tend to dwell in the past rather than the
present and future. If you do this, you will date
yourself. Discuss your plans to take adult education courses in order to upgrade your skills. Talk
about your career ambitions within the company.
Inform them of your interest in the latest technologies, etc.

They talk too much about themselves, about their
past troubles and personal problems. This makes
them appear to be difficult or cantankerous.

They exude a lack of self-confidence. They come in
with a beaten down expression. You can't convince
an employer with such an attitude.

Some go to the other extreme and overcompensate
for any fears and insecurities they may have. They
try to come across as Superman and Wonder Woman,

and oversell themselves. It's foolish to represent yourself as something you aren't. You won't fool anyone but yourself.

Be realistic about what you can and cannot do. Say, for example, "I certainly can't lift 175 pounds anymore, but I can lift more 50 pound weights in one day than when I was younger, because I've learned how to pace myself. I can do more with less effort, because I've learned how to be more efficient in my movements."

Or, "I've learned to channel my energies so that I don't waste as much as I used to. I can manage my time better, and in the process I've increased my stamina. For example, I used to work without a break until I collapsed. Now I've learned to take short breaks before exhausting my reserves of energy; consequently, I can work for a much longer period of time."

Or, "In my last job, I was out sick only once in two years."

Some of them haven't learned how to turn a disadvantage into an advantage. If you have a health problem like arthritis or diabetes, for example, don't try to hide it if the matter of your health comes up during the interview. Don't try to explain it away either. Your attitude means more than any disability that can be compensated for. Be open and positive about it.

Say something to this effect, "Although I've had this condition for the past four years, I've learned to compensate for it by strengthening my other abilities. I can't use my right hand as well as I used to, but I've learned how to write with my left hand and now I can do better with it than I could with my right one."

"I've learned to avoid accidents by not taking unreasonable risks. I'm more careful than I used to be when I was 25; consequently, I have fewer accidents now and I make fewer mistakes."

"I've learned to concentrate more on my work, and my thoughts don't wander as much from the task at hand."

Another common mistake is that they focus too much on their own needs instead of pointing out how their abilities and experience will benefit the company. In other words, they take an egocentric, or selfish, approach. The employer isn't in business to do them a favor. This is the impression they give if they say, for example, "I have bills to pay...kids in college...a mortgage on the house," and so on. Then they go into the story of what a tough life they've had, trying to win sympathy.

Some of them are too age conscious. If the interviewer is about the same age as they are, they try to establish a common bond on this basis. A 60-year old interviewer does not want to be reminded of his age. If you make him aware of his approaching retirement, you're finished. If, on the other hand, the interviewer is much younger, any talk about your age may be viewed as condescension. It's as if you were saying, "I have seniority over you. I have much more life experiences."

AFTER THE INTERVIEW

Even if the job looks like a sure bet, don't cancel any other interviews you have lined up, and keep looking. It does happen that the funds for a job are suddenly withdrawn, or the job itself is cancelled as an economizing measure. This happened to a man who was offered a job as department head in a state agency. He had already put his house up for sale and made other arrangements when the telegram bearing the bad news arrived. Fortunately, he had a good lawyer and the job offer was restituted.

Write a brief thank you note which restates your interest in working for the company and summarizes important points covered during the interview. Some experts advise attaching a one page, post-interview resume which highlights your special qualifications for the job. Then, follow up your letter with a phone call to see if it was received and learn the employer's decision. Some employers say this can be the deciding factor.

If you are not offered the job, some experts advise you to send another letter expressing your continued interest in working for the company. Ask whether there are other departments which might need someone with your background in the near future. Ask if the interviewer can suggest another employer who might be interested in someone with your qualifications.

PSYCHOLOGICAL TESTS

Some employers administer tests of skills and aptitudes, personality and interests, and general intelligence to job applicants who pass the first screening. These tests are administered in order to ensure that the applicant has the requisite skills and aptitudes for the job and the personality traits which make for good teamwork.

Are you aware that you may not get the job because you score too high on an intelligence test? It's true! The science of personnel psychology is so advanced that it's possible to know the range of I.Q. scores which suit the cognitive demands of different occupations. If your score indicates that the job you're applying for is not challenging enough, you're more likely to get bored and quit at the earliest opportunity.

Large firms which have personnel departments are more likely to administer psychological tests. Some job placement agencies also administer tests in order to assure employers that the persons they recommend possess the requisite qualifications. Many government jobs require a minimum passing grade on civil service examinations.

There's no need to be scared. Hiring decisions are not based on test scores alone. Other factors are taken into account, and often these carry more weight. If an applicant's other qualifications are excellent, a below average score is often disregarded. Employers know that a single test score is an inadequate measure of a person's suitability for a job.

If possible, learn in advance if the job requires taking a test. You can do this by phoning the company's personnel department or by reading about the occupation in the Occupational Outlook Handbook. If it's a civil service job, contact the Federal Job Service office.

Be smart and prepare in advance. The tests are not difficult, but some people, especially older applicants who haven't taken a test in years, suffer from text anxiety. Another factor which weighs against older job applicants is that many of these written, multiple choice tests are timed. So, borrow a stopwatch and practice speeding up your rate of response to a few tests.

Aptitude tests are relatively easy for most persons. They assess basic skills in spelling and vocabulary, reading comprehension, simple arithmetic and mathematics, reasoning, and the ability to follow directions. (That's why it's important for you to read the job application form carefully, and to answer the questions completely and clearly.) You don't even have to write out your answers. All that's needed is to mark the right answer among a given set of answers. The score is based on the number of correct choices you make in a set period of time.

In a reading comprehension test, all you have to do is read several, short paragraphs and then mark the correct answer from among four or five given answers. Its purpose is to assess how well you understand what you have just read. The numerical reasoning tests estimate your ability to apply what you learned in elementary and high school to solve simple problems encountered in everyday life.

Taking timed, multiple choice tests is a skill in itself which is easily learned. One of the skills involved is knowing how to optimize the correct number of choices you make in the allotted time.

You can find sample tests to practice on in the public library and in school career guidance and placement offices. Also, see if the local Federal Job Service office is still administering such tests free of charge. The best way to get rid of test anxiety is to practice taking them in a stress-free situation.

It's important to listen carefully to the instructions given before the test begins. If there's something you don't understand, ask questions no matter how stupid or trivial they seem to you. If you wait until after the test starts, you'll lose valuable seconds which can lower your score.

Remember, every second counts in a timed test. Have everything you might need during the test on hand so you can work steadily: handkerchief, chewing gum, eraser, pencils, etc.

When a difficult question appears, don't waste time pondering over it. Answer all the easy questions first, skipping over the difficult ones, marking these lightly so that when you are ready to go back to them, you'll waste no time finding them.

It's very likely that the job you are applying for does not require taking any tests. If it does, you will find them quite simple.

GOOD LUCK!

At the age of 100, Giuseppe Prezzolini continues to write several reviews and articles a month for European newspapers.

"I just wanted to learn more," said 98 year old Jesse Byam, of Michigan, explaining why she returned to high school so late in life. Years ago, despite good grades, she had to drop out of school in the 10th grade. In 1982, she graduated as a straight-A student.

Shelomo Dov Goitein, age 82, receives a lifetime award of $60,000 annually from the John D. and Catherine T. MacArthur Foundation. The award will enable the noted authority on Islamic civilization to continue his outstanding scholarly work.

At 85, Roger Sessions wins the Pulitzer Prize for his "Concerto for Orchestra," which the Boston Symphony Orchestra introduced the year before. Mr. Sessions is still busy teaching and composing music.

"Mr. Plastic," as 88-year old Herman Mark is known, is still experimenting with new safety synthetic fabrics. He travels an average of 100,000 miles a year to conduct his research and give lectures.

At the age of 86. Esther van Wagoner Tufty continues her busy life as a Washington based newspaper reporter.

At the age of 80, Barbara Cartland, continues to churn out heart throbbing love stories.

Actress Ruth Gordon changes careers at the age of 85, when she offers her first novel, "Shady Lady."

John Payne, who made his first movie in 1937, retires as an actor and returns to school to earn a Ph.D.

At 68, Violet Ashton publishes her first book.

11

BEST JOB PROSPECTS FOR THE EIGHTIES

According to career counselors and labor market experts, your best chances of finding a job or making a successful career change in this decade lie in the following areas:

- Occupations which have a critical shortage of skilled workers.

- Traditional occupations which employ large numbers of workers and in which worker turnover is relatively high.

- Occupations in which mature workers are acknowledged to be better workers and age discrimination is minimal.

- Civil Service Jobs - These generally have no upper age limit, since government policy favors the hiring of persons in "disadvantaged" categories. This includes persons 45 years of age and older, females of all ages, members of minority groups, and the handicapped.

- Companies which have a good record of hiring, promoting and/or retaining mature workers.

HOW TO BEAT THE COMPETITION

LEARN WHICH INDUSTRIES OFFER THE BEST EMPLOYMENT PROSPECTS FOR SOMEONE WITH YOUR SKILLS. Did you know that the same occupation generally has widely different levels of opportunities in different industries? During the recent recession, some industries were thriving and hiring office workers and salespersons like crazy while others, notably the automobile, rubber, steel and textile industries, were laying off thousands of workers at all levels.

If you lost your job as sales representative with an automobile manufacturer, for example, try transferring your skills and experience to another industry which is hiring more workers, such as electronics, pharmaceutical, or cable television. If you're an engineer who has been replaced by a recent graduate, you can transfer your skills to non-technical settings, such as hospitals, banks, insurance companies, research laboratories, government agencies, and consulting firms. If you're in training and development, your skills are needed in the thriving health industry. Other categories of workers who are in demand in a variety of industries include secretaries, janitors, receptionists and word processors.

LEARN BETTER WAYS TO DO YOUR JOB, OR ENROLL IN A COURSE TO BRING YOUR SKILLS UP-TO-DATE.
Whenever there's a surplus of job seekers in a particular occupation, employers tend to get fussy. They demand specific training and more "hands on" experience. "They no longer hire just any kind of computer programmer," said a Jobs Service counselor. "They look for programmers who are experts in a specific language and specific hardware."

Many job descriptions are being revised to include the changes brought about by technological and scientific discoveries. All you may need to upgrade your present skills is just one evening course. A typist, for example, can learn word processing in just one week. The demand for word processors is currently so great that many companies and placement agencies are offering free training.

Although jobs for liberal arts graduates are hard to find these days, reports the Bureau of Labor Statistics, those who have acquired some knowledge of the skills and/or jargon of the new technical fields can find jobs more easily.

IF JOB PROSPECTS IN YOUR COMMUNITY ARE POOR, GO WHERE THE OPPORTUNITIES ARE MUCH BETTER
The Census Bureau reports that by 1990, over half of the nation's population is expected to move to the South and West. And, for the first time since 1820, small towns and rural areas in every region are gaining population faster than the big cities and metropolitan areas. Companies in these communities need qualified workers in all occupations, including those which have poor nationwide employment prospects.

Before you start packing, however, there are some facts you should know about forecasts which are based on statistics. Data from the Census Bureau and the Bureau of Labor Statistics is at least one year old by the time it gets reported in the newspapers. Meanwhile, unanticipated, short-term changes may occur which invalidate a forecast which looks ten years or more into the future.

For example, California has been one of the fastest growing states in terms of jobs and population growth. In mid-1982, however, its growth began to decline as a result of the spreading economic recession and internal factors such as an astronomical increase in housing costs. Even senior level managers and professionals were turning down job offers in the state because they couldn't afford to live there.

Although Texas has had a phenomenal job growth rate, migrants who are unskilled or have unwanted skills have been no better off than they were in the depressed areas of the Northeast and Midwest. In 1982, the State's Human Resources Department distributed a brochure to newcomers which read, "Dead Broke in Texas?"

A better way of learning where jobs are more plentiful is to look at statistics based on local economic conditions and at employment trends within a region or state rather than nationwide. You'll probably be able to find towns and cities which have better prospects not too far away home. For example, not all parts of the Sunbelt have experienced a booming economic growth rate. At one point, Alabama had the second highest unemployment rate in the nation.

In Michigan, Illinois and Ohio, new developments are thumbing their collective noses at the poor employment projections for these states. In 1981, despite its above average unemployment rate, Ohio had acute shortages of engineers, computer technicians, tool and die makers, and accountants. While workers in the declining manufacturing industries of Cleveland were being laid off, employers were recruiting workers for the new service and medical technology industries. And in Detroit, building contractors were reporting shortages of technicians, hydrologists and geologists. All across the depressed automobile manufacturing states, electronics and other high technology companies were opening their doors to qualified workers and so were the service industries.

The Illinois Bureau of Employment Security reported shortages of workers in the repair, health and business services, and projected a 45% increase in the demand for air conditioning, heating and refrigeration repairers. The health and data processing industries were predicting even greater increases in jobs for skilled workers. And in all of of these industries, clerical workers, secretaries, receptionists and other support workers were also in demand.

WHEN MOVING TO ANOTHER COMMUNITY IS THE ONLY WAY TO SAVE YOUR CAREER. It can also be an opportunity to escape disagreeable relatives, a high crime area and an unbearable climate. Before you start packing, however, it's wise to make a few inquiries about the place which beckons you.

How does the local pay range for your occupation compare with the living costs? The pay range for an occupation often varies widely among regions and from rural to urban areas. Pay rates in cities, for example, are often higher than in rural areas, but so is the cost of living. In recent years, the increase in the cost of living in traditionally high wage states, such as New York and California, has been greater than the increase in salary levels. In 1981, despite the fact that professions in California paid as much as 20% higher than in other areas, the state had difficulty recruiting needed workers because the average price of a house was $100,000 to $150,000.

Another problem that must be considered is the difficulty of finding a buyer for your home while interest rates remain high. In the New York metropolitan region, for example, some corporations resorted to buying and listing the homes of executives who had to be transferred. One firm advertised a free luxury automobile to buyers of these houses.

If you must move while the real estate market is depressed, you may have to rent your home, have it managed by a real estate broker, or sell it at a loss until things get back to normal. Another factor to consider is the high cost of moving to a new community.

A move to a boom area does not necessarily guarantee that you'll find the kind of job you want. The competition may be tougher than you imagined because companies which have plenty of job openings, such as those in the computer industry, usually skim the cream of the crop. The experts advise you not to go out of state unless you're certain a job is waiting for you. See chapter 3 for information on how this can be done.

ADJUST YOUR SALARY DEMANDS TO THE REALITIES OF THE JOB MARKET. "Even in fields where there are plenty of jobs, we see highly skilled, well educated, older persons being rejected time after time," said a Jobs Service counselor. "This is because they expect a salary at a higher level than the one they earned in their previous job. They don't realize they're competing with recent graduates who have more up-to-date skills and lower salary requirements. Let's face it, employers prefer those with up-to-date skills."

FIND OTHER OCCUPATIONS WHICH CAN UTILIZE YOUR SKILLS AND EXPERTISE.

See chapter 3 for a definition of job "families." Look in the 1982-83 <u>Occupational Outlook Handbook</u> to find your job family. Many dismissed middle managers and technical experts, for example, find work as consultants, either as freelancers or as members of consulting firms. Others transfer to companies where their skills and experience are in greater demand, such as financial services and information services. Many find sales positions in high technology firms.

Artists are having a rough time finding work these days, but with a certificate or degree which combines their art skills with psychology, many are able to find jobs working with emotionally and physically handicapped children or as art therapists in psychiatric hospitals, nursing homes, and rehabilitation programs.

Despite the strong demand for engineers, many who are past 45 years of age are having difficulty finding a job in their specialty. However, there are plenty of opportunities in related fields where their skills and experience are highly valued. For example, there is a critical shortage of mathematics and science teachers in technical and high schools. Colleges are also desperately in need of mathematics and science teachers. There are plenty of part-time and full-time positions available which do not require a teaching certificate. Many of the private schools are hiring qualified persons who lack a certificate, and the public schools in some states have waived this requirement temporarily while the new teacher studies for a certificate after work.

With a few courses in management, an engineer may
be able to move into the exploding field of telecommunications, especially cable television. This
industry is so new that there are few college
courses available on the subject, and most of the
workers presently employed received their training
on the job. The computer industry is also in need
of persons who combine the skills and knowledge of
engineering with a few courses in finance and
management.

WHICH EMPLOYERS HAVE A GOOD RECORD OF HIRING MATURE PERSONS ?

It's difficult to know with any degree of certain-
ty which employers have a more enlightened policy
toward workers 45 years of age and older. One way
to find out is to ask persons you know who are in
a position to get this information. Another is to
look in the public library for news about companies which have had age discrimination charges
brought against them. They are generally eager to
prevent another such occurrence because of the bad
publicity involved. Ask the librarian how to find
this information

MANY COMPANIES HIRE RETIREES ON A PART-TIME OR
TEMPORARY, FULL-TIME BASIS. If you are not nearing
retirement, you may find that companies which have
such a program are more willing to hire persons
over 45 years of age as a result of having had
good experiences with older employees. SRI International, Exxon, Monsanto and Shell are a few of
the large corporations which hire as consultants
retirees who had been employed at the technical,
professional and managerial level. Traveler's
Insurance Company uses retirees to fill mostly
temporary clerical assignments. In 1982 the home
office was considering converting 300 jobs into
job sharing positions for 600 retirees.

COMPANIES WHICH DO RESEARCH ON A CONTRACT BASIS
generally need specialists to work on short notice
and on a temporary basis. The Avionics division of
Honeywell, Minneapolis, hires its middle management and executive retirees as consultants for
short term projects. It recently started a computerized skills bank which matches needed skills
with available retirees. Several calls a month
come in from other employers in the city who are
looking for older persons to fill full or part-
time positions in consulting, accounting, engi-

neering and other jobs. Grumman Corporation, in Long Island, has a successful program of hiring retired technicians, engineers, technical writers and other persons with needed skills.

SOME EMPLOYERS HAVE SPECIAL PROGRAMS TO PROMOTE THE HIRING OF MATURE WORKERS. Some hire only for part-time assignments. Among these are Walt Disney Productions, Atlantic Richfield Company, Continental Illinois Bank and Trust Company, Burger King, Harris Trust and Savings Bank in Chicago, The Sun Company Inc., Polaroid Corporation, the Toro Company in Minneapolis, Textron Inc. in Rhode Island, Control Data Corporation in Minneapolis, Hazeltine Corporation in Long Island, Xerox Corporation, Pepsico in Purchase, New York and MacDonald's fast food restaurants.

Many banks hire retired and older workers for positions ranging from teller to top management. Bankers Life and Casualty Company in Chicago has hired persons over 65 years of age with excellent results. One of them was an 85 year old woman. A secretary who had to leave her job in another company because she had reached its mandatory retirement age of 65 found another job at Bankers Life and Casualty which does not have a mandatory retirement policy. In the six years she has been with the company, she has had several promotions.

Insurance companies have long had fair employment policies for middle age and older workers. In 1982, over 100 chief executive officers from the industry sent a letter to the White House promising to increase the hiring, training and retraining of older workers.

The real estate industry also finds maturity and experience to be assets. Many employers are known to hire older persons, including retirees, as sales persons and brokers.

The Aerospace Corporation of Los Angeles was so impressed with the performance of a group of retirees and older workers who were hired to solve a tough assignment from the U. S. Air Force that it now has a policy of hiring qualified older persons. The assignment was to learn why some Atlas missiles were failing, a problem its younger employees were unable to solve efficiently due to their relative inexperience. The older workers came up with a plan which will save the Federal government millions of dollars.

Other companies have had such excellent results with older workers that they hire them almost exclusively. One of these is Burpee Seeds Subsidiary of General Foods which hires workers age 56 to 85 to work on a flexible work schedule.

ACS of America Inc., a computer software firm which is based in Bradenton, Florida, hires and trains retirees to write computer programs on a piecework basis. They can choose to commute or work in their homes, using a terminal installed by the company. The reliability and work performance of the older workers has been so good that the company is planning to expand the program in Florida and other states. The company plans to advertise its openings in the local newspapers and through senior citizens' groups. The company's New York address is 633 Third Avenue, New York, NY 10022.

The American Express central office, which is located at American Express Plaza, New York, NY 10004, is currently involved in a pilot program with the Private Industry Council of New York City (see Jobs Training Partnership Act). The company employs homebound, handicapped persons to do word processing, full-time, in their own homes. The workers are screened and trained by the Private Industry Council. The program had been in operation only nine months when a company spokesperson was interviewed. She reported that it has been highly successful and that the work performance is excellent. However, future plans to expand the program to other branches were uncertain at the time because of strenuous union objections.

Community and junior colleges, under the auspices of the Older Americans Program, also utilize the skills and experience of senior workers. A recent survey indicates that almost half the reporting colleges hire older persons; three-fourths in paid positions and one-third in volunteer jobs.

The colleges also offer training in areas which senior employment centers are finding most open to the older job seeker: clerical, office and sales; consumer education; health occupations, especially those involving services to the elderly; arts and crafts; repair services; and various specialized tasks such as inspectors, paperwork in police and fire departments, paralegal work, and as instructors in adult education classes.

State and city governments are also involved in creating permanent, part-time and flexitime work for retirees. These include Massachusetts, New York, California, Florida, Illinois, Pennsylvania and others.

SMALL COMPANIES AND FAMILY OWNED BUSINESSES ARE GENERALLY MORE RECEPTIVE TO THE HIRING OF OLDER WORKERS. A 1983 study by the Brookings Institution found that businesses with fewer than 100 employees created 51% of the nation's new jobs between 1976 and 1980. Surprisingly, several studies report that large corporations are not a factor in job creation.

Small businesses are more likely to hire seasoned workers because they generally cannot afford to provide training for new employees or pay salaries that are competitive with the salaries of large corporations. For the same reason, they are more likely to consider older workers and retirees for management and research positions.

Small companies are more likely to hire generalists who can function at more than one task rather than specialists who fit into a narrow niche. They are also ideal for persons who prefer an informal work environment. Another advantage is that you can see the results of your decisions and actions since you're more likely to be involved in more than one phase of operations.

Some experts say that a small company is more likely to hire someone they like, even during a recession, since they aren't as restricted by rigid financial controls. Some economists warn that new, poorly established companies are more likely to go bust during a recession. Yet, during New York City's economic crisis, which lasted from 1969 to 1974, small businesses (those with fewer than 10 workers) weathered the crisis better than the large ones. (Who was it that said if you line up all the economists in the world, they will each point in a different direction?)

Before you accept a job in a small, family owned business, try to meet as many of the family members as possible. And be sure to get a written contract rather than verbal promises regarding fringe benefits, promotions, job security and the like.

Small companies tend to be in the service industries. They are more difficult to locate because
they aren't listed in the well known business
directories. The best way to locate them is
through the Standard Directory of Advertisers
which gives information about a company's size.
Also check the names of the company's officers. If
several have the same surname, it is more likely
to be a small, family owned business.

JOB FAIRS which are sponsored by a consortium of
local governments and private employers for the
purpose of promoting the hiring of older persons
are an excellent source of locating companies
which are more willing to hire the mature job
seeker. See chapter 3 for more information.

OCCUPATIONS AND INDUSTRIES WHICH HAVE THE BEST JOB PROSPECTS

This section summarizes the industries and occupations which, according to the Bureau of Labor
Statistics, are expected to have the best employment prospects for the 1980's. Only those which
seem most promising for mature job seekers are
mentioned here.

For complete information on these and other occupations, (including those with poor job prospects,) read the Occupational Outlook Quarterly,
which is published by the Bureau of Labor Statistics, and Job Openings, which is published monthly by the Employment and Training Administration,
both of the U.S. Department of Labor. You can also
get this information from the nearest Job Service
Center.

The number of job openings in an occupation depends on its size, the percentage of workers who
leave it, and its growth rate. Generally, large
occupations have more job openings than small
ones, occupations with a high turnover rate have
more openings than those with low turnover, and
occupations with a fast growth rate have more
openings than those with a slow growth or declining rate.

Large, slow growth occupations generally have more
job openings than small, fast growing ones. This
is because more new workers are needed to replace
those who leave for various reasons. For example,
of the 10 occupations projected to have the best

prospects, only two are expected to grow faster than the average. All are large, with a 1980 employment of a million or more workers. Nine do not require a college degree, and about half accept workers who have no special training or experience. Generally, they are the low skill, entry level occupations which employ clerical, sales and service workers. The large number of openings is due to the large size and high turnover rates of these occupations.

Everyone has read about the terrific job opportunities for programmers and systems analysts. These are rated as having a much faster than average growth rate. Yet they will have fewer openings than the kindergarten and elementary schoolteacher occupation, which has a slow growth rate. The occupation of bookkeeping is expected to grow slowly over the next few years, yet it, too, offers more job opportunities than the smaller, fast growing computer occupations because of its larger size and higher turnover rate.

SOME PEOPLE USE STATISTICS THE WAY A DRUNK USES A LAMPPOST, FOR SUPPORT RATHER THAN ILLUMINATION
So said some wag. You are not advised to do the same; that is, base your career decision too literally on statistical data provided by the Department of Labor or any other source. The reasons are as follows.

- Every day people get jobs, even in occupations with a gloomy job forecast. They manage to do this through persistence, patience, and the use of "old boy" networks. With the exception of occupations that will become obsolete, there will always be openings due to the need to replace workers who leave.

- Economists cannot measure precisely the ten year outlook for every occupation; they can only make estimates. Too many unpredictable variables are involved, such as a severe drought in the farm belt, an outbreak of war, foreign competition and new inventions and discoveries.

For example, in 1981/82 the Bureau of Labor Statistics predicted a phenomenal growth in the computer industry. By mid-1983, however, jobs were drying up and recent graduates were taking volunteer jobs as programmers in order to gain experience. The reasons are the prolonged recession and an unexpectedly high number of persons who had heard about the excellent job forecast and enrolled in computer programming courses. At present, colleges and universities don't have enough room for all the people who want to study programming.

Furthermore, the statistics reflect the outlook for the nation as a whole. Generally, an occupation has widely varying job prospects in different regions and states, even within a single state. For example, during the recent nationwide shortage of jobs for elementary and secondary school teachers, there were plenty of openings in the sunbelt states because of the influx of young couples with children.

Within a single occupation there may be different markets for persons with different specialties and qualifications. For example, as secondary schools in the nation are closing down and terminating teachers for lack of students, there is a critical shortage of mathematics and science teachers.

You can learn about the market for your occupation in your state and locality by contacting the state department of labor and/or the local Job Service Office.

OCCUPATIONS WHICH MAY BE DIFFICULT TO GET INTO, are those which are involved in the rapidly changing, high technology and energy research fields. They need up-to-date skills more than they need experience. This also includes occupations which face terminal obsolescence as a result of technological change. Clerical workers involved with billing, payroll and inventory, secretaries who lack word processing and computer literacy skills and keypunch operators will have greater difficulty getting a job.

AGE DISCRIMINATION exists to varying degrees in most industries and occupations. In civil service jobs, for example, it is minimal or absent. In others, it begins as early as 35 to 40. Generally, these are the ones where a youthful image is associated with the product or service, such as publishing, airlines, television, and businesses which involve guest contact, such as hotels, motels and gambling resort areas. The older worker should avoid these.

THE BRIGHT PROSPECTS

"People who have skills in areas where there is a labor shortage, such as machinists, tool and die makers, and certain skilled construction trades, should have no difficulty finding a job, regardless of age. The employer's main criterion for these openings is, 'Can the person do the job?' We've placed persons who are in their eighties, full-time, in such occupations, and their employers are happy to have them," said a Job Service counselor in 1983.

"There is a growing shortage of young (age 16 to 24) workers which will create a boom in the hiring of older workers for entry level jobs and jobs which have a chronic labor shortage. This means better opportunities for returning housewives with little experience in paid or volunteer jobs and for retirees who aren't ambitious to scramble up the corporate ladder of success.

There are also excellent opportunities for mature workers and retirees who have high level skills which are in short supply. In white collar jobs there is still a strong demand for secretaries, computer operators, accountants and more. Even teachers are now being hired if they have a background in special education, mathematics and science. We're placing teachers 55 years of age and older in such openings," he added.

Entry level jobs that are not affected by the new technology, such as sales clerks, janitors and waitresses, will still be plentiful. In 1981, New York City's Department of Employment placed over 30,000 persons in jobs as secretary, sales clerk, janitor, waiter, accounting clerk, customer service representative, data entry clerk, dental assistant, cable TV installer, and machine operator.

JOB OPPORTUNITIES WILL BE CREATED BY THE EXPLODING OVER-65 POPULATION. The Bureau of Labor Statistics reports the number of persons over 65 will increase from 26 million in 1983 to 35 million by the year 2000, and occupations which involve products and services for this age group will have plenty of openings. These include the following.

- ENTERTAINMENT, RECREATION AND HOTEL SERVICES: Since the elderly will have more time for leisure activities, jobs involving travel and hotel services and organizing and conducting social and sports activities for this age group will be plentiful.

- PUBLIC TRANSPORTATION will be in greater demand and so will workers in this industry, such as bus drivers and office workers.

- HEALTH CARE: nurses, physicians, laboratory and pharmaceutical technicians, homemakers, social workers with training or experience working with the elderly, and others in this category should have little difficulty finding a job. One study predicts a severe shortage of professionals specializing in geriatrics.

- FINANCE AND BANKING will need people to help manage pension funds.

- PET CARE AND PRODUCTS: Since the number of elderly persons who own pets will increase, any occupation involved in providing pet services and products has a bright outlook.

- ADULT EDUCATION courses in two and four year post-secondary schools will be in greater demand and so will teachers.

Some experts think we will become an age irrelevant society, that skills and aptitudes will count more in hiring decisions because there is such a desperate need for certain skills as the economy is shifting...It's like anything else in the marketplace, it's a matter of supply and demand. Where there's a shortage of skilled talent, the older job seeker will have better opportunities, absolutely. -- reported to the U.S. House Select Committee on Aging.

THE FASTEST GROWING INDUSTRIES may be a good hunting ground for mid-life and "young-old" job seekers for the following reasons.

- They have a shortage of certain skills.

- There are no firmly established "old boy" networks which exclude outsiders.

From the mature job seeker's point of view, they have two, main, drawbacks. The employees, including managers, are predominantly young, and the pace is fast. Yet, there are more opportunities for flexitime and work at home jobs which are

232

generally acknowledged to be better suited to homemakers and older workers.

THE HIGH TECHNOLOGY AND SCIENTIFIC INDUSTRIES have some of the brightest job prospects. By 1990, there will be about 2.5 million workers in these industries, which include computers, optical fibers, robots, medical instruments, laser, communications equipment, semiconductors, and miniaturized integrated circuits.

EMERGING OCCUPATIONS are those which have been created by the high technology revolution within the last ten years or so. They offer opportunities to persons of any age who have the right combination of skills because there are relatively few persons who possess the needed skills at present. The major drawback is their relatively small size, which means fewer job openings at present.

Here are some of the emerging occupations reported by the Bureau of Labor Statistics.

- Child advocates
- Energy efficiency technicians
- Industrial hygiene technicians
- Fiber optics workers
- Geriatric and gerontological technicians
- Housing rehabilitation specialists
- Halfway house managers
- Case managers for the mentally disabled

Also needed are laser/electro/optics technicians whose duties include the operation and repair of laser systems. Electronics technicians or engineers possess the skills needed for this occupation: the ability to perform tests and measurements using electronic equipment and the ability to prepare and understand shop drawings and schematics.

Another emerging occupation is the toxic waste specialist which requires a background in environmental health, toxicology and biology. Only a few colleges offered programs in this field in mid-1982, and the number of job openings far exceeded the number of qualified workers.

Robotic engineers and technicians will be in demand, writes Gail Martin.[1] Robots are expected to take over more and more tasks in the manufacturing and agricultural industries. They will work on assembly lines, spray and dust farm crops, till the ground, milk and feed cows, fabricate high rise buildings, paint spray bridges and do other menial, repetitious and boring tasks.

They are so new that experts find it difficult to predict the impact of robotization on employment. Some believe there may be a net gain in jobs because of emerging occupations to produce, program, service, operate and maintain robots. Others predict millions of workers might be replaced. Almost everyone predicts that, ultimately, the nation will need a workforce with a higher level of skills than are now available, and that unskilled workers will be those least able to find work.

The following are some of the new occupations in this field.

- Robotics engineers and manufacturing engineers experienced in robotic applications.

- Engineers with related skills to do research and development.

- Robotic maintenance workers are expected to make up the largest segment of robotics occupations.

- Robotic operators to operate and monitor robots. Very little training is required for this occupation and, frequently, robot manufacturers or vendors provide the training. According to a Carnegie Mellon University study, anyone who has experience in machine maintenance can easily learn to maintain them.

- Robot manufacturers will need workers in machine construction, and in computer and software development. They'll also need experienced salespersons to market them.

Community colleges and vocational schools are developing programs to train workers for this new industry. For a list of these, write to the Bureau of Labor Statistics or contact the department of education in your state.

COMPUTER PROGRAMMERS write the instructions used by computers to perform their miracles. In 1983 the starting salary for persons with a bachelor's degree in computer science was $24,485 and with four years experience it was as high as $43,500, reports a Michigan state survey. Between 1980 and 1990 job openings are expected to grow between 49 and 60 percent, writes Thomas Nardone of the Bureau of Labor Statistics. Nevertheless, beginning programmers are having difficulty finding jobs for the reasons stated above.

Two years or less of training is sufficient for a job involving the use of computers for business applications. In fact, an applicant with a 2-year certificate and experience in accounting, finance and management is more likely to be hired over someone with a bachelor's degree in computer science who has little or no business background. Furthermore, employers value a high quality 2-year certificate more than a college degree earned in a mediocre or substandard college. Mr. Nardone advises taking a double major in data processing and business or a science or engineering field in order to increase your prospects of finding a job.

A bachelor's degree in computer science, mathematics, engineering or the physical sciences is the minimum requirement for a job involving scientific or engineering applications. For some jobs in these fields, a graduate degree is required.

As a result of new programming languages which involve the use of English, persons who specialize in BASIC, FORTRAN and other computer languages may find getting a job harder than those who combine computer courses with business, health, engineering or other training. Many software and computer businesses, for example, prefer to hire such generalists because of their ability to apply their computer expertise to practical applications.

Some large companies have their own computer training program. A.T.& T., for example, administers an aptitude test, such as the Wolfe-Spence Programmers Aptitude Test, to determine whether an applicant has the ability to learn programming. Those who are accepted take courses at company time and expense and are then placed in programming jobs.

he computer revolution has spawned many other occupations. Some of the following were little known a decade ago.

COMPUTER ENGINEERING SPECIALISTS, such as computer assisted design (CAD) engineers, robotics engineers, and software engineers will have little difficulty finding work. Electronics engineers who know how to develop more powerful computers are also needed. Software engineering is new to the high technology industry. It requires skills and training in administration, business management and programming.

According to an American Electronics Association report in July 1983, over the next five years job openings for software engineers will increase 115%, electronic engineers will jump 107%, and computer analysts and programmers will increase by 103%. A bachelor of science degree in computer science, electrical engineering or mathematics is a must.

INSTRUCTORS are needed by organizations which use computer technology to teach their employees computer literacy and how to overcome "computerphobia." A bachelor's degree in any field gives you an advantage over job seekers who don't have one, but it isn't necessary. Jobs can be found in private industry, consulting firms, hardware and software manufacturers, such as Digital Equipment, Wang, and IBM, and in computer stores which need persons to explain to the consumers how to use their new "toy."

This is a good field for liberal arts majors who are facing a greatly restricted job market for their skills. Many graduates in music, psychology, English literature and other disciplines find the transfer to this new occupation relatively painless and much more profitable than teaching in a school system.

COMPUTER REPAIR job opportunities are expected to grow 93% by 1990. All it takes to qualify is a 2-year technical certificate or associate degree. Job opportunities are expected to be greater in this field than for 4-year graduates in computer science.

MARKETING AND SALES jobs in the hardware and software retail markets are also expected to mushroom. It's a good field for someone with marketing, business, engineering or sales experience. College graduates with majors in music, psychology and mathematics have been highly successful in this occupation.

A few computer courses to learn the basics of programming and how computers work may be all you need to qualify. If you're a computer hobbyist, you probably already understand the jargon and possess the technical bent needed for the job. This is an occupation in which communications skills, assertiveness, and the ability to work in teams are highly prized. Team selling is quite common in high technology equipment.

The Bureau of Labor Statistics predicts the demand for sales persons of all types will rise to 7.6 million by 1990, making it one of the fastest growing occupations. Persons who combine sales skills with technical know-how practically have it made in the high-technology and health industries.

WORD PROCESSORS are "smart" typewriters which store, edit, retrieve and print documents more accurately and faster than humans can. Some experts say word processing will eliminate a high percentage of typist, clerical and lower level secretarial jobs. Mail clerks, for example, are already being replaced by electronic sorting and mailing. But, they will never replace the executive or administrative secretary. Placement agencies report that more employers are requesting secretaries with some knowledge of word processors.

Word processing is currently a high paying skill because of the shortage of office workers who can do it. It's excellent for part-time work. In 1982, a temporary word processor in the New York metropolitan area could earn $600 a week. The pay is higher for evening and night work. Many people moonlight after regular work hours as word processors.

It's also ideal for at-home work assignments. An increasing number of companies provide the training at their own expense, and install the terminals in their employees' homes. American Express in New York City, for example, is involved in a program with the Private Industry Council which trains and employs handicapped persons to do word processing at home. Contact the Job Service Center in your community to see if something similar is available.

Word processing is easy to learn, especially if you already know how to type. If you know someone who has a home computer, you can learn from the manuals provided by the software manufacturer. Or,

you can enroll in an intensive, one-week course.
Better yet, apply for a job at one of the large,
placement agencies which train you and then place
you on assignments.

If you want information on other computer occupations and their requirements, write to the following:

- American Federation of Information Processing
Societies, 210 Summit Avenue, Montvale, NJ 07645.

- Data Processing management Association, 505 Busse
Highway, Park Ridge, ILL 60068.

- Association for Educational Data Systems, 1201
Sixteenth Street N.W., Washington, D.C. 20036.

- Send for the free brochure, Your Career in Computer Science, issued by the Bell and Howell Education Group, 2201 W. Howard Street, Evanston, ILL
60202 and enclose a stamped, self addressed envelope.

EMERGING INDUSTRIES
These industries deal with new scientific discoveries such as lasers; ceramics; optical fibers;
bioengineering; and nuclear, solar and wind energy
sources. Some experts, for example, believe we
are entering the age of ceramics since ceramics
materials will replace metals and plastics as the
major components of products such as automobiles,
microwave ovens, and fuel cells. Laser equipment
is already being used in bioengineering, food,
information storage and other industries. Solar,
wind and nuclear energy producing industries are
expected to rival the petroleum industry.

These are such new fields that it's hard to predict their impact on the employment market. They
are small and slow growing at present, which means
the number of openings is not as great as in the
much larger, traditional industries. But the handwriting is already on the wall. A 1981 survey by
the American Electronics Association reports that
by 1985 the demand for laser technicians will grow
by 228% nationwide, with regional increases up to
1,000% (in the New England area).

Experts predict a severe shortage of technicians,
engineers, operators, repairers, and inspectors.
Support workers such as computer programmers,

salespersons, managers, marketing people, janitors, secretaries, clerks, receptionists, technical writers, nurses, accountants, bookkeepers,
lawyers, advertisers, market researchers, financial analysts, public relations people, and others
will also be needed.

The telecommunications industry is also expected
to have an explosive growth as more American
households acquire cable TV and home computers
which enable them to do all their banking, shopping and mailing from home, as well as read the
newspaper, enroll in college courses and do a host
of other activities which at present require going
outside the home.

This industry will be hiring workers at all levels
of skills, training, and expertise - from semi-
skilled to specialists trained to deal with the
special needs of this industry. These include
cable TV installers and technicians, independent
producers, freelance directors, actors, graphic
artists, cameramen, set designers and carpenters.

The field is so new that many of the people in it
have learned on the job. For this reason, also,
entry level jobs are plentiful, and talented women
find it especially easy to rise to the top. This
is because the "old boy" networks have not had
time to establish themselves.

There are so many new jobs that college graduates
with majors in the liberal arts find it relatively
easy to get hired and win rapid promotions, since
persons with above average reasoning ability and
communications skills are needed. However, the
industry is so new that the average age of employees is less than 35, which suggests that age
discrimination may be greater in this field than
in others.

OPPORTUNITIES IN THE TRADITIONAL OCCUPATIONS

TEACHING - For the past few years there has been a
shortage of teaching jobs, from kindergarten to
college level, but not in every region nor in
every subject. By 1986/87, however, a serious,
nationwide shortage of kindergarten and elementary
teachers is expected which will be felt most a-
cutely in the Sunbelt states. This is due to an
increase in the nation's birthrate which is expected to continue as the number of women of

childbearing age, members of the post World War II baby boom generation, reaches its peak. However, the teenage and college age population is declining sharply. There will be a shortage of jobs in high schools and colleges, especially for teachers of music, social studies and languages.

Teachers of mathematics and science are needed at all levels. The shortage is so critical that some states are offering bonuses of up to $2,000 a year and others are offering free certification courses to anyone trained in the field of mathematics and science. If you have a bachelor's degree in any one of the liberal arts and an interest or aptitude in mathematics or science, you can probably find a job in a school system that offers free, concurrent education courses leading to a teaching certificate. Private schools are more likely to do this since they are less bound by red tape than the public schools.

Teachers of emotionally handicapped, learning disabled, and neurologically impaired children are also needed. The number of openings is likely to increase within the next few years, if an ominous July 1983 report of a 25% increase in the number of babies born with physical or mental disabilities over the preceding year continues to hold true.

LIBERAL ARTS GRADUATES - According to the Bureau of Labor Statistics, there will be 15 million new college graduates entering the labor force this decade, but there won't be enough jobs available that require a college degree. The majority who will be pounding the pavements will be those with liberal arts degrees. In order to find a job, they must be willing to accept opportunities in fields other than their own or take courses in a high technology field to supplement their skills.

However, a liberal arts degree is still valued by many employers as the foundation for mid and upper level positions. The higher up the occupational ladder, the more valuable a liberal arts degree becomes. A high school music teacher who quit his job to enter the business world is now a sales executive for a microcomputer manufacturer. He not only loves his new career, he's earning three times the salary he earned as a teacher.

According to the Bureau of Labor Statistics, liberal arts graduates are less likely to be unemployed than blue collar workers and white collar workers who lack a college degree. In March 1982, when the overall unemployment rate was 9%, it was only 3.2% for college graduates and 11.2% for workers who lacked a degree. The earnings of college graduates are also higher than the earnings of non-graduates. So, despite a shrinkage of openings in occupations liberal arts graduates have traditionally entered - publishing and teaching, for example - they are still better off than persons who have not graduated from college.

Liberal arts graduates can increase immeasurably their chances of landing a good job by taking courses in business or computer science. This expertise, plus their proven skills in communication and research and their above average reasoning and learning ability, add up to a powerful combination of assets. They should have little difficulty finding jobs in banks, insurance companies, non-profit organizations, government, publishing houses, loan companies, advertising agencies, and retail establishments.

Technical writing is another field where the communications skills of liberal arts graduates will be sorely needed for at least the next decade. Technical writers can earn as much as an engineer does. With some knowledge of the jargon and technology of microcomputers and software, or any other high technology industry, a person with a degree in liberal arts can find a job as technical writer for a manufacturing firm, retail organization, consulting firm, trade and professional association, research institute, or the publisher of microcomputer and technical magazines and books.

In 1983, Wang Laboratories, a large computer manufacturer in Massachusetts, employed a division of 60 writers and 25 editors, and not one of them had a computer science background. Employers want writers with a limited computer background because they can write in a manner the average layman understands. General Electric, Western Electric and Eastman Kodak are other kinds of high technology companies that need writers for their publications.

The health industry also needs liberal arts graduates as writers. Physicians, dentists, pharmacists and other medical professionals are as frightened of the printed word as are executives

in the world of business and high technology, says
a successful science writer. He reports that many
physicians are semi-literate and need writers to
do their lectures and journal articles. There is
big money in writing for the medical profession on
a free lance basis, he says. There are also tremendous opportunities for writers in pharmaceutical companies. "Tell them you're a medical writer
and get on the phone and bug the hell out of
them," he advises.

SALESPERSONS will be in greater demand as the
economic recovery gains momentum and Americans
start spending more. The Bureau of Labor Statistics predicts about a 45% increase in business for
travel agents, tour operators and accommodations
appraisers. The sale of merchandise, real estate,
stocks, bonds, and insurance is also expected to
rise sharply as inflation slows down and interest
rates decline. Real estate in particular should
show a sharp rise due to the prolonged housing
shortage and the large number of baby boomers with
children who are looking for homes to buy.

Sales work involves the following categories:

- RETAIL SALES - This is the lowest paying of
  the group, and it has a disproportionate
  number of women employees.

- SECURITIES SALES involves buying and selling
  commodities in the stock market for investors.

- MANUFACTURERS' SALES involves selling products to other businesses. Once the private
  domain of men, more women are entering this
  field.

- WHOLESALE TRADE workers are wholesalers who
  distribute goods to supply stores.

- REAL ESTATE SALES

- INSURANCE AGENTS

Many employers in these industries prefer to hire
experienced, mature workers. Real estate, for
example, has been a haven for the older, displaced
worker and career changer. All you need to become
a real estate salesperson is a license which you
can get after completing a 45 hour evening course
and passing an easy examination. A broker's license requires passing a written examination after

completing an additional 45-hour course. There are no other formal entry requirements.

Merchandise retailing is a high pressure, youth oriented industry, but some employers prefer to hire as middle managers experienced persons in their fifties, writes Elizabeth Fowler of the New York Times. There are growing sales opportunities in medical group practice, fast food retailers and in the communications industry, particularly retail stores that sell computers, telephones and other equipment.

Financial planning is a new occupation in which experienced, mature persons are needed who have a good understanding of investments, cash flow, taxation, estate planning and the ability to integrate all of these into a money management service to middle and upper income persons. According to Leonard Sloane in a recent article in the New York Times, most financial planners are paid through commissions from the financial products sold or by a combination of commissions and fees. Some are able to earn their total income on a fee-only basis.

At present there are no state licensing requirements and anyone can use the title of financial planner. Mr. Sloane advises persons who are seriously considering this career to enroll in a home study course offered by the College for Financial Planning in Denver, Colorado or the American College in Bryn Mawr, Pennsylvania as a way of acquiring professional status. The study program is from 18 to 24 months long and requires the passing of examinations in such subjects as tax planning and estate planning.

THE SERVICE INDUSTRIES

These will employ more Americans than the traditional high-employment manufacturing, construction and mining industries. There will be openings for just about anybody - professional, technical, managerial and administrative level workers down to entry level occupations such as clerical and maintenance work. According to Samuel M. Ehrenhalt, a regional commissioner of the Bureau of Labor Statistics, many of the jobs are concentrated in urban areas. These industries include the following.

Education

Recreation and Amusement

Nonprofit Membership Organizations

Personal Services (legal, automotive repair, eating and drinking places, janitorial, etc.

Social Services

Business Services (banking/financial insurance, management, securities, real estate, bookkeeping, retail and general merchandise, auditing, accounting, etc.

THE HEALTH INDUSTRY

From 1970 to 1979, the number of persons employed in hospitals, physicians' and dentists' offices, convalescent institutions, medical centers, nursing homes and other health facilities increased 55%, reports the Bureau of Labor Statistics. The major reason is the increase in the over-65 population, which is growing twice as fast as the population as a whole.

Despite excellent prospects, finding a job in this field depends on keeping up with the rapid changes in the science and technology of medicine and biology. For example, job opportunities for technicians who know how to use CAT scanners, ultrasound devices, laser instruments, radiological or sonography equipment, and a host of other innovations which hardly existed a decade ago, are expected to double in the next decade. All it takes to prepare for these jobs is a two year certificate or less.

However, some lower skilled occupations are becoming obsolescent, and in other occupations hiring is expected to slow down as computerization spreads through the industry. These include doctor's assistants and food service and laundry workers.

Hospitals and community health centers need persons with skills and experience in marketing, management, and sales analysis and strategy. Administrators are needed in family planning centers, convalescent and nursing homes and in programs for the physically and mentally disabled. A new specialty, occupational gerontology, combines skills in management with knowledge of retirement planning, labor relations, and the needs of older adults.

Sales opportunities in this industry are also expected to increase. Community health centers and for-profit hospitals are expected to have openings in marketing, pharmaceutical sales and medical sales. In 1982 alone, the Eli Lilly Company in Indianapolis employed about 1,200 sales representatives. About half of them had some sales background, and all were required to have good skills in communication and human relations as well as the ability to learn complex medical and pharmaceutical data. Women are entering this field in significant numbers.

Applicants with a bachelor of science degree in pharmacy, nursing, and the biological and chemical sciences are given priority in hiring decisions. Top salespersons made about $50,000 in 1982.

A 65% increase in the number of openings for occupational therapists and a 51% increase for physical therapists is forecast within the next few years. This is an excellent field for older persons, particularly homemakers who already possess the basic nurturing and human relations skills needed for this kind of work. The average salary for therapists in 1982 was about $21,000 a year, and some earned up to $30,000. Part-time work is plentiful in this occupation. The requirements include a bachelor's degree from an accredited college and a passing grade on a state licensing examination.

New York University has an arrangement with the United Cerebral Palsy Association of New York State, in which persons admitted to the University's master's degree program in occupational therapy can earn from $14,500 to over $17,500, depending on experience, while they study for the degree. Candidates in their fifties have been accepted.

If you love to travel, there is a Traveling Therapist Corps which places you on assignments in medical facilities across the nation. The assignments last a minimum of 6 to 12 weeks. Free round trip fare and free or shared cost housing are provided.

The occupation of registered nurses heads the list of 55 most promising occupations issued by the Bureau of Labor Statistics. Nursing schools are recruiting older persons, women who have raised families, and members of minority groups. Homemakers are especially valued because they have the managerial and nurturing skills required in this occupation. Qualified handicapped persons are also accepted, and assignments and work settings are being restructured to accommodate their disabilities. Nen are also entering the nursing field as salaries and opportunities to climb the ladder improve.

To be a licensed nurse you must have a minimum of a bachelor's degree. If you wish to become a nursing instructor or administrator, you need a Master's degree or a Doctorate. Nurses have a wider range of specialties to choose from nowadays: nurse midwifery, mental health nursing, nursing administration, pediatrics, geriatrics, instructors, and others.

The starting salary for registered nurses in 1982 ranged from $19,500 to $25,277 in the New York metropolitan area, depending on the level of education, experience and night shift. Nurse researchers and college faculty can earn up to $40,000, depending on academic rank and administrative duties.

Most hospitals now offer a 5-week vacation with liberal sick leave and continuing education benefits which may include free tuition towards a higher degree. Flexible and alternate week work schedules, including full and part-time work, are also available. Other benefits include life insurance, pension plan, free or rent subsidized apartments, a tax deferred annuity program, credit union and employer paid health plan coverage.

Travel opportunities for nurses are great! There are assignments to any part of the world which last up to several years. Advertisements appear weekly from Saudi Arabia, Southern California, Palm Beach, ski resort areas and other places. As a member of the Traveling Nurse Corps, you can fly to any place in the nation you choose and stay four weeks or more in each place. It offers full salary and free or subsidized housing and other benefits.

To be a licensed practical nurse, you do not need a bachelor's degree and many states don't even require a high school diploma. Generally all that's required is one year of study which combines internship with classroom attendance. Many licensed practical nurses continue their studies while working part-time and become registered nurses.

Nurses' aides generally receive on-the-job training and do not require a high school diploma, although it is preferred. They serve meals to patients, take temperatures and do other chores.

Social workers and counselors will also be in demand to provide counseling and related social services to patients receiving care in their homes and to schools, recreation centers and businesses. More of them will be needed as the new focus on health maintenance rather than on treating illnesses becomes widespread.

Home health aides will also be needed in this expanding program of caring for the aged, disabled and the sick within the community setting. This occupation lends itself well to part-time work.

The shortage of persons trained in radiation therapy, nuclear medicine technology, ultrasound technology, respiratory therapy, and in the use of sophisticated devices such as CAT scanners is expected to increase in time. With a two year certificate or associate's degree, technicians can earn more than liberal arts graduates. Training for these fields can be obtained in community colleges and in the adult education divisions of some institutions of higher learning.

A woman of my age, I see many things, I see the earth aging around me. The trees I knew as saplings that have grown so tall and so old. I feel, how shall I say it, synthese - a synthese. I have more energy now than I ever did, because I don't get depressed so often...I feel in control of my life...I can experience solitude and the feeling that everything is possible. - French actress Jeanne Moreau, at 54.

1. Martin, Gail. "Industrial robots join the work force," <u>Occupational Outlook Quarterly,</u> Fall 1982. Bureau of Labor Statistics, U.S. Department of Labor.

According to the Bureau of Labor Statistics, the following
are some of the occupations which will have the most job
openings in this decade:

	1980 employment	Projected Growth 1980-1990	Percent Growth
Secretary	2,469,000	700,000	28.3%
Nurses aide, Orderly	1,175,000	508,000	43.2
Janitor, sexton	2,751,000	501,000	18.2
Sales Clerk	2,880,000	479,000	16.7
Cashier	1,597,000	452,000	28.4
Licensed Nurse	1,104,000	437,000	39.6
Fast-food worker	806,000	400,000	49.6
Office clerk	2,395,000	377,000	15.8
Waiter, waitress	1,711,000	360,000	21.1
Primary teacher	1,286,000	251,000	19.5
Accountant, auditor	833,000	221,000	26.5
Automotive mechanic	846.000	206,000	24.4
Typist	1,067,000	187,000	17.5
Practical nurse	522,000	185,000	35.5
FASTEST GROWING HIGH TECHNOLOGY JOBS			
Data processing mechanic	83,000	77,000	92.3
Computer operator	185,000	133,000	71.6
Computer analyst	205,000	139,000	67.8
Office machine servicers	55,000	33,000	59.8
Computer programmer	228,000	112,00	48.9

248

- 12 -
WHY NOT BE YOUR OWN BOSS?

More people than ever before are leaving the insecurities of a quirky job market to start their own
business. They include workers whose skills are
obsolete and retirees who have little worthwhile
to do and less money to do it with. In 1981, there
were 6.8 million such adventurous souls, an all
time high, and their numbers are growing faster
than the number of people who work for a paycheck.

There are many advantages to being your own boss.
You're no longer chained to the office clock or
subject to petty office politics. If you love to
solve problems, you'll have plenty of opportunities to do so. No more bureaucratic stranglehold
on your creativity and spontaneity. No more job
burnout. Your talents, experience and skills are
employed to earn a profit for yourself, not someone else. If you can't hold a 9-to-5 job because
of a physical handicap or some other reason, a
home business is one of the best ways to earn a
living.

Your work is portable; you can take it anywhere
you like. Would you like to earn your living in
the midst of swaying palm trees, warmed by the
tropical sun? One woman in her fifties left the
blizzards of Buffalo to open a leather crafts shop
in the airport of a Caribbean island, and she
loves it. Many persons who prefer snow country and
sports have set up a mail order or service business in or near ski resort areas.

You can arrange your work schedule to suit your
"biological clock," and you'll happily discover
that you can be more productive with less sleep.
Whether you are at your peak at sunrise or sundown, YOU decide when to work, not someone else. A
woman who turned her hobby of jewelry design into
a home business works best at a time most of us
are asleep. During the late morning and early
afternoon hours, she takes her phone off the hook
so that she can sleep without interruption.

You can take breaks whenever you want, for as long
as you want. You can work to music, dressed in
your pajamas, and take care of your pets and
garden during breaks.

If your goal is to become rich, you have a better chance of succeeding as an entrepreneur than as an employee. All you need is a hot idea for a product or service which has a big demand and the willingness to put in the required time, energy and capital investment. If, on the other hand, you want just enough to get by so that you'll have plenty of time for fun and friends, you can reduce your work schedule with no worries about being fired.

Many persons have become successful beyond their wildest dreams working at what they like to do best. Coralee Kern started a home based MAID TO ORDER service after she came down with a disability which forced her to quit a job that barely paid enough to feed herself and her children. Within a few years, it was grossing over $300,000. Another woman started what was to be a sideline party planning service in her small apartment. It soon outgrew her expectations and her apartment, grossing well over $250,000 annually.

A former marketing executive quit a high salaried job to open a crafts shop, The Potter's Wheel, in an old garage in Massachusetts. Within two years he was earning more working at his hobby than he did as an executive. Anne P. Hyde and Janet Jones-Parker decided to chuck the frustrations of the corporate world to start their own management recruiting business, Management Women, Inc. They chipped in $3,000 apiece, rented a small room in a swanky Manhattan hotel, and soon had a business which brought in a six figure annual income.

Kim Cohan was a 16 year old high school dropout when he founded MicroSharing with his inexpensive home computer. After converting it to a coin operated machine, he persuaded the local public library to install it. Several years later, libraries across California had coin operated computers, and Kim was on his way to joining the legion of teen age millionaires.

Emily Chiarello, of Sioux City, Iowa, invented a hot air solar heating system to trim her energy bills. It worked so well that she formed a business, Alternate Energy, Inc., to sell her plans by mail order. There were so many interested customers that she decided to manufacture them.

One woman spent $200 on a tray of beads, some nylon string and leather thongs which she turned into a half million dollar business making and selling unusual necklaces. She hired neighborhood kids to string them, and then she sold them to local boutiques and clothing stores. The customers snapped them up as soon as they went on display. Soon, she had a staff of 15 sales representatives selling her jewelry to every major store in the nation.

WHAT ARE THE BASIC QUALITIES NEEDED FOR SUCCESS IN BUSINESS?

Many successful entrepreneurs started out with no college degree, no prior business experience, no big bank account. All they had was a good idea at the right time and the personal qualities to make a go of it.

Let's suppose you have an idea for a product or service for which there is a big demand, but which is not being met adequately, or at all. It might be installing self-cleaning swimming pools in Palm Beach, Florida, doing word processing for professionals and small businesses in Manhattan, or preparing income tax forms for Spanish speaking residents of El Paso, Texas. All you may need is a few months of evening classes or a home study course, and you're set. (The way things are these days, persons who have a technical school training have a better opportunity to make a million than college graduates.)

Take a temporary job in the type of business you plan to open and learn from observation how a successful, small business is run. Money magazine describes how Raymond Haldeman took a job as catering director on an entertaining yacht. After learning all he could, he started his own hugely successful catering business in his kitchen with a $30 investment and some old pots and pans.

YOU PROBABLY ALREADY HAVE THE BASIC QUALITIES NEEDED FOR SUCCESS IN BUSINESS - natural intelligence, energy, and a special talent, skill or expertise which will sell. The other attributes which set winners apart from losers can be easily acquired. According to the Small Business Administration, they include the following.

WINNERS ARE SELF-STARTERS. When there are problems to be solved and decisions to be made, they don't need anyone to lean on. They would rather do the creative work themselves and delegate the details to others, rather than complete work which is assigned to them. You had better think twice about going into business for yourself if you feel more secure working under supervision. Or, you might consider a franchised business where everything is arranged for you.

WINNERS ARE NOT AFRAID TO TAKE CALCULATED RISKS. Successful entrepreneurs, like successful corporate executives and investors, are gamblers. They gamble on the future. But first, they try to get as much information as necessary in order to prepare a business plan. Then, on the basis of this information and some intuition, they take action. They require no blueprint for success, only guideposts. Not all small business ventures involve taking a substantial risk, however, and there are proven techniques for reducing the risks involved.

WINNERS ARE SELF-CONFIDENT, otherwise they wouldn't be able to surmount the inevitable disappointments and emergencies. "For every business success I've had, there have been five setbacks," said the owner of a small bath shop in Greenwich Village, New York. "You just have to keep pursuing what you want until your get over the barriers."

Self-confidence is more than a passive belief in your abilities. It's based on careful research, followed by a step-by-step plan of actions to take before you start the business and during its initial phases.

It means having contingent plans to fall back on when things go wrong, such as an unexpected illness, a breakdown in some vital equipment, or an unanticipated expense. For example, it means making copies of your computerized customer list just in case the computer breaks down as you're about to make a shipment.

It involves a realistic assessment of things going wrong when you least expect them to, and making alternative plans, just in case. If, for example, your dream is to sell grandma's fabulous homemade bread by mail order, you might also have in reserve a plan to market pizza-size cookies in the event your customers are lured away by a competitor.

It involves devising ways to boost your morale whenever exhaustion and unexpected setbacks make you feel like chucking everything, such as treating yourself to a sinful chocolate pie at the end of a bad day, or keeping "shop" open until you make a sale.

WINNERS ENJOY HARD WORK. They are willing to break their collective neck and sacrifice their social life to get their business going. A curious thing happens to people when they start working for themselves. They put in longer hours and more effort than when they work for others.

WINNERS ARE WELL ORGANIZED. Any successful entrepreneur will tell you that starting the business took far more time and work than anticipated. According to the Small Business Administration, one major reason why businesses fail is that people aren't willing to put in the time required to attend to details and work out an efficient plan of action BEFORE opening the business. This is the only way to keep from being swamped by an a mountain of things that had to be done last month.

WINNERS ARE FLEXIBLE. They make periodic revisions in their plan in response to the many, inevitable changes that occur in the course of doing business. That's what makes it so exciting. For want of a nail, a shoe was lost. For want of a shoe, a horse was lost; and for want of a horse, a battle was lost.

WINNERS ATTEND TO EVERY DETAIL. Suppose you plan to sell homemade candy. It's not enough to have a scrumptious recipe and an eye catching advertising pitch. You need to select the periodicals whose readers are most likely to want to buy your advertised item. You need to shop around until you find where to get the best quality ingredients at the lowest price. You must to attend to a hundred seemingly trivial details, such as choosing the right color ribbon on the package, which can make the difference between success or failure.

WINNERS ARE PATIENT. They know it may take up to one and a half to two years to complete the preliminary steps needed to get a business started: selecting a product or service, finding suppliers, developing a record keeping system, designing the packaging and advertising, selecting the best markets, etc.

WINNERS ENJOY SOLVING PROBLEMS. You don't need a high I.Q. to be a creative problem solver. In

fact, some of the most creative people have mediocre I.Q. scores. However, they do have an uncanny
ability to generate lots of ideas, many of which
seem crazy, impractical and unworkable. People
laughed when Galileo announced that the earth
revolved around the sun. The idea of humans flying
in the air like birds was another hilarious inspi-
ration.

Creative persons see opportunities where merely
intelligent people see nothing. They are able to
spot a consumer need that isn't being met or think
of ways to improve a service or product that
someone else is selling. Obstacles which discourage most people are fascinating challenges to the
creative person.

Many of the best money making ideas are ridicu-
lously simple. A classic example is Henry Ford's
assembly line. More recently, someone made millions selling a cleverly packaged "Pet Rock" with
a list of humorous instructions on how to take
care of it. The man who conceived the cotton swab
after watching his wife laboriously wrap absorbent
cotton around a matchstick also made millions.

A retired teacher decided to cash in on the current increase in semi-literacy among American high
school and college graduates. She started a learning skills service to teach people how to write
reports, overcome math anxiety, take examinations,
and improve their reading speed and comprehension.
The genius of her idea was in its timing.

WINNERS MAKE AN EARNEST EFFORT TO LEARN THE ESSEN-
TIALS OF RUNNING A SMALL BUSINESS. "Eighty five
percent of small businesses in this city fail.
It's not just the difficulties with the economy.
So many people don't know the basics of running a
modern business," said 82-year old Sidney H. Kush-
in, a commissioner in New York City's Economic
Development Administration. If you don't know a
thing about operating a business, there are many
free and low cost services available in your community to help you learn.

You're never too old to make a million.
- 83 year old Nora Wolfson, who created the best
selling "Maison de Nora" fudge sauce just 3 years
earlier.

SOME BUSINESS IDEAS THAT HAVE WORKED

You'll create a better service or product if you
narrow you list of possibilities down to what
interests you most and what you enjoy doing most.
Here are some ideas which have made money for
people. Some of them are best suited for a part-
time business which provides a supplementary income, others to a full-time commitment as a main
source of income. They are listed not as ideas for
you to imitate, but to spark better or additional
money making ideas of your own. Many of the products and services can be sold by mail order.

Run a public relations firm from home. Learn how
to do it by reading as much as you can absorb in
the public library. Then, get a job in a successful public relations firm, any kind of a job, as
long as you're there to see how it's done.

Enroll in a real estate salesperson's course and
get your license. Then work full or part-time for
a local broker. Later on, you can enroll in a real
estate broker's course and become a broker yourself. You never have to retire and you can work
from home.

Handpaint china and miniatures. Sell privately
and/or to gift shops.

Paint oil or watercolor portraits for Father's
and Mother's Day. Sell by mail order.

Screenprint T-shirts with clever and/or personalized sayings.

Print bumper stickers with cute and off-beat sayings.

Make one-of-a-kind jewelry: hand-painted porcelain
jewelry, heirloom buttons made into earrings, etc.

Silverplate heirlooms, antiques.

Make one-of-a-kind Christmas wreaths from local
materials - pine cones, herbs, vines, berries,
etc.

Make customized director's chairs with hand painted or silk screened canvas.

Make colorful, appliqued seat covers for bar stools, kitchen stools, director's chairs, etc.

Start a house-sitting service. One woman's business has expanded to the point that she hires over 20 retirees to housesit for periods of up to a year. If you live in or near a college town, you'll have plenty of calls from professors who go off on long sabbaticals.

Start an organizing/relocating business for people who are moving out of town and haven't got the time to do the necessary chores themselves: packing and unpacking, writing and mailing change-of-address cards, taking things to be sold to flea markets, cleaning up, mailing packages, etc.

Handpaint or cross-stitch your customers' favorite songs, poems, or sayings.

Offer to paint customized wall murals.

Repair and restore art objects, figurines, china and glassware.

Give private music lessons. Play for church events and parties.

Do freelance photography for the local newspaper, private parties and other special events.

Make sound videotapes of weddings, confirmations, parties, etc.

Make video portraits in sound and color for gift giving.

Make documentary style sound movies for weddings, birthdays, anniversaries, bar mitzvahs, etc.

Videotape wills.

Operate an after-six and weekend secretarial service.

Do freelance bookkeeping for local professionals and small businesses.

Operate a data processing service. Get a home computer and maintain mailing lists for small businesses and professionals.

Prepare income tax reports for small businesses and professionals.

Operate a computerized accounting service for professionals and small businesses.

Mount old photographs, diplomas and other memorabilia on wooden plaques.

Do custom tailoring. Turn old fur coats into jackets; narrow wide neckties, etc.

Sew replicas of early American quilts.

Make customized lampshades.

Make dress patterns for dolls packaged with fabric and instructions.

Reproduce business cards and memorabilia in brass or silver.

Encase medals and mementoes in plastic.

Plan and run conventions and fairs for organizations in your community.

Be a party coordinator. Send the invitations, prepare and serve the food, take photographs, arrange for entertainment, and clean up later.

Organize and operate tours of your community and interesting surrounding features.

Be a freelance bartender at private parties.

Organize and run bargain hunting tours to discount shops, factory outlets and flea markets.

Turn your home into a boarding home for the elderly.

Provide a messenger service to the elderly to get groceries, library books, medicines, take clothes to the cleaners, etc.

Do freelance home repair. There is a big demand for this. In 1982, an estimated 78% of Americans owned their own homes and remained there after retirement.

Do freelance practical nursing.

If you have a degree in nursing, become a health consultant. Match the needs of the homebound with the right equipment and practical nursing services so that they can remain at home.

Become a distributor of specialized health supplies to physicians. One woman built a profitable business distributing a special harness for persons suffering from a herniated disc.

Create an entire kitchen plan, from linoleum to lamp fixtures to pots and pans, for contractors and persons building their own homes. Then, order the items from various distributors and have them delivered to the client. One housewife saw the need for someone to design, plan, and coordinate the purchase and delivery of the many items needed to set up a complete kitchen, and made a fortune.

Sell exotic food by mail order: smoked turkey, snack pack for college students, freeze dried backpack meals for campers and hikers, pizza-size cookies made from a family recipe, etc.

Sell unusual recipes through the classified ads. Swedish rye bread, Cherokee Indian teas, aphrodisiac snacks, and other such items are being sold every day. (Be aware that services which provide food and food recipes are vulnerable to lawsuits, and that there is insurance to protect such businesses.)

Sell to gourmet shops unusual, home made cookies, sauces, herbal teas, fruitcakes, candies, etc.

Cook and cater exotic ethnic dinners for parties at customers' homes.

Prepare and cater romantic champagne brunches, candlelight dinners, etc.

Take a brief course at the local technical college and then do freelance repair of air conditioners, refrigerators, microwave ovens or electric typewriters. One of the hottest businesses going is the repair of home computers and printers.

Provide a child escort service for working couples. Gertrude MacLean started the highly profitable Universal Aunts & Uncles, a London based service which chaperones children during school holidays. She also arranges sightseeing trips for them, hires proxy mothers, and advises on a broad range of matters such as where to find heraldry experts and how to dress for garden tea parties. The business employed over 400 "Aunts" and "Uncles" in 1983.

Learn to build, install and/or repair home solar energy equipment.

Offer to do kitchen installations on a freelance basis at a lower cost than your competitors.

Restore antique or cane furniture.

Provide services for working singles and couples: shop for groceries, pay bills, walk the dog, register the car, wait for servicemen and deliveries, pick up packages at the post office, buy and deliver gifts, return merchandise, etc.

Do freelance gardening and landscaping.

Plant a herbal garden and make herbal teas for sale. Make and sell kitchen herb window boxes.

Design, purchase and care for plants in local business and professional offices.

Publish a hobby newsletter.

Write and self-publish a cookbook. (See precaution on selling foods above.)

Search for hard-to-find books.

Operate a real estate search service. Make data and photograph searches on sites, buildings, sales and transfers, original owners, etc.

Get a home computer, a printer and word processing software, and offer to compose, type and print dissertations, reports, letters, legal documents, and mailing lists for local businesses, students and professionals.

If you know a foreign language, add a translation service to your services.

Do library and on-site research on various topics for people who don't have the time to do it themselves.

Become a distributor of micro-computers. A former fashion model began distributing the made-in-

England Sinclair computers from her apartment, and within a year she had grossed more than a million.

Organize an ensemble with some musician friends and play at special events.

Buy a tuxedo and become a strolling violinist for parties, receptions, etc.

Use your talents as comedian, artist, dancer or musician, and offer a unique "singing telegram" service.

Help disorganized or harried persons plan a more efficient budget.

Become a shopping consultant and help coordinate wardrobes for people who don't have the taste and class that you have.

Learn how to operate an electrolysis machine and remove surplus hair from people.

Operate a telephone reminder service for busy persons who can't afford to hire a full-time secretary to remind them of important events.

Organize a unique dating service for singles: fine arts lovers, football freaks, college graduates, the over'60s set, etc. A former meteorologist set up a dating service which grossed over $7,000 a month in 1983.

Organize a gourmet club in your community which provides good eating out and the opportunity to meet interesting persons. Judy Moscovitz's The Single Gourmet has proven so popular that there are branches in several cities in Canada and the U.S.

If you have a large house and live in a city or tourist area which has many visitors, become a Bed & Breakfast host or hostess. Enroll in the Bed & Breakfast League, Ltd for about $50 and receive valuable advice on how to do this. The address is 2855 28th Street NW, Washington, D.C. 20008

Become a cat or dog breeder.

Breed poodles. Sew cute costumes, and train several to perform at children's parties. A retired actress living in Astoria, New York, includes a retired vaudeville actor dressed as an organ grinder with a trained monkey.

Operate a pet motel which provides personalized service for owners who don't want to board their pets in kennels. The Canine Country Club in Virginia Beach provides whatever the individual pet usually receives in order to adjust to the new environment - fresh vegetables, poached eggs in the morning, a goodnight kiss, a slice of Edam cheese every evening at nine, even an early morning recitation of the 23rd Psalm.

Offer to do professional dog grooming in the pet owner's home.

Offer to do pet sitting in the pet owner's home.

Operate a used book store in your garage or basement.

Do the same with used video cassettes.

Open a gourmet shop in your home to sell specialty and ethnic foods that are lacking in your community.

Buy and sell antiques. Start with a few good pieces and some business cards. Attend antique fairs and flea markets. In 1982, people were earning up to $500 a day in this business.

Teach small groups of adults your special skill: how to build a log cabin, make and install a solar heating panel, pave a tennis court, construct a greenhouse, build a windmill, etc.

Teach creative and exotic cooking to local bachelors and brides-to-be.

Give private knitting, crocheting or sewing lessons,

Teach Yoga or other relaxation techniques.

Take tennis or golf lessons to perfect your technique and become a teaching pro.

If you own a home computer, learn to program your own games, and rent yourself and your computer out to entertain at parties. There's a man in California who is doing this under the name of "The Wizard."

HOW TO BRAINSTORM FOR GOOD BUSINESS IDEAS

Make a list of all the things you know or do especially well. Then narrow the list down to a manageable number of possibilities. If you can't think of anything, ask yourself the following question.

IS THERE A MARKET (DEMAND) FOR A CERTAIN PRODUCT OR SERVICE THAT ISN'T BEING MET?

Look around your community to see if there is a need or an interest which is not being met by an existing business. For example, in 1982 there were approximately 1,000 "mom-and-pop" high technology enterprises in Long Island, New York, each of which grossed a minimum of $500,000 yearly. They assemble or manufacture space-age items such as fiber optics and computer chips for the rapidly growing industry on the Island. Some of these entrepreneurs, like Ellen Math, who had been a high school teacher, are mid-life career changers.

In 1981 there were over 2,000 highly profitable, low cost newsletters which were being published as mom and pop enterprises. Although most of them summarized federal regulatory changes and other Washington events for business persons, others catered to specialized interests. Some of the best selling newsletters that are bringing in a six figure income started out on the kitchen table.

For example, a couple with a small needlecraft shop started out by mimeographing a one page news-letter as a free service to their customers. It became so popular, they began publishing and sel-ling an expanded version on a subscription basis. After learning there were 50 million other TV soap opera addicts in the nation, a woman in Texas started a newsletter which summarizes the daily TV shows for subscribers who miss a show. It was a huge success.

IS THERE A GOLD MINE IN YOUR COMMUNITY WAITING TO BE EXPLOITED?

If you live in a large city or a small community that has interesting geographic features, there are many services and products which visiting tourists and business persons will buy. For exam-ple, you can operate sightseeing tours. People are making money and enjoying themselves at the same time by operating tours to ethnic restaurants, museums, discount shops and factory outlets, sce-nic countryside spots, etc. Someone living in Long

Island has organized a gourmet club which meets
regularly for a feast at interesting restaurants.
Georgie Clark, owner of <u>Georgie's River Rats,</u> has
been taking tourists on white water trips down the
Colorado River rapids since 1944. Others have fun
making money as organizers of camping, backpacking, horseback, and skiing weekends for small
groups.

Is there abundant, free or low cost local material
which can be transmuted into an exotic or gourmet
gift item that is unavailable elsewhere? A woman
living in the Northwest creates Christmas wreaths
from the pine cones in her area. She also sells
instruction kits by mail. Another persons sells
fragrant fireplace starters made of pine cones.

Someone living near the English Channel creates
beautiful, one-of-a-kind night lights made of sea
shells mounted on driftwood bases. Another entrepreneur is making a small fortune selling four,
gift wrapped, giant Idaho potatoes encased in a
cedar lined box for 20 dollars plus shipping.

Is there a service that's needed in your community
which isn't being met? Think of all the people who
have bought home computers and printers which
need low-cost repair.

Now that there is a national concern over food
additives and other contaminants which may cause
health problems, how about making and selling
natural food products from your home and/or by
mail order?

Studies indicate more than 25% of the 1.5 million
or more elderly persons now in nursing homes could
live at home if they had home care services. They
need someone to provide transportation to clinics
and senior centers, shopping services, physical
therapy and similar services.

*Retirement at 65 is ridiculous. Why, when I was
65, I still had pimples.* - George Burns at 85.

IS THERE A PRODUCT OR SERVICE WHICH IS BEING SOLD
THAT I CAN PROVIDE MORE EFFICIENTLY, AT LOWER COST
AND HIGHER QUALITY?
For example, two housewives started a wallpapering
service in a community which already had such a
service. They beat their competition by providing
greater reliability and a willingness to do rush
jobs which their competitor failed to do.

Another example is the simple, singing telegram. Who would image such a service to be as highly profitable as it is today? Take a look in the classified ads of a city newspaper and see how many clever people are offering a fascinating twist such as composing and singing custom made lyrics, dressing up in fancy costumes to suit the occasion, and strip tease singing telegrams. Eastern Onion, of Las Vegas, Nevada, started out small. Now it grosses over $8 million a year and has more than 42 franchises.

QUESTIONS TO ASK YOURSELF AFTER YOU DECIDE ON A BUSINESS IDEA

HOW WILL IT AFFECT MY FAMILY'S LIVING ARRANGEMENTS? WHERE CAN I EXPAND IF IT OUTGROWS MY HOME? (If you plan to operate a home based business.) Mary Ellen Pinkham, author of a best selling, self-published book on household hints, ordered 500,000 copies of her book which took up every available space in her home. She even had to store them in the refrigerator.

WHAT KIND OF BUSINESS AM I REALLY GOING INTO? The Small Business Administration reports that many people go broke because they fail to be specific about the kind of business they plan to start.

There's the case of a man who opened a small radio and television shop. As the neighborhood grew, so did his business. That is, until another appliance shop opened and began taking away his customers. If he had persisted in thinking of his business as a retail store, he would have gone broke. Instead, he correctly predicted an increased demand for quality repair work, and decided he was in the electronic repair business. His profits skyrocketed.

Another example is the changeover of barbershops to "unisex hair styling" services as a result of the decrease in demand for shaves with the introduction of the electric shaver.

WHAT LEGAL STRUCTURE SHOULD MY BUSINESS HAVE? There are three main types of business structures: sole proprietorship, partnership, and corporation. The Small Business Administration advises people who are starting out to select the sole proprietorship. Then, as business expands, a partnership or corporation may be more advantageous.

THE SOLE PROPRIETORSHIP involves just one person as owner and operator. There are fewer legal
restrictions in establishing it. All you'll probably need is a license or two. Little or no government approval is required, and it's less expensive
than the other two legal structures. As sole pro-
prietor, you keep all the profits and make all the
decisions. Government control is minimal and there
is no special taxation to contend with.

The disadvantages include unlimited liability,
which means that you are responsible for all
debts. However, there is insurance available for
personal injury and physical loss. Another disadvantage is that, generally, a sole proprietorship
has greater difficulty obtaining long term loans.

THE PARTNERSHIP is an association of two or
more persons who act as co-owners of the business.
They draw up a partnership agreement which covers
such matters as how to divide profits and losses,
handle business expenses and separate debts, the
death of a partner, sale of partnership interest,
settlements of disputes, and the authority of each
partner.

The advantages of a partnership over a sole proprietorship include the greater, combined assets
of each partner and the fact that two heads are
involved in decision making, thereby lessening the
possibility of errors of judgment.

Among its disadvantages is the difficulty in buying out of a partnership unless arranged for in
the written agreement. A partnership has an unstable life. If one partner is eliminated, the partnership dissolves. However, the business can continue on the basis of right of survivorship and
the creation of a new partnership. There is insurance to minimize such risks. Another disadvantage
is that, compared to a corporation, obtaining long
term financing is more difficult.

Consult with the Small Business Administration
about the best legal structure for your business
in order to avoid problems later on.

MAKE A BUSINESS PLAN

The following is a brief summary of pamphlet
2.022, Business Plan For Small Service Firms which
you can get, free, from the Small Business Admin-

istration (SBA). It is presented here to show you what's involved in setting up a small business, not as a complete guide to follow. For that you should write for the free pamphlets listed in the appendix. You should also make an appointment to speak with an advisor in the Small Business Administration.

Not everyone needs to start off with as detailed a plan as is described in the pamphlet. It depends on the type of business, how much you plan to invest in it, the expected volume of sales, how much money you need to borrow (if any), and whether you plan to hire workers and/or rent an office.

Some people have started out with less than several hundred dollars for the printing of business cards and flyers, and the rest of the operation was fueled by their ingenuity. They generally have small scale, local businesses such as private tutoring and home repair services. After business picks up, the use of a more detailed record keeping system is recommended.

One purpose of a business plan is to help you estimate what it will cost to set up your business and whether you need to borrow money. You also need a plan if you request a loan from a bank or the Small Business Administration.

A business plan includes the following items.

FIXTURES AND EQUIPMENT - Make a list of all the equipment and furniture you will need. Get price estimates. The formula to use is:

Type of Equipment = Number Needed X Unit Cost

PARTS AND MATERIALS - List the essential items you'll need to start the business, and then estimate the first year's cost of these items according to this formula:

Item = Amount Needed For 12 Months X Unit Cost

You can get an estimated cost of the items you'll need by phoning several suppliers. Also find out how many days or weeks it takes to deliver these, whether the supplier will ship a few items or if you have to buy a dozen or more, how long delivery will take, and who pays for the freight costs. This last item can be expensive. Also look into the obsolescence policy and warranty policy.

OVERHEAD - These items include rent, utilities, office help, insurance, interest, telephone, postage, accountant's fee, lawyer's fee, licenses or other local taxes, and wages and salaries of employees, if you'll need them.

The next step is to translate your business plan into dollars. First, estimate the dollar volume of business you anticipate in the first 12 months. Next, estimate the cost of doing this volume of business, using the figures you have obtained from the formulas above.

A START-UP BUDGET helps you to see the dollar amount of your monthly expenses and whether the estimated sales will be enough to pay your bills on time. To do this, you need to figure out the monthly cost of any of the following items which pertain to your business.

    Advertising
    Office Supplies
    Licenses & Permits
    Starting Inventory
    Fixtures & Equipment
    Decorating & Remodeling
    Deposits for Utilities
    Legal & Professional Fees

A GOOD RECORD KEEPING SYSTEM will help you to see from month to month if your plan is making a profit or a loss. It should be set up before you begin business, because later on you will be so swamped with things to do that you won't have time to give it proper attention. It's wise to have an accountant or the Small Business Administration help you set up a good control system.

It should provide the following additional information.

  - What needs to be done on a daily, weekly, and monthly basis.

  - The amount of stock you have on hand.

  - Your sales and disbursements.

  - An inventory of the parts and materials used in your business.

A good record keeping system will help prevent delays in providing service and let you know at a glance if there is any loss due to theft, errors or waste. It also helps you tie up fewer dollars on your inventory since it shows what needs to be ordered and when. It will also show whether you are paying your bills on time so that you'll get a suppliers discount, and the amount of tax money to set aside and when it should be paid so that you'll avoid penalties.

HOW TO CUT COSTS

First, list the the essential items needed to start your business and get an estimate of their cost: office supplies, advertising, postage, telephone, car maintenance, materials, etc. Even the insignificant items should be included because these add up in the course of doing business: rubber bands, glue, scotch tape, paper clips, erasers, pens and pencils, notebooks, etc.

Resist the temptation to buy expensive items which you can get later on with your first profits. You don't have to set up a complete office or shop in the beginning.

Purchase small quantities of business cards, flyers, letterhead stationary, and brochures at the outset. When business picks up, you can order larger quantities.

The wording and design of a brochure or flyer can be very expensive if you have it done by an advertising agency. If you have time, you can do one yourself by studying the many samples which come with the junk mail. Analyze what attracts your attention, the spacing, the advertising pitch, etc. Then discuss your needs with a local printer who can run off about 2,000 for less than $600. The printer may have design samples which you can adapt to your own needs.

Make an inventory of what you already have lying around in your home that you can use.

Improvise whenever possible. Instead of spending hundreds of dollars on a desk, make one yourself out of second hand filing cabinets and an old door which you can buy at the lumber yard for a few dollars. Cover large boxes with pretty contact paper and make your own storage boxes. Use any wicker baskets lying around for the same purpose. Save magazine covers and use them as filing folders. Use your imagination.

Find out if the people you know are willing to sell, lend or barter their second hand equipment.

Browse at flea markets and garage sales. Look in the used-for-sale classified ads. You can find good, used filing cabinets, lamps, desks, chairs, etc. at the Salvation Army shops and used furniture stores. Cleaned up and with a bit of paint, they'll look good as new.

If your list of essentials includes expensive equipment, such as a home computer, copier, word processor or special oven, it might be cheaper in the long run to lease rather than purchase. Leasing differs from renting in that later on, when you can afford it, you can purchase the item at a price reduced by the leasing costs. Leasing expenses are tax deductible. Look in the Yellow Pages for supply companies which lease the equipment you need.

Print and duplicate your own flyers, mail order pamphlets and price lists and save on printing costs. The cost of a home computer with word processing software and a printer has come down to $600 recently. Desktop photocopy machines can be purchased second hand, and the price of a new one has been slashed considerably.

If you purchase new electronic equipment from out of state you may be able to save thousands of dollars and you won't have to pay a state sales tax. A recent survey showed that the majority of persons who purchased from out of state mail order houses were able to set up their equipment and have it running right away. However, you may not get free consultation if you should have difficulty understanding the instructions or some other problem. A local dealer who charges the full retail price or more will provide this service as part of the cost. However, some mail order houses also offer toll-free consultation services to their clients. (It is not advisable to buy second hand equipment from out of state.) Electronic equipment is advertised in computer and electronic magazines.

See if your friends, neighbors and relatives are willing to volunteer or barter their services for something you can provide.

Make deliveries or purchases yourself, or hire students at the minimum wage to do so. It's much cheaper than parcel post and private courier service.

If your business requires being out a lot, a telephone answering service will pay for itself by bringing in more orders. Or, you can buy an inexpensive telephone answering machine and deduct its cost and depreciation from your income tax.

If your business requires much use of the phone, ask the telephone company for information on a total phone package which includes call forwarding. It may cost less than the combined costs of commercial rates and a telephone answering service and it will look more professional.

Operate the business from your home at the outset. Rent an office or shop only when there is no more space to breathe. You'll save thousands of dollars on commuting costs, rent, clothes (You can work in your old jeans), meals out and office insurance. (Home policies are much less expensive.)

IRS DEDUCTIONS are allowed for home business expenses, but you must prove they are necessary to your business. Among the items you are allowed to deduct are: a percentage of phone service and utility bills, furniture and remodeling expenses, even the expense of buying and feeding a guard dog. You can charge yourself rent for the portion of your home used for business and deduct that also. Depreciation expenses are also deductible.

The following guides are free and obtainable from your local IRS office. The Small Business Administration can also help you estimate the costs and deductible expenses of working from your home.

BUSINESS USE OF YOUR HOME - IRS publication 587.

TAX GUIDE FOR SMALL BUSINESS - IRS 334.

HOW TO RAISE MONEY WITHOUT ASKING FOR A LOAN

Make a list of things you own which can be sold: jewelry, sports equipment, sailboat, stereo set, camper, etc.

See if relatives or friends are willing to invest in your business or go into partnership with you and share the costs.

Borrow against your life insurance policy. You may be able to borrow the entire cash surrender value at a lower interest rate than the bank rate.

Borrow against your stock holdings.

Sell your gold and silver items and jewelry, your coin or stamp collection.

Look in the attic and garage for anything, even "junk," which is more than 50 years old. People are getting good money for old beer cans, movie star photographs, piano music sheets, matchboxes, old dolls, hats, etc. Visit an antique fair and see for yourself what's rolling in the money.

Although some persons advise taking out a second mortgage on your home, proceed with extreme caution in today's shaky real estate market. Wait until interest rates stabilize and, even then, do this as a last resort and only if your business is a sure winner.

Before you quit your job, apply for credit cards at your bank. Join the employee's credit union and borrow as much as you can just before leaving. Don't let them know you intend to quit soon.

GETTING A LOAN

Recent regulations make it possible for you to get a loan from savings and loan associations and savings banks as well as commercial banks and credit unions.

It's easier to get a loan if:

- Your business is already in operation.

- You invest a sizeable amount of your own money. The more you are willing to risk in your business, the more assurance the creditors will have that it's going to be a success.

The only person who should see you in your birthday suit, besides your spouse or lover, is your banker.

- Apply for a loan at a bank where you already have an account. Get to know your banker on a first name basis. Lenders are understandably reluctant to give credit to strangers.

- Get several copies of the loan application form and study it carefully when you get home. Gather all the information required and fill it out COMPLETELY, ACCURATELY, and IN DETAIL. This helps convince the lender that you are a well organized person who is likely to succeed.

- After your loan application is reviewed, you'll be called in for an interview. Be prepared to clarify information you gave on the form and answer further questions. Use the opportunity to convince them of the worthiness of your business plan and your ability to make it succeed.

Some of the questions you may be asked include these:

What kind of business are you planning?

How much money do you expect it to earn the first year?

What experience do you have in business and management?

What makes you think it will succeed?

Have you made a preliminary market survey?

Have you chosen a business location?

Why do you think this location is good for your business?

How much money will you invest in your business and how much do you need to borrow?

How will you use the money?

What collateral can you put up to prove that you will repay the loan?

When do you expect the business to begin paying for itself?

You may be asked even more questions than these. The Small Business Administration advises you to be prepared for the interview and learn some of the buzzwords of the banking industry so that you'll be able to understand the questions and respond more effectively.

You might be eligible for a grant or low cost loan from a foundation if you are a woman or a member of a minority group which is considered disadvantaged. For information on such foundations, look at Gale's Directory of Foundations or contact the Small Business Administration.

Knowing how to apply for a loan can make the difference between acceptance and refusal. The Small Business Administration recommends the following ways to learn how to do this.

- Enroll in their Pre-Business Workshop.

- Talk things over with a SCORE volunteer. (Retired business persons who work with SBA offices to provide valuable advice to those wishing to start a business.)

- Read their free, easy to read and understand publications. (See the list in the appendix.)

BEFORE THE INTERVIEW YOU SHOULD:

1. Write a detailed business plan. Estimate your earnings for the first year.

2. Review your business experience and management skills. Include any relevant volunteer experience as well.

3. Prepare an estimate of how much money you can afford to invest in the business and how much you need to borrow. Explain how you intend to spend the loan.

4. Prepare a financial statement listing all your personal assets and debts.

5. Itemize all the collateral you can put up as security for the loan. Give the current market value for each.

If your request for a bank loan is refused, ask the bank to give you a loan under the Small Business Administration's Loan Guaranty Plan or ask your banker to discuss your loan application with the SBA. If this doesn't work, visit the SBA office for advice on what to do next.

CREDIT UNIONS are cooperatives which operate like banks. They offer a savings plan, credit cards, checking privileges, and loans at a lower interest rate and on easier terms than banks. Many are employee cooperatives. If you are unemployed, it may still be possible to join a credit union that is owned by persons who share a common characteristic such as a profession or trade, residence in a community, even a common surname like Smith. The SBA can tell you how to get such information.

SMALL BUSINESS INVESTMENT COMPANIES (SBIC) are private credit companies which are licensed by the Small Business Administration. They make straight loans in the form of equity-style investments in your business. In return, they want a share of your profits. Their interest rates are low and they have little or no collateral requirements. For a list of SBICs, write to The Small Business Administration, Washington, D.C. 20416.

SUPPLIERS also "lend" money to their customers in the form of liberal credit terms.

BEWARE OF PRIVATE, UNLICENSED LOAN COMPANIES or you could lose your shirt as thousands already have. Before signing anything, check with the SBA and the Better Business Bureau.

DO YOU KNOW WHO YOUR CUSTOMERS WILL BE?

MARKET RESEARCH is an objective and accurate way of learning how well your product or service will sell before you spend a fortune. YOU'VE GOT TO SELL WHAT YOUR CLIENTS WANT, NOT WHAT YOU WANT TO SELL THEM. That's the essence of market research. If you can estimate the number of potential customers who want what you're selling, you have a good chance of being successful. If you can pinpoint where they live and what their lifestyles are, so much the better.

Market research can supply the answers to the following questions.

1. What do people need or desire to have?

2. What kind of people are more likely to buy my product or service? (Who are they in terms of sex, age, marital status, education, career, lifestyle, ethnic origin, religion, number of children, income, etc.)

3. Where do they live?

4. When is the best time of year to sell my service or product?

5. How does my product or service compare with what my competitors are offering? What do my potential clients like and dislike about my competitor's product or service?

Ideally, market research should be done BEFORE you open for business and PERIODICALLY thereafter. It's the only way to keep abreast of changes in your clients' tastes and needs and learn what they like or dislike about your product or service.

YOU CAN DO YOUR OWN MARKET RESEARCH IF YOU ARE STARTING OUT SMALL. Large companies spend a fortune to have market research firms find the answers to such questions, but you can do it yourself inexpensively.

First, you need to ask the right questions. You will have to break down large questions into smaller and more specific ones. Here are some examples:

1. Who is more likely to purchase your product or service - working couples? the elderly? couples with children under the age of five? persons with incomes above $45,000? single parent households? - and so on.

2. How many potential clients are there and where do they live?

The public library has census reports and other survey data which have the answers you need. They contain information on the number of people in the nation in each of the following categories: sex, age, marital status, ethnic background, race, religion, education, income, number of children in households, average housing costs, etc.

The reports also tell you where each category of persons are located nationwide - by region, state, city, and local census tracts. You can look up, for example, the geographic distribution of Spanish speaking persons. You can get even more specific, such as Spanish speaking residents in a certain census tract who originate from Honduras.

Let's assume you want to sell gold plated tooth-
brushes as gifts for people who have everything.
You would look in the census reports for the
following data.

1. The number of households above a certain income level.

2.   The localities in which they tend to cluster.

3. The average housing costs in these localities.
You can estimate the disposable income in a census
tract by subtracting these costs from the median
income.

Suppose, instead, you want to start a home repair
business for elderly home owners in your community. First, you would look up the number of persons
above a certain age who live in your census tract.
Then, you would make an on-site inspection of the
community to get an idea of the age of the housing
stock. The older it is, the greater the need for
your service.

If you intend to serve the local market, you need
to answer other questions as well.

1. Is there a strong economic base? For example,
are there lots of welfare families living there?
Are nearby industries operating full or part-time?
Have any businesses or industries moved out or
closed down recently? Are new ones scheduled to
open in the near future? Are some of the larger
department stores moving out? Do you see many
houses that are boarded up? Does the area look run
down?

THERE IS SOME INFORMATION THE CENSUS REPORTS CAN-
NOT PROVIDE For this you will need to do a more
sophisticated study which involves creating and
mailing questionnaires to selected samples of the
people you hope to serve.

For example, suppose you plan to design and sew
clothing for premature babies which you intend to
sell nationwide by mail order. First, you would
need to know if this product is sold in the local
stores or by mail order. (It is.) Next, you want
to know if there is a reasonably large market out
there and how large it is. Is it large enough to
be worth your while? The census reports only give
the number of babies born, regardless of whether
they are premature or not.

The special information you need can be found in surveys conducted by hospitals or private market research firms. Your friendly, local librarian can help you track down this and other exotic information. There are also publications available at the SBA office which give more complete details on how to do your own market research.

WHERE TO FIND CENSUS AND OTHER SURVEY DATA

1. THE PUBLIC LIBRARY has the U.S. government census reports, American Demographics magazine, The New York Times Index, The Wall Street Journal Index, and other publications.

2. UNIVERSITIES AND FOUR YEAR COLLEGES have libraries which contain much of the information you want. Their business administration departments also have information or can tell you where it can be found. Some departments offer free or low cost consultation to the public. It may also be possible to get a graduate student to do a low cost, sophisticated market research study for your business as a study assignment.

3. TRADE ASSOCIATIONS

4. THE SMALL BUSINESS ADMINISTRATION

5. CHAMBER OF COMMERCE

6. MANUFACTURERS and DISTRIBUTORS of the supplies and equipment you need.

MARKET RESEARCH DOES NOT HAVE TO BE COMPLICATED.

Some small business ventures need only a simple observation of the community. For example, if you're thinking of starting a tutoring service for grade school children in the community, you would need to know approximately how many middle and upper income families live there. (Lower income families are not likely to be your clients.) You also need to know how many children there are in this age category. An on-site observation of the neighborhoods, schools and playgrounds can give you an overview of your potential market.

Margaret Rudkin began selling baked goodies by mail order in 1937. Twenty years later, her Pepperidge Farm business was sold to the Campbell Soup Company for $28 million.

You also need to know if others are offering the same service and, if so, how you can improve on what they are doing. There is no sense in starting a tutoring service if the community is saturated with them, UNLESS YOU HAVE A WAY OF BESTING THE COMPETITION.

You can find out how many there are by looking in the Yellow Pages and newspaper ads. Send for their brochures or phone to inquire about their service. If you can "borrow" a child, arrange for a few tutoring sessions and make a note of what is being done, how it is being done, and the setting. Then think of ways you can make your service superior.

Trade journals, newspapers, and the local Chamber of Commerce can also provide information on what others in your line of business are doing.

Here are some questions you need to answer.

- How many others are providing the same service?

- How many of them appear prosperous?

- Are there too many for the size of the market?

- What advantages will my service/product have over theirs?

- How many businesses of this type failed in the past few years?

- Why did they fail?

- What price do my competitors charge?

If the competition looks formidable, add a new twist or go into another business. Provide a more reliable, efficient, cheaper, better quality, more interesting and attractive service or product. Conduct a more clever advertising campaign. And they will be the ones to worry.

ATTRACTING CLIENTS

After you have defined your market and sized up your competition, the next step is to learn how to promote and advertise your product or service. Here again, the census and other survey data can be helpful. In order to create your advertisement and get the most for your advertising dollars, you need to know your prospective clients - their sex, educational level, age, occupation, hobbies, preferred reading material, income level, etc.

This information will help you to select the magazines, newspapers and journals your clients are most likely to read. For example, if you plan to make and sell dehydrated food packets for backpacking trips, the most logical place to focus your advertising dollar is on magazines which cater to sports and outdoor enthusiasts. You can also place ads in the newspapers and general interest publications which environmentalists and sportsmen are most likely to read, such as National Geographic.

People of a certain income and educational level (the two are correlated) tend to read certain types of newspapers and magazines. For example, highly educated, upper income professionals, managers and executives are more likely to read The Wall Street Journal, The New York Times, and similar publications. Mary Ellen Pinkham, self published author of the best seller, Mary Ellen's Best Household Hints, initially advertised in the National Enquirer, knowing that more American housewives read this publication than the Saturday Review and similar publications.

This information also helps you to know which clubs and associations your prospective clients are likely to join so that you can focus your direct mail campaign more productively.

Ask your friends, neighbors and relatives to recommend clients and spread the word about your business. Consult real estate brokers, the local cop, bus and cab drivers, the meat market manager, and others in your community who are in a position to know about your potential clients.

Study the traffic flow in your community (if your business serves the local market) in order to learn where the volume of traffic is highest. Then you'll know where to distribute your business cards, flyers, free samples, and/or brochures. One woman hired students, dressed in fancy costumes which she sewed herself, to roller skate back and forth along the main street and distribute her flyers. This attracted the attention of the local newspaper and gained her additional, free publicity in the form of a personal interest article.

The site of your business should also be considered. If you plan to sell from your home, your clients are not likely to go out of their way to find you if it's far from the nearest main thoroughfare. Think of other methods of distribution. For example, rent a van and distribute door-to-door or at a highway stop. Sell through mail order, local flea markets and garage sales, or pick up and deliver.

Here are additional questions you need to answer if you plan to have clients come to your place of business.

- Is there adequate lighting, heating, air conditioning?

- Is there nearby public transportation?

- Is parking space available?

- If your business is in a remote location, will the savings in rent make up for the inconvenience to your customers and increased advertising cost?

After you open for business, you should do a periodic evaluation of your market. Old clients move out and new people with different needs and tastes move into a community. You may learn, in the nick of time, that the clients who loved your product or service are moving out in droves and a new type of resident is coming in with different needs and tastes.

Has the neighborhood started to change? Is there a nationwide demographic change, such a a migration from big cities to smaller communities, or from the Northeast to the Southwest? If so, WHO is doing the moving - middle income people? young families? a certain racial or ethnic group? You need to keep abreast of such changes in order to direct your advertising and promotion more effectively and adapt your product or service to the needs of your new market.

A nationwide census is done every ten years, so you will need information on demographic changes in off-census years also. You can do this by making periodic, on-site observations in your community, as described above; by keeping up with events reported in business periodicals, newspapers and trade or professional journals; and by regularly contacting the local Chamber of Commerce and Small Business Administration office.

You can also keep up-to-date by joining your trade, business or professional association. Attend conventions, seminars and trade shows in your line of business. Subscribe to their newsletters or journals.

Get to know your local real estate broker and banker on a first name basis. They know the latest events in the community. Join the local Chamber of Commerce.

PROMOTION AND ADVERTISING

The difference between the two is that promoting your business takes more time and energy, but it costs less, often nothing at all. Promotion methods include word-of-mouth by satisfied clients, feature stories about your business in the local newspaper, radio and television appearances, lectures, distributing free samples, and more. Advertising includes direct mail, space and classified ads, and radio and television commercials.

ADVERTISING

This is very expensive, so it must be done right. You must know who your potential clients are, which publications they read, how to pitch the wording of the ad to their interests and needs, and the best months or seasons to advertise.

Newspaper and magazine ads include the relatively inexpensive, but small, classified ads and the very expensive space ads. Focus your advertising dollar on the periodicals your clients are more likely to read. In addition to the general interest publications, there are thousands of special interest magazines and newsletters to consider.

Some experts believe newspaper ads aren't worth the cost because the audience is too general, especially in big city newspapers. But, for a business which serves a local community, the local newspaper can reap rich rewards. One woman who started a local house cleaning service received hundreds of orders immediately after placing a seven dollar ad. Place ads in large, national newspapers only if your product appeals to a general, nationwide audience. This is how the Pet

Rock and the Four Famous Idaho Potatoes were sold.

In which newspaper or magazine should you advertise? You can get a general idea of the type of
reader each publication attracts by browsing
through their ads. Also look at their circulation
figures. You can find this in the references listed below or by writing to the periodical. Be sure
to ask for the ABC data (Audit Bureau of Circulation) which is based on the number of purchases
rather than the number of readers. Also ask for a
reader profile, which gives census-type information.

SPACE ADS

These can be placed anywhere in the publication,
whereas classified ads are found only in the classified section, which is usually in the back. In a
classified ad you pay for the number of words,
whereas in a space ad you pay for the space utilized. Some experts believe space ads in newspapers
are not worth the expense, but a space in the
Yellow Pages, in a business or professional directory, or a community newsletter will probably draw
a continuing response.

For a professional looking ad, consider hiring an
advertising agency to design one for you. The cost
will probably be in the hundreds of dollars, but
it will probably be worth it.

CLASSIFIED ADS

Small, classified ads have made a lot of money for
some persons. By repeating the ad, you can multi-
ply your response rate. Classified ads can also be
used to develop your own list of names for direct
mailing.

Decide which is the best section to place your ad.
Where would you look if you were a client? Study
the different placements of ads to find the best
one for your own.

WRITING A CLASSIFIED AD

This takes a special expertise which this book
cannot go into in detail. The Small Business Administration can guide you. Some of the references

listed below and in the appendix will be helpful.

There are some cardinal rules to follow. One is to study the ads in the periodicals and dailies and determine what it is that captures your attention and what turns you off. Adapt somebody's ad to suit your needs. There is no copyright infringement as long as the artwork and wording is not a point-by-point imitation. In fact, you will notice that most of the ads are variations on a theme.

Revise your ad repeatedly until you are completely satisfied. Then ask friends and relatives to rip it apart with criticism. Then revise again, and boil it down to the barest minimum of powerful words.

DIRECTORIES OF MAGAZINES AND NEWSPAPERS

You can find these in the public library. Here are a few suggestions.

- Ayer Directory of Publications

- Ulrich's International Periodicals Directory

- Bacon's Publicity Checker

- International Yearbook

- Broadcast Yearbook

- Trade and Professional Association Directory

TEST YOUR AD

First place it in the inexpensive publications. Start with small ads and work up to larger ones which cost more. If an ad gets a poor response in one publication, try another. Compare the results.

Ads placed at different times of the year or different days of the week bring in a different response rate. The worst days are just before and after the holidays. Use your own good judgment. Which day of the week attracts the greatest number of readers? If you said Sunday, you're absolutely right. Which day of the week brings the worst response rate? Studies show that Fridays and Mondays are poor days.

Write two or three versions of an ad and place it in the same publication to see which one pulls the most. Place the same ad at the same time in several publications. Try placing the same ad in different sections of a publication. Select the section which your clients are more likely to read: women's section, sports, automobile ads, etc.

FREE OR LOW COST ADVERTISING

This can be obtained by placing your ad in the community newsletter or bulletin board, school newspapers, church bulletin boards, give-away shopper's guides, local Chamber of Commerce newsletter and more.

You can also carry small quantities of your flyers, brochures and/or business cards wherever you go and distribute them. Flea markets, fund raising events, conventions and trade shows, exhibitions, street and school fairs, church bazaars, shopping malls, supermarkets, and any other gathering of large numbers of people are opportune occasions. One woman started a tutoring service without spending a penny on advertising. She got all the clients she needed by distributing her business card to teachers and parents at the local schools.

DIRECT MAIL

This is expensive, but well worth the cost if it's done right. It involves mailing a letter, brochure, order form and reply envelope to a list of selected persons. They may be friends, neighbors, past customers, and members of associations and clubs to whom your product or service would appeal. One woman developed a successful mail order business of selling herbs and herbal food items by first selling directly to customers who came to her home. As the number of customers grew, so did her list of names and addresses. When she had enough to close "shop," she began selling only through direct mail and classified ads.

Although direct mail is more expensive in the short run, it often gets better results than ads placed in publications. The secret is to have a mailing list of persons who are more likely to want your product or service. Another secret is to periodically winnow out the fish that don't bite. You can do this by coding the addresses so that you can trace the results of your mailings.

The mail order business is booming, thanks to an increase in transportation costs and the number of working wives. There are millions of people who don't have the time or transportation facilities to shop for specialized goods and services. Where else, for example, can a New Yorker buy Cherokee Indian bread except through mail order?

Since your own list of names probably isn't long enough to make direct mailing profitable, you might consider renting a mailing list from a publication. The one where you got good results from your space or classified ads is the logical place to start. You can also rent them from list brokers. They can be found in Klein's Directory, the Yellow Pages, Standard Rate and Data Service Directory, and Direct Marketing Magazine.

A man who was thinking of starting a fiber optics manufacturing business in his garage first tested the market by renting a mailing list of 8,000 potential buyers. He wrote a simple flier which described the product, and mailed it out. He knew he had a winner when 6,000 replies came. Then, and only then, did he invest the money and time to open his business.

You can save money on large quantity mailing by using the following - brochures or letters which can be folded and mailed without envelopes, printed postcards and using your business card as a promotion flyer by advertising on the back. The post office will give you more information.

TELEPHONE SALES

This can be used effectively by a business which caters to the local market, and it's cheaper than direct mail. You can get the addresses and phone numbers of residents in the community from the reverse telephone directory which you can buy from the telephone company or find in the library.

RADIO OR TELEVISION APPEARANCES

These give your business free exposure. Talk shows, contests, quiz shows, and the like are always hungry for new faces. You'll need an interesting "handle" however, something you have done in the past or something connected with your business which makes local news.

FEATURE ARTICLES IN THE LOCAL NEWSPAPER, COMMUNITY NEWSLETTER OR COMPANY NEWSLETTER

These, and anything else which is distributed locally, can also provide free advertising. Some people write their own article and send it to the newspaper, knowing it's more likely to be accepted if it requires little or no editing.

USE A VARIETY OF ADVERTISING AND PROMOTION METHODS

Do this only if you can afford it, and focus on those which bring the best response rate. Mary Ellen Pinkham first placed an ad in the National Enquirer. Then she got on the mailing lists of gift shops across the country. She sold 1.5 million copies through the gift shops alone. When she appeared on the Good Morning, America show, her sales hit the ceiling.

SOME PROBLEMS YOU MAY ENCOUNTER AFTER STARTING A BUSINESS

LONG HOURS/SHORT INCOME

Some entrepreneurs succeed beyond their wildest dreams. Many more, however, discover they are working longer hours for a modest income, especially during the first year or two. There are ways to reduce the burden.

- Delegate some tasks to family members.

- Hire students as low-cost assistants.

- Pay others to do some of the chores: income tax preparation, accounting, packing and mailing, delivering, cleaning, etc. If you don't have the cash to pay for these services, barter your service or product for what you need.

YOUR HOME BUSINESS INTERFERES WITH
YOUR FAMILY LIFE.

Many people get so involved with the unending
business of starting a business that they have
little time for their families. When the business
expands, the family's living quarters are taken
over by an accumulation of equipment, supplies and
even a few employees. Here are solutions which
have worked.

- Organize your time and tasks more efficiently.
Prepare a detailed schedule of things that must be
done on a daily, a weekly, and a monthly basis.

- Ask family members to share your work.

- Add an extension to the house.

- Rent additional office space nearby: neighbor's
garage or basement, a desk in a local real estate
or insurance office, etc.

- Move your business to the garage or basement

- Get a camper and park it in the yard.

YOUR SOCIAL LIFE BECOMES A FADING MEMORY

Working for yourself is lonesome business. After
the initial euphoria of being your own boss is
over, you'll feel isolated from the world. You'll
miss getting dressed in the morning and the human
interactions of public transportation and the
office. Here is what others have done about this
problem.

- Combine business with pleasure whenever possible. Make frequent trips to the library to read
business forecasts and the latest news on your
type of business. Do some of your paper work in
the library, at the beach or park.

- Take mini-holidays: long walks around the neighborhood, to the shopping malls, etc. While you're
at it, distribute your flyers, business cards, and
other promotion materials whenever feasible.

- Enroll in an adult education course which will
give you greater business expertise. Take a course
in home computers.

YOUR HOME BUSINESS IS NOT TAKEN SERIOUSLY

Women, especially, find this to be a problem. Some
male clients take a patronizing attitude toward
them. The problem can be serious enough to result
in a loss of potential clients. Here what some
experts advise you to do.

- A professional image is important. You can't
expect clients to take your business seriously if
you greet them dressed in hair curlers and old
clothes. Wear a business suit whenever you meet
clients. Read chapter five for more suggestions on
how to improve your professional image.

- In the TV movie, A Woman Called Golda, Israel's
prime minister is seen conferring with a visiting
American congressman in her kitchen where she
brews him a hot cup of tea and serves her homemade cake. You are not advised to follow suit.
Instead of meeting clients in your living room or
kitchen, "borrow" an office from a friend until
you can afford to rent your own. Rent a desk in
the local insurance or real estate office. Meet
clients in the lobby of a classy hotel.

- Get a separate business phone which only you or
a telephone answering service will answer. Never
have children or teenagers answer business calls
for you.

- Get business cards and good quality stationery
with your business logo on it. If you can't design
a professional looking logo yourself, the printer
can recommend a local artist to design one for you
at a reasonable cost. Use the logo on everything:
business cards, stationary, mailing labels, order
forms, etc.

"THE DEVIL MADE ME DO IT" AND SELF-DISCIPLINE

Comedian Flip Wilson draws laughs whenever he uses
this excuse, but it will only draw tears from you.
Working for yourself invites the temptation to
take time off from your work. It requires enormous
self-discipline to stick to a schedule when you
are feeling rotten or whenever distractions occur.
No one is looking over your shoulder, so why not
take off? The problem is that a few minutes here
and there add up until you discover that you won't
be able to meet the deadlines. Here is what others
have done about it.

- Establish a routine and stick to it until it becomes a habit. A well-known writer keeps her 4:00 A.M to noon work schedule religiously, despite severe bouts of arthritis. Such determination contributes to her success as much as her talent does.

- Adjust your schedule to suit your biological clock (the hours when you are in peak form). A jewelry designer who works from sundown until three in the morning notified her friends not to make social calls in the evening so that she wouldn't be bothered while working.

- Move your workplace to a quiet part of the house. A freelance artist with small children uses the attic as the only undisturbed part of the house to do her work. A writer who lives in cramped quarters installed fluorescent lights in a large closet and uses it for serious writing.

- Reward yourself each time you resist the temptation to take a break from your schedule. Punish yourself whenever you do.

NEW, SMALL BUSINESSES ARE THE MOST VULNERABLE

Although nearly 50% of new businesses failed in 1981, more succeeded, and some did so sensationally. From October 1979 until July 1980, the national bankruptcy petitions increased 72%, and almost all of them were small businesses. According to the Small Business Administration, three out of four small businesses fail within the first year, and nine out of ten within ten years.

Some of the causes of failure are preventable. Many people, for example, start a business without the savings needed to weather a prolonged rise in interest rates or reduced consumer spending. Many are single product or service businesses which lack the diversification needed in order to respond to increased competition and changes in consumer tastes. They have more difficulty getting loans during rough times and they often resort to bank loans at higher interest rates than the big firms have to pay.

THERE ARE WAYS TO REDUCE THE RISKS

Consult with the Small Business Administration before starting your business, and continue to consult them on a regular basis thereafter.

Since a small business is more vulnerable, it must be more efficiently run than a large one. Here are some ways to improve its organization and management.

- Make a long range business plan, based on the most reliable information and advice.

- Improve the efficiency of your record keeping and time management.

- Calculate how much you can afford to spend each year, and spend not one penny more. Set aside some of the first year's profits for expanding the business.

- Diversify. Plan to sell other products or services when the demand for the current one slows down, so that the earnings from one will offset losses on the other.

- Someone asked a man who made a fortune during the Great Depression while everyone else was going broke how he did it. He replied, "Good judgment." And how does one acquire such good judgment?. "Experience," was his reply. And how did he get such valuable experience? "By making mistakes," he said. Learn from your mistakes. Don't give in to them.

When I went home from the Navy in 1953, I did not have a job. I did not have a home. I lived in the government housing project....I did not make enough money the first year to pay my rent. Later, I went to the Small Business Administration and they not only gave me a loan, they gave me constant annual advice and help. They would send a distinguished, retired gentleman down to Plains to spend two or three days, at no cost to me, to go through my warehouse business which was just getting started, and to give me advice on how to handle my accounts receivable, how to keep records, how to borrow money, how to market my products better. — President Jimmy Carter

THE SMALL BUSINESS ADMINISTRATION

WHAT IT CAN DO FOR YOU

The SBA is an independent government agency which was created to help and protect the interests of small businesses. It offers a variety of valuable services and has a wealth of information which is either free or at very low cost. It can help you to improve your management skills, obtain government contracts, make or guarantee a loan, and more. In 1980 it established the Women's Business Enterprises office to assist women in starting their own business. The main categories of assistance are in management, financial service, and procurement.

The management assistance program includes courses, conferences, workshops and clinics which are often co-sponsored with local Chambers of Commerce, banks and other lending institutions, and universities and colleges. Many of the training sessions are geared to the needs of newcomers to the world of business. For example, the pre-business workshops show the participants how to apply for a loan. If you want to discuss the advisability of starting a business or if you need help in choosing a business location or making a business plan, the Management Assistance people are the ones to see.

The Small Business Institute (SBI) program offers long term counseling to new and troubled small businesses located in or near colleges or universities. The students and faculty of the business administration departments do the counseling.

Financial assistance in the form of various loan programs is also available. To be eligible, a person must show proof of having been turned down by a commercial bank or two savings banks in communities with a population of no less than 200,000. There are special loan programs for the physically handicapped, for people who are considered socially and/or economically disadvantaged, and for businesses suffering from the effects of Federal renewal or other construction programs. See the appendix for a list of publications issued by the SBA.

What you have read in this chapter is not the whole story, but it should be enough to help you decide if you want to go into business for yourself. Good Luck!

BY PERMISSION

The following authors and publications were the source of the additional quotations listed on the pages indicated.

page 6
A. Edward Friedmann quotation is from Lawrence Van Gelder's "From Buying Gems to Polishing Thesis." © 1983 by The New York Times Company.

page 28
Jacob Landers quotation is from Anna Quindlen's "69, Out of Law School and in the Thick of Life." © 1980 by The New York Times Company.

page 100
Tony LoBianco quotation is from Stephen Kinzer's "How Ethnic Childhoods Shaped 'Bridge' Actors." © 1983 by The New York Times Company.

page 109
Satchel Paige quotation is from Joseph Durso's "Satchel Page, Black Pitching Star, is Dead at 75." © 1982 by The New York Times Company.

page 160
Benjamin Buttenweiser quotation is from Deirdre Carmody's "More and More Workers Hit Stride." © 1982 by The New York Times Company.

page 195
Joke involving "Solly Wishnick," the waiter, is taken from Stan Burns & Mel Weinstein, The Book of Jewish World Records, Pinnacle Books, New York City, 1978.

page 247
Jeanne Moreau quotation is from Glen Collins, "Jeanne Moareau Enters a Sweet Season."   © 1983 by The New York Times Company.

A P P E N D I X

HOW TO START A SELF-HELP JOB BANK
IN YOUR COMMUNITY

A job bank for people in your community who are 45
years of age and over can provide mutual support,
friendship, and a network of potential job contacts. Your group can also put pressure on private
industry employers and local government officials
to help unemployed, older persons. It can mount a
public relations campaign to persuade local employers to hire more older workers. Others have
done it and so can you. All you need is the help
of like-minded individuals who are willing to put
in the time and effort. This is how the famous,
Forty Plus Clubs got started. The following resources will show you how it can be done. It's
much easier than you think, and it's lots of fun.

ORGANIZATIONS WHICH HELP LOCAL SELFHELP GROUPS
GET STARTED

Note: Many of the following organizations operate
with volunteer staff and small budgets. Send a
self-addressed, stamped envelope so they can expe-
dite a reply to your request for information.

NATIONAL SELF-HELP RESOURCE CENTER
1722 Connecticut Avenue, NW, Washington, D.C.
20009. Phone number:(202) 3871088. Works with
neighborhood organizations to develop expertise in
local planning, information networking, skills
banks and community organization.

NATIONAL INSTITUTE ON AGING, WORK AND RETIREMENT
c/o National Council on the Aging, 600 Maryland
Avenue, SW, Washington, D.C. 20024. Phone number
is (202) 4791200. Promotes opportunities for middle aged and older workers. Provides information
and assistance to persons and groups seeking
employment. Sponsors seminars, workshops, research.

NATIONAL ASSOCIATION OF OLDER WORKER EMPLOYMENT
SERVICES, c/o National Council on Aging (see a-
bove) Provides services to members of the National
Council on Aging who deliver employment services
to workers age 40 and over. Helps improve employment opportunities for older workers. Serves as an
advocate for older workers and older worker em-

ployment services. Establishes contacts with private industry to involve its members in association business. Identifies training and retraining needs of older workers. Provides technical assistance, information exchange, training, and a forum for discussion of older worker issues. Also gives assistance to communities and organizations seeking to establish older worker employment services.

OPERATION ABLE
36 South Wabash Avenue, Chicago, ILL. 60603; phone number is (312) 7823335. It's a consortium of placement professionals, local government agencies, and public and private employers whose purpose is to help middle aged and older persons find jobs. Operates a job bank, a yearly job fair, and publishes a newsletter, "Networking," which is a treasure house of tips on how to start and operate a job bank.

SENIOR JOB BANK
P.O. Drawer 2217, Fort Myers, FLA 33902. Phone number: (813) 3341281. It began as a job bank to help persons 55-plus who are over the income guidelines for the Senior Aide Program. Send for their pamphlet, "You Should Have a Senior Job Bank." It gives step-by-step directions on how to start your own job bank.

THE SELF-HELP CENTER
1600 Dodge Avenue, Suite S-122, Evanston, ILL 60201. Phone number is (312) 328-0470. A nonprofit organization which assists self-help/mutual aid groups in the Chicago area and nationwide. Provides a free telephone referral service to persons seeking information on how to start a self-help group. Offers direct assistance, either on a consultation basis or as part of funded projects. Publishes directories of groups in the Chicago area. Maintains a library of publications on self-help groups.

NATIONAL SELF-HELP CLEARINGHOUSE
Graduate Center, City University of New York, 33 West 42nd Street, New York, NY 10036. The phone number is (212) 840-7606. Does research on self-help groups and publishes materials which you may find helpful. Publishes a newsletter, "The Self-Help Reporter," which reports on news and research activities relating to self-help groups.

LEARNING EXCHANGE
Box 920, Evanston, IL 60201. Phone number is (312)

273-3383.

O.W.L. (OLDER WOMEN'S LEAGUE)
3800 Harrison Street, Oakland, California 94611.
Phone: (415) 658-0141. Primarily for women age 45
to 65. A self-help network dedicated to programs
to change negative stereotypes of older women and
to political activism on their behalf.

LEAGUE OF WOMEN VOTERS
1730 M Street, NW, Washington, D.C. 20036. Send
$1.00 for their Media Kit, Pub. # 163, which
gives tips on how to do public relations for your
organization.

AARP BROADCAST SERVICES DEPARTMENT
1909 K Street, NW, Washington, D.C. 20049. Offers
support services to get the news about your organization on radio and television.

SUGGESTED READINGS ON SELF-HELP GROUPS

Help: A Working Guide to Self-Help Groups by Alan
Gartner & Frank Riessman (Watts, 1979)

Organizing: A Self-Help Guide For Grass Roots
Leaders by Si Kahn (McGraw Hill, New York, 1981)

Self-Help Groups For Coping With Crisis: Origins,
Members, Processes and Impact by Morton A.
Lieberman, Leonard D. Borman and Associates. (Jos-
sey-Bass Publications, Inc. San Francisco, 1979)
Discusses how groups are started and structured,
how self-help groups work, and how to evaluate
their impact.

The Family Circle Guide to Self-Help by Glen
Evans. (Ballantine Books, 1979) Includes the ABC's of
starting your own self-help group.

Neighborhoods: A Self-Help Sampler (171Q2) can be
purchased for $6.50 from the Superintendent of
Documents, Washington, D.C. 20402. Describes the
experiences and techniques of effective self-help
organizations throughout the nation.

Second Career Opportunities For Older Persons: A
Program Guide - available from the Institute of
Lifetime Learning, 1909 K Street, NW, Washington,
D.C. 20049. Written for organizations that provide
information and plan activities to help older
people develop and promote jobs. Offers advice on

how to set up job fairs, job placement services,
employment workshops, and more.

Starting a Group in Your City - How to run meetings, find local resources, file charges of discrimination, your legal rights, and more. Send $1
to Working Women, 1224 Huron Road, Cleveland, OH
44115.

HOW TO FIND A JOB THROUGH NETWORKING

Networks are the modern equivalent of the "Old
Boy" system of finding a job through personal
contacts. Networks exist in every community. They
may be well structured organizations with the
specific purpose of helping persons who share
certain characteristics find jobs. They can be
informal contacts such as the local banker, your
lawyer, neighbors, friends, relatives, doctor,
people you meet in job placement offices, ex-
spouses, anyone who is in a position to help you
locate a job opening or knows someone who can.

Most of the existing, well organized networks are
for members of groups that are considered disadvantaged, such as women and racial, ethnic and
religious minorities. The paucity of men's groups
listed below is not due to the author's bias. Men
seem to be lagging in this form of self-help
enterprise at present.

OFFICE OF INFORMATION, EMPLOYMENT AND TRAINING
ADMINISTRATION, U.S. Department of Labor, 601 D
Street, NW, Washington, D.C. 20213. Phone number
is (202) 376-6730. (for older workers and veterans)

PRESIDENT'S COMMITTEE ON EMPLOYMENT OF THE HANDI-
CAPPED, Vanguard Building, 1111 20th Street, NW,
Washington, D.C. 20036. (For handicapped persons)

REHABILITATION SERVICES ADMINISTRATION, U.S. Department of Education, Room 1427, 330 C Street,
SW, Washington, D.C. 20201.

(There is a Directory of Organizations Interested
in the Handicapped which lists over 150 voluntary
and public agencies involved in the rehabilitation and employment of the handicapped.)
DIVISION OF VETERAN'S AFFAIRS
Empire State Plaza, Agency Building 2, Albany, NY

12223; phone number is (518) 474-3725.

FORTY PLUS CLUB
15 Park Row, New York, NY 10038. Phone number is (212) 233-6086. This is a self-help group for professionals and persons in executive and management whose previous earnings were $25,000 and over in 1983. See the index for the various places in this book where it is discussed.

OLDER PERSONS EMPLOYMENT NETWORK
RSVP Office Complex, Ithaca, New York

NATIONAL CLEARINGHOUSE ON AGING
Department of Health and Human Services
Washington, D.C. 20201. Phone: (202) 245-0188.

STATE COMMISSIONS AND OFFICES ON AGING
These can give you information on job training and opportunities in your community, employment agencies and, often, career counseling and job placement services at little or no cost. Look in your phone book for the address and phone number of the nearest office.

NATIONAL ASSOCIATION FOR HUMAN DEVELOPMENT
1750 Pennsylvania Avenue, NW, Washington, D.C. 20006. Phone: (202) 393-1881. Research and training programs on maintaining physical and mental health; career education, job training and a placement bureau.

NATIONAL CAUCUS AND CENTER ON BLACK AGED
1424 K Street, NW, Suite 500, Washington, D.C. 20005. Phone: (202) 637-8400. Maintains a Rural Senior Employment Program and a training and education division, among others.

WOMEN'S BUREAU, U.S. Department of Labor, Washington, D.C. 2020. Issues publications of interest to women workers and women's action groups. Its purpose is to work for equality in employment for women. Conducts outreach projects. Does research on women in the workforce. Among the free or low cost publications you can send for are "Job Options for Women in the 80's;" "Women are Underrepresented as Managers and Skilled Crafts Workers;" "Handbook on Women Workers."
CATALYST
6 East 82nd Street, New York, NY 10028.
See index for sections in this book where this important organization for women is discussed. Catalyst also issues free and low cost publica-

tions for women who are exploring new careers. Here is a sample: "Women in Banking," "Women in the Corporate World," "Women Entrepreneurs," "Women in Management," "Women in the Skilled Trades," "Women in Government and Politics," "Returning Women."

WOMEN IN MANAGEMENT
525 North Grant, Westmont, ILL 60559. Phone number is (312) 963-0079. A support network of women in professional and management positions. Issues a monthly newsletter.

NATIONAL FEDERATION OF BUSINESS AND PROFESSIONAL WOMEN'S CLUBS, 2012 Massachusetts Avenue NW, Washington, D.C. 20036. Phone number is (202) 293-1100. Promotes the interests of business and professional women and extends their educational opportunities. Sponsors the Business and Professional Women's Foundation which gives scholarships and fellowships.

NATIONAL COMMISSION ON WORKING WOMEN
1211 Connecticut Avenue, NW, suite 301, Washington, D.C. 20036; phone number is (202) 887-6820. Focus is on non-professional and non-managerial women who have low paying, low status jobs. Action programs designed to help solve their problems. A national exchange for ideas, information and research. Sponsors career seminars.

WOMEN'S DIVISION, AMERICAN ASSOCIATION OF RETIRED PERSONS, 1909 K Street, NW, Washington, D.C. 20049. Serves as a clearinghouse for all national women's organizations. Coordinates programs for older women.

ADVOCATES FOR WOMEN, 414 Mason Street, San Francisco, CA 94102. Phone number is (415) 391-4870. An economic development center to improve the status of women. Also has offices in Berkeley and Hayward, California. Provides job listings, career counseling, employment workshops, skills training, job hunting tips, tutoring for blue collar employment, and more. Its publications include a guide for women's organizations to develop an affirmative action counseling service.

CAREER ADVANCEMENT NETWORK, 3805 North High Street, Suite 310, Columbus, Ohio 43214. Phone number is (614) 267-0958. Promotes development of contacts to advance women in employment. Runs workshops, seminars, training sessions, and a referral service to programs sponsored by other organizations or educational institutions.

WOMEN IN SALES ASSOCIATION, 21 Cleveland Street, Valhalla, New York 10595. Phone number is (914)946-3802. For women working in the occupation or aspiring to a sales career. Provides networking, career guidance, job referrals. Issues a monthly newsletter.

NATIONAL NETWORK FOR WOMEN IN SALES, P.O Box 95269, Schaumberg, ILL 60195. Phone number is (312) 577-1944. For women in sales or seeking a sales career. Sponsors monthly programs. Operates a placement services and job bank. Maintains resume file. Conducts job fairs. Provides scholarships to women studying marketing and sales at a 2-year college. Issues a monthly newsletter.

WOMEN EMPLOYED, Five South Wabash, Suite 415, Chicago, ILL 60603. Phone number is (312) 782-3902. Helps women improve their employment opportunities. Assists women in asking for higher salaries and obtaining back pay settlements. Advice on how to deal with office politics. Job referrals, seminars on resume writing, interviews, etc.

DISPLACED HOMEMAKERS NETWORK, INC.
755 8th Street, NW. Washington, D.C. 20001. See index for information on this valuable network throughout this book. The "Displaced Homemaker Program Directory" contains a national listing of centers and programs providing services to displaced homemakers. Contains over 400 programs. Issues "Network News," a bimonthly newsletter which reports on local and national news relating to the Displaced Homemaker Program.

NATIONAL ORGANIZATION FOR WOMEN (N.O.W.) in some states offer career counseling sessions, assertiveness training as well as a network of peers to help women advance in the world of work. The address is 84 Fifth Avenue, New York, NY 10011. Phone: (212) 989-7230.

SUGGESTED READINGS ON THE TOPIC

Directory of Special Opportunities for Women (Garrett Park Press, Garrett Park, Maryland, 1981.)

Is Networking For You? A Working Woman's Alternative To The Old Boy System by Barbara Stern. (Prentice Hall, 1980)

Networking by Mary Scott Welch. (Harcourt, Brace, Jovanovich)

Working Woman - see the March 1980 issue for a list of about 300 networks.

Women's Organizations: A New York City Directory can be obtained from Department Y, New York City Commission On The Status of Women, 250 Broadway, suite 1412, New York, NY 10007. Send a $5.95 check payable to the CSW Fund, Inc. Listings include educational programs, professional groups, networks, ethnic and racial groups, older women's groups, religious affiliated organizations, and many more categories.

The Complete Guide to Getting a Better Job, Advancing Your Career & Feeling Good As a Woman Through Networking by Carol Kleiman. (Lippincott & Crowell)

National Directory of Women's Employment Programs published by Wider Opportunities for Women (W.O.W.), 1649 K Street, NW, Washington, D.C. 20006. Lists over 140 women's job action and advocacy organizations in the nation. If it isn't in the library, you can order it from W.O.W. The price in 1979 was $7.50 plus postage.

FLEXIBLE WORKSTYLES AND VOLUNTEER WORK

ASSOCIATION OF PART-TIME PROFESSIONALS
P.O. Box 3419, Alexandria, Virginia 22302. Phone number is (703) 370-6206. Promotes job opportunities for persons interested in part-time professional jobs. Operates a placement service for part time professionals, permanent part-time work, job sharing, free lancers and consultants. Public awareness activities to educate the public on the advantages of increased flexibility in work. Information resource center. Conducts workshops and research. Issues "A Part Timer's Guide to Federal Part-Time Employment" and other materials.

NATIONAL ASSOCIATION OF TEMPORARY SERVICES
119 South Asaph Street, Alexandria, Virginia 22314; phone number is (703) 549-6287. The professional organization for temporary job placement agencies. Sets standards for the industry and issues a code of ethics. You can contact them if you have any questions or complaints about an

agency in your community, or to get a list of reputable agencies in or near your community.

FLEXIBLE CAREERS AND ASSOCIATES
Santa Barbara, CA.

FLEXIBLE CAREERS, INC.
37 South Wabash, Chicago, ILL 60603

NEW WAYS TO WORK
149 Ninth Street, San Francisco, CA 94103. Phone: (415) 552-1000. Provides information, training and support to persons and groups interested in flexible ways to work. Sponsors job sharing workshops. Publishes many "how to" materials.

FLEXIBLE WAYS TO WORK
c/o YWCA, 1111 SW Tenth Street, Portland, OR 97205

FOUR-ONE-ONE
7304 Beverly Street, Annandale, Virginia 22003. Phone number is (703) 354-6270. A national clearinghouse on community volunteer programs. Lists national organizations and agencies involved in human services and community needs.

ASSOCIATION OF VOLUNTEER BUREAUS
801 North Fairfax Street, Alexandria, Virginia 22314.

VOLUNTEER: THE NATIONAL CENTER FOR
CITIZEN INVOLVEMENT
P.O. Box 4179, Boulder, CO 80306. Phone number is (303) 447-0492. A clearinghouse for dissemination of information on volunteer programs.

AMERICAN ASSOCIATION OF EMERITI
c/o Lawrence Mirel, founder, 918 16th Street, NW, Washington, D.C. Phone number is (202) 463-7880. See index for section where it is discussed.

NATIONAL EXECUTIVE SERVICE CORP
122 Third Avenue, New York, NY 10017. Phone number is (212) 867-5010. Provides paid consulting and volunteer work opportunities for retired executives. Some of the assignments are overseas.

NATIONAL COUNCIL OF SENIOR CITIZENS
925 15th Street, NW, Washington, D.C. 20005. Phone: (202) 347-8800. Organization of 4,000 senior citizen clubs, associations, councils and other groups. Sponsors educational workshops and leadership training institutes and voluntary ser-

vice activities in local communities.

SUGGESTED READINGS

CATALYST
6 East 82nd Street, New York, NY 10028, publishes
the following pamphlets:
  - Volunteers and Volunteerism
  - Alternative Work Patterns
      A. General Reference
      B. Job Sharing/Paired Employment
      C. Part Time Employment

Working Less But Enjoying It More, is a job-
sharing publication available from NEW WAYS TO
WORK (see above)

NON-PROFIT EMPLOYMENT SERVICES FOR MATURE PERSONS

Some of the network and self-help organizations
mentioned above also provide job banks and job
referrals for their members or clients. The following organizations supplement those mentioned
elsewhere in this book. This listing does not
exhaust the number of services that are available
in this country. There are probably many more. If
your community is not represented here, the listing will give you a broad picture of the kinds of
services available and their titles which you may
be able to find in your local telephone directory.

GREEN THUMB
1012 14th Street, NW, Washington, D.C. 20005.
Phone: (703) 276-0750. Funded primarily by the
U.S. Department of Agriculture. Provides job
placement and part-time community service employment for persons 55-plus who are at or near the
poverty income level and who live in rural areas.
Conducts on-the-job training to place older workers in energy related industries.
ALL CRAFT FOUNDATION, 25 St. Marks Place, New
York, NY 10003; phone number is (212) 228-6421.
Trains low income women to enter the skilled construction trades (3 months learning and practice
in carpentry, plumbing, electrical work, cabinet
making, etc.) Provides counseling and job placement.

SENIOR EMPLOYMENT SERVICES
Wilmington Senior Center, Inc., Wilmington, Dela-
ware

OVER 60 COUNSELING AND EMPLOYMENT
4700 Norwood Drive, Chevy Chase, Maryland.

CALIFORNIA ABLE, INC.
787 Crossbrook Drive, Moraga, CA 94556

SENIOR ACHIEVEMENT AWARD
8780 S.W. 48th Street, Miami, Florida 33165

ALLIANCE OF BUSINESS, INC.
3 Computer Drive, Computer Park, Albany, New York
12205

EMPLOYMENT PROGRAMS
New York City Department of Aging

SPECIAL PROGRAMS AND SERVICES AND EMPLOYMENT RE-
FERRAL SERVICES
Richland-Lexington Council on Aging, Columbia, SC.

SAGE ADVOCATE EMPLOYMENT SERVICE
New Haven, Connecticut

SENIOR PERSONNEL PLACEMENT BUREAU
22 Church Street, New Rochelle, NY.

YONKERS EMPLOYMENT SERVICE FOR SENIORS
365 Broadway, Yonkers, NY.

RETIREMENT JOBS, INC   SENIOR ENTERPRISES, INC.
San Francisco, CA   Indianapolis, Indiana

JOB DEVELOPMENT SERVICE   SECOND CAREERS PROGRAMS
Arlington, Virginia   Los Angeles, CA.

SENIOR CITIZENS SERVICES   ELDER HIRE
Memphis, Tennessee   Cambridge, MASS

EXECUTIVE AND MANAGEMENT RECRUITING FIRMS

THE AMERICAN MANAGEMENT ASSOCIATION
135 West 50th Street, New York, NY 10020. Issues
the "Executive Recruitment Organizations and Executive Job Counseling Organizations," which can be
purchased from the Association.

CONSULTANT NEWS
Templeton Road, Fitzwilliam, NH 03347. Issues a
"Directory of Executive Recruiters" which lists
over 1,800 search firms in the U.S. and overseas.

PERFORMANCE DYNAMICS, INC.
Publishing Division, 300 Lanidex Plaza,
Parsippany, NJ 07054. Issues "The Performance
Dynamics Worldwide Directory of Job Hunting Con-
tacts: A Guide to 2,400 Employment Recruiters."

THE JOB HUNT

SUPERDIRECTORIES AND DIRECTORIES
Superdirectories list all the directories that are
available for various industries, associations,
employers, and publications. Use the following
when you run out of leads.

Guide to American Directories (B. Klein Publications, P.O. Box 8503, Coral Springs, FL 33065)

Directory of Directories (Gale Research Company,
Book Tower, Detroit, MI 48226) Facts on over 5,000
current directories in business and industry,
health and medicine, finance and banking, insurance, science, energy, public affairs, real estate, labor, agriculture, mining, sports and more.
Over 2,000 different fields are covered.

Encyclopedia of Associations (Gale Research Company) Lists trade, business, professional, labor,
scientific, educational, voluntary and social
organizations.

National Trade and Professional Associations of
the United States and Canada (Columbia Books Publisher, New York) Lists names, addresses and phone
numbers of over 4,000 business and professional
associations.

Federal Government (U.S. Library of Congress)
Lists information resources in the U.S. and government sponsored information analysis centers.

Business Organizations and Agencies Directory
(Gale Research Company) Guide to private and public organizations which provide information on
business and industry.

Directory of International Business, Travel and
Relocation (Gale Research)

Medical and Health Information Directory (Gale
Research Company) is a comprehensive guide to
health related organizations and publications.

Encyclopedia of Business Information Sources

Employer Directory (published by Albin)

Training and Development Organizations Directory (Gale Research Company)

The American Bank Directory lists about 18,000 banks and gives addresses, phone numbers and names of executives.

International Directory of Computers and Information System Services

The New 1983 National Directory of Addresses and Telephone Numbers (Concord Reference Books, 135 West 50th Street, New York, NY 10022)

Rand-McNally International Banker Directory (Rand-McNally & Co.) lists over 37,000 banks, giving officials and statement figures.

Moody's Banks and Finance (Moody's Investor Service) Lists over 9,700 banks and financial institutions, giving names of directors, officers and other top level personnel.

Standard Directory of Advertisers and Agencies

Wall Street Index

U.S. Industrial Outlook

Corporate Annual Reports

Business Periodicals Index

Dun and Bradstreet
Lists about 31,000 business which have a net worth of between $500,000 and $1 million. Gives addresses, phone numbers, number of employees, names of directors.

Standard & Poor's Register of Corporations, Directors and Executives (Standard & Poor's Corp.)

Standard Rate and Data lists all business periodicals.

Writer's Market (Writer's Digest, 9933 Alliance Road, Cincinnati, OH 45242) lists over 5,000 markets for writers, editors, typists, word processors and anyone else who wants to work in the publishing industry.

Writer's Digest (see above) also publishes market directories for photographers, artists, song writers, and craft workers.

Writer's Handbook (The Writer, Inc., 8 Arlington Street, Boston MA 02116) lists over 2,000 places to sell manuscripts.

OTHER SOURCES OF INFORMATION ON JOBS, THE JOB MARKET AND EMPLOYERS

FEDERAL INFORMATION CENTER PROGRAM
General Services Administration, 18th and F Streets, NW, Washington, D.C. 20405; phone number is (202) 566-1937. Provides assistance to those "lost in the maze of Federal programs and services." There are centers in 41 cities and 43 other cities which have toll-free phone lines to the nearest center. Look it up in your phone book.

OFFICE OF PERSONNEL MANAGEMENT, FEDERAL JOB INFORMATION CENTER
P.O. Box 52, Washington, D.C. 20044.

SUGGESTED READINGS

International Employment Opportunity Digest (International Publications, P.O. Box 29344, Indianapolis, IN 46229. Phone number is 317/357-6567). A quarterly subscription is $15.

Job Openings (Superintendent of Documents, U.S. Government Printing Office, Washington, D.C. 20402). A monthly Government newspaper based on computerized listings of job openings with the United States Employment Service. It gives job titles, number of vacancies, where they are located, and the range of salaries offered. Civil Service examination announcements also give short descriptions of the work, education and experience requirements and starting salaries. Send $18 for an annual subscription. Copies are available for review at your nearest local Job Service Office. You can get a free, single copy from the Consumer Information Center, Dept. No. 533J, Pueblo, Colorado 81009

Telesearch: Dial the Best Job of Your Life by John Truitt (Facts on File Publications, 460 Park Avenue South, New York, NY 10016)

Occupational Outlook Handbook, 1982-83 edition, (published by The Bureau of Labor Statistics, U.S. Department of Labor. Price in 1982 was $9, but you can probably find it in your local library.) A 496 page "encyclopedia of careers" which gives detailed information on over 250 occupations. The Handbook is published every two years. Information is given on the following:
    What the work is like
    Job prospects to 1990
    Personal qualifications, training and educational requirements
    Working conditions
    Related occupations
    Earnings
    Chances for advancement
    Where to find additional information

Reprints from the Occupational Outlook Handbook, 1982-83 edition. These are leaflets on "Job Families," or related occupations. Useful to the job hunter who wants to learn about a specific occupation or job family. Send for a free list by writing to any regional office of the Bureau of Labor Statistics. You can look this up in the telephone directory under "U.S. Government." The price for each reprint is $2.25.

Occupational Outlook Quarterly describes emerging occupations, training opportunities, salary trends, career counseling, and the latest research findings of the Bureau of Labor Statistics. The price is $8 for a one year subscription.

Directory of Occupational Titles defines job titles and activities for over 35,000 occupations. (Does not give information on outlook, salaries, education and training requirements or employers.)

The above listed publications from the Bureau of Labor Statistics can also be obtained from the Superintendent of Documents, U.S. Government Printing Office, Washington, D.C. 20402

Encyclopedia of Careers and Vocational Guidance (J. G. Ferguson Publishing Co.) covers national information on all aspects of job responsibilities, education and other requirements, job outlook, and salary for over 350 occupations.

Employment Opportunities for the Handicapped
(World Trade Academy Press) After each occupational description it gives the types of handicaps
which would not interfere with job performance.

Computer and Mathematics-Related Occupations. Send
$2.25 to the U.S. Government Printing Office.

Job Options for Women in the 80's. Send $3.50 to
the U.S. Government Printing Office.

The Job Outlook in Brief (in the Spring 1982 issue
of Occupational Outlook Quarterly. Trends and
prospects in this decade for more than 250 different occupations. Send $2.75 to the U.S. Government
Printing Office)

Peterson's Guide to Engineering, Science and Computer Jobs (Peterson's Guides)

The American Almanac of Jobs and Salaries by John
B. Wright (Avon Books). Gives job descriptions,
salary ranges and advancement opportunities for
most levels and many occupations in banking, service, transportation, retailing and other industries as well as for traditional professions.

The Federal Employment Handbook by William C.
Robinson (Monarch/Simon and Schuster) describes
about 450 white collar, civil service occupations.

CATALYST also issues pamphlets on a wide range of
occupations. Write to them for a free list. See
index for address and other information.

Job Finding Techniques for Mature Women published
by the U. S. Department of Labor. Send a stamped,
self addressed envelope to the Superintendent of
Documents, U.S. Government Printing Office, Washington, D.C. 20402.

Everything a Woman Needs to Know to Get Paid What
She's Worth by Caroline Bird and David McKay (Bantam Books)

The Working Woman Success Book by the editors of
Working Woman magazine (Ace Original, 1981) Describes how to start out in the working world, how
to change jobs, etc.

CATALYST (14 East 60th Street, New York, NY 10022) issues the following guides:

- Resume Preparation Manual: A Step-By-Step Guide For Women

- Marketing Yourself: The Catalyst's Women's Guide to Successful Resumes and Interviews

Personal Resume Preparation by Michael P. Jaquish.

The Professional Job Changing System by Robert J. Jameson (includes psychological testing, stress interview questions, and a resume checklist)

Tea Leaves:A New Look At Resumes by Richard Bolles (by the author of the best seller, What Color Is Your Parachute? - a 24 page guide)

Write to the non-profit COUNCIL FOR CAREER PLAN-NING for booklets with samples of resumes and application letters. For a free brochure which describes the booklets and their prices, write to the Council at 310 Madison Avenue, New York, NY 10017.

Choosing to Work by Leonard Cohen (Reston Publishing Company, Reston, VA) A step-by-step guide to writing resumes, cover letters, interviews, etc. Includes a section on how older workers, the physically handicapped and minorities can overcome employee biases.

The Perfect Resume by Tom Jackson. A variety of resume types for different job titles and experience levels.

Professional Resume/Job Search Guide by Harold Dickhut. Examples for persons in selected business specialties, e.g. accounting, sales, law.

Resume Writing by Burdette E. Bostwick. Samples of different kinds of resumes, e.g. chronological, functional, and of broadcast letters.

Salary Strategies by Marilyn Moats Kennedy (Rawson Wade Publishers) Excellent guide on how to determine the salary range for your occupation and experience level, how to bargain for more.

OUT-OF-TOWN JOB MARKETS

Before you pack up and rush off, take out a subscription to the newspapers of the communities you are considering. It's the best way to get a picture of quality of life, cost of living, housing prices, and the job market.

Job Bank guides to Metropolitan New York, Chicago, Boston and San Francisco published by Robert Adams. Lists major firms and employment agencies in each area.

Finding Your Best Place to Live in America by Thomas Bowman, George Giuliani, and Ronald Minge (Red Lion Books, West Babylon, NY 11704)

National Job Finding Guide by Heinz Ulrich and J. Robert Connon (Doubleday & Company, New York). An encyclopedic reference guide to finding a job out of town. Lists names and addresses of newspapers with the most help-wanted ads, employment agencies, executive recruitment firms, trade and professional journals that carry help-wanted ads, a geographical index of 800 major corporations and their employment practices, job seekers' clubs, networks for women, the handicapped, and members of minority groups.

SELF-ASSESSMENT FOR A CAREER CHANGE

COUNSELING CENTERS

COUNCIL FOR CAREER PLANNING
310 Madison Avenue, New York, NY 10017. An affiliation of colleges and universities to provide career counseling, placement and job opportunity resources. Outreach projects include aid to disadvantaged women, minority women, older women and youths.

American Board of Counseling Services, Directory of Approved Counseling Agencies is published by the American Personnel and Guidance Association, Two Skyline Place, 5203 Leesburg Pike, Falls Church, VA 22041. Phone: (703) 820-4710. It includes employment and career counseling services of all kinds and is revised annually.

Directory of Educational and Career Information
Services for Adults is published by the National
Center for Educational Brokering. The 1978 edition
listed over 215 centers in 41 states. The sites
include libraries, community agencies, adult education divisions of high schools and community and
four year colleges as well as state agencies. Ask
your librarian for a more recent edition.

COLLEGES AND UNIVERSITIES have career counseling
and placement divisions for the use of their enrolled students and graduates. Two year colleges
often have such services available for any mature
resident of the community, regardless of whether
he or she is, or has been, a student. You may be
eligible for their services (and to use the library of career information) even if it's been
decades since you graduated.

CATALYST (see above) will send you a free brochure
which lists accredited career counseling and job
placement centers in your state.

DISPLACED HOMEMAKER NETWORK provides information
on free or low cost counseling and job placement
in or near your community. (For women who meet
their eligibility criteria) Write to their headquarters at 755 8th Street, NW, Washington, D.C.
20001.

JOB SERVICE OFFICES in or near your community may
still be offering career counseling and skills and
interests testing free of charge.

STATE VOCATIONAL REHABILITATION AGENCIES offer
career and job placement services to people with
handicaps. Some offer free literature on the job
market and job hunting tips.

WOMEN'S CENTERS AND ORGANIZATIONS, such as N.O.W.
offer career counseling sessions for little or no
charge. See the network organizations listed above
or in the index.

SUGGESTED READINGS

Group Career Dynamics: Participant Workbook by
Andrew A. Helwig (Group Career Dynamics, Logan,
Utah). Includes a series of exercises to help you
do a self-assessment and develop a career plan.
Employs the learning style preferred by mature
adults. Has been used in Job Factories, Job Clubs
and other self-help groups. Can be used by indivi-

duals and groups. A trainer's manual includes information and exercises and instructions to conduct a 3-to-4 day career workshop on self assessment, resume preparation, communication skills, practicing telephone canvassing of employers, etc.

The Hidden Job Market for the 80's by Tom Jackson and Davidyne Mayleas (Times Books) includes nearly 50 self-assessment quizzes and helps you to match your strengths to "job families."

Matching Personal and Job Characteristics is published by the U.S. Department of Labor. How to choose the right career; includes easy to use chart for comparing your background and personality traits with the characteristics of 281 occupations. Send $2.75 to Consumer Information Center, Dept. H, Pueblo, CO 81009.

Life Work Planning by Arthur Kern and Marie Kern (McGraw Hill) is a workbook of exercises which help you analyze your strengths, clarify your goals, set priorities and develop a plan of action for achieving your career goals.

What Color Is Your Parachute? by Richard N. Bolles (Ten Speed Press, Berkeley, CAL). This best seller includes the Quick Job Hunting Map and discusses other topics such as how to deal with rejection, where to get help, who has the power to hire you, and more.

Where Do I Go From Here With My Life? by John C. Crystal and Richard N. Bolles (Ten Speed Press) A workbook for job hunters and career changers written by two of the leaders in the field.

The Quick Job-Hunting Map by Richard N. Bolles (Ten Speed Press). A series of exercises which help you to analyze your skills, find the right career, and learn how to find a job.

Second Career Opportunities for Older Persons published by the American Association of Retired Persons' Institute of Lifetime Learning. Write to the Institute of Lifetime Learning, Box 2400, Long Beach, CAL 90801 for a free copy.

"Getting a New Job," chapter 6 in Life After Layoff: A Handbook for Workers in a Plant Shutdown (Utah Center for Productivity and Quality of Working Life, Logan, UT) This is a 38 page chapter, taken from the larger handbook, which gives a step-by-step outline of how to find a new job. Includes worksheets and examples on how to decide on a job and job hunting tips.

Focus on Choice: A Program Guide helps undereducated women improve their self-esteem and develop life planning skills. Write to the Fort Wayne Women's Bureau, P.O. Box 554, Fort Wayne, IN 46801.

CATALYST issues a series of pamphlets and books for women who need guidance in self-assessment, life planning and job search skills. Among these are What to Do With the Rest of Your Life which is published by Simon & Schuster. Write to Catalyst for a free list of their publications: 6 East 82nd Street, New York, NY 10028.

A Counselor's Guide to Occupational Information is published by the U.S. Department of Labor. It lists pamphlets, brochures, monographs and other career guidance publications issued by Federal agencies. Send $4.00 to the Superintendent of Documents, U.S. Government Printing Office, Washington, D.C. 20402.

I Can: A Tool for Assessing Skills Acquired Through Volunteer Experience (Council of National Organizations for Adult Education, Ramco Associates, 228 East 45th street, New York, NY 10017.

DISCRIMINATION IN EMPLOYMENT

SOURCES OF INFORMATION AND ADVOCACY

EQUAL EMPLOYMENT OPPORTUNITY COMMISSION, 2401 E Street, NW, Washington, D.C. 20506. Phone: (202) 756-6040 or 634-6814. Contact them if you have a complaint to file.

OFFICE OF PUBLIC AFFAIRS, 2401 E Street, NW, Room 4202, Washington, D.C. 20506. Write to them if you need information.

DEPARTMENT OF HEALTH AND HUMAN SERVICES, OFFICE FOR CIVIL RIGHTS, 200 Independence Avenue, SW, Washington, D.C. 20201. Phone: (202) 426-7307.

DEPARTMENT OF JUSTICE, EQUAL EMPLOYMENT OPPORTUNITY OFFICE, 10th Street and Constitution Avenue,

NW, Washington, D.C. 20530. Phone: (202) 633-3696.

OFFICE OF THE SECRETARY, WOMEN'S BUREAU, U.S. DEPARTMENT OF LABOR, Washington, D.C. 20210. Enclose a stamped, self-addressed envelope.

Also contact the human rights agency in your state. You can look up the exact title and the address in the phone book. In New York State, for example, it is called "Division of Human Rights," and is located at Twin Towers, 99 Washington Avenue, Albany, NY 12210. Phone: (518) 474-2705.

LEGAL SERVICES FOR THE ELDERLY, 132 West 43rd Street, New York, NY 10036. Phone: (212) 595-1340. Does research, provides litigation services and educational programs relating to problems affecting the elderly.

EEO INSTITUTE
4801 Massachusetts Avenue, NW, Suite 400, Washington, D.C. 20016. Phone: (202) 364-8710. Does research on equal employment opportunity. Offers advice to women, blacks and other minorities, and to the handicapped. Sponsors seminars and para-professional training.

AMERICAN CIVIL LIBERTIES UNION,, 132 West 43rd Street, New York, NY 10036. Phone: (212) 944-9800. Activities include test court cases, opposition to repressive legislation, public protests on inroads of civil rights. Sponsors projects on equal employment opportunity, women's rights, and more.

NATIONAL SENIOR CITIZENS LAW CENTER
1424 16th Street, NW, Suite 300, Washington, D.C. 20036. Phone: (202) 232-6570. Acts as advocate on behalf of the elderly poor. Maintains library and publishes weekly newsletter, handbooks and guides.

NATIONAL EMPLOYMENT LAW PROJECT
475 Riverside Drive, New York, NY 10027. Phone: (212) 870-2121. Areas of concern include employment discrimination and employment rights of the handicapped. Focus is on the poor.

PRIVATE LAWYERS are expensive, but some offer free or low cost services to members of disadvantaged groups, among which are women and the elderly. Check with the Lawyer Referral Service of the American Bar Association. You may find a local office listed in your phone book. Or, you can write to the Association's address: 1155 East 50th

Street, Chicago, ILL 60637. Phone: (312) 667-4700.

NATIONAL LEGAL AID AND DEFENDER ASSOCIATION, 1625 K Street, NW, Washington, D.C. 20006. Phone: (202) 452-0620. It publishes a directory of member attorneys and paralegals who handle civil and criminal matters. It also maintains lists of attorneys who specialize in a specific area of the law. Fees are often based on ability to pay. The directory cost $6 in 1983.

LEGAL COUNSEL FOR THE ELDERLY, 1909 K Street, NW, Washington, D.C. 20049. Phone: (202) 331-4215. Offers free legal services to residents of Washington, D.C. who are age 60-plus.

EQUAL RIGHTS ADVOCATES (ERA), 1370 Mission Street, San Francisco, CA 94103. Phone: (415) 621-0505. Deals with sex discrimination. Brings class action suits on behalf of plaintiffs, focusing on employment issues such as equal pay, nontraditional work, discriminatory practices, etc. Offers legal advice to victims of sex discrimination.

N.O.W. LEGAL DEFENSE AND EDUCATION FUND, 132 West 43rd Street, New York, NY 10036. Phone: (212) 354-1225. An affiliate of the National Organization of Women. Provides legal assistance to women to combat discrimination based on sex, religion, race or national origin.

WOMEN'S EQUITY ACTION LEAGUE (WEAL), 805 15th Street, NW, Washington, D.C. 20005. Phone: (202) 638-1961. Works for legal and economic rights for women through research, public education, litigation and legislation advocacy. Areas of interest include problems of older women, discrimination in employment and education, access to training programs. The Washington, D.C. office provides work experiences for retirees, job hunters, career changers, etc.

COMPARABLE WORTH PROJECT, 488 41st Street, No. 5, Oakland, CA 94609. Phone: (415) 658-1808. Supports comparable pay for working women through networking, education and advocacy.

N.O.W. (NATIONAL ORGANIZATION FOR WOMEN), 425 13th Street, NW, Suite 1048, Washington, D.C. 20004. Phone: (202) 347-2279. Purpose is to combat discrimination against women in government, industry, the professions, education, etc. Committees include Disabled Women, Discrimination in Education,

Discrimination in Employment, and others.

WOMEN'S LAW FUND, 620 Keith Building, 1621 Euclid Avenue, Cleveland, OH 4115. Phone: (216) 621-3443. Provides legal assistance to women who have administrative charges pending before state and Federal government agencies. Provides representation in court proceedings. Purpose is to eradicate discrimination in employment, education, government benefits and more.

WOMEN'S LAW PROJECT, 112 South 16th Street, Suite 1012, Philadelphia, PA 19102. Phone: (215) 564-6280. A non-profit law firm working to eradicate sex discrimination through litigation, individual counseling and representation of women's groups. Provides telephone counseling and referral services. Conducts test cases and class action litigation in employment and other forms of discrimination based on sex.

WOMEN'S LEGAL DEFENSE FUND, 2000 P Street, NW, Washington, D.C. 20036. Phone: (202) 887-0361. Has attorneys and paralegals on staff. Provides volunteer legal representation on legal issues concerning women. Provides advocacy on behalf of women's rights in employment, education and other areas.

SUGGESTED READINGS

Sue Your Boss: Rights & Remedies for Employment Discrimination by Richard E. Larson (Farrar, Straus & Giroux) Mr. Larson serves as the national staff counsel of the American Civil Liberties Union.

Job Termination Handbook by Robert Coulson, president of the American Arbitration Association. (Free Press, Riverside, NJ 08370)

Legal Rights Calendar published by the Legal Counsel for the Elderly. Features concise and easy to read facts on age discrimination, how to choose a lawyer, tax benefits, consumer credit rights, financial protection and other matters concerning the elderly. Send a check for $4.95 to: 1984 Legal Rights Calendar, P.O. Box 19269 L, Washington, D.C. 20036.

The Rights of Women by Susan Deller Ross, special counsel for sex-discrimination litigation in the Civil Rights Division of the Department of Justice, and Ann Barcher, lawyer for the Port Author-

ity of New York and New Jersey. Published by the
American Civil Liberties Union. Discusses such
areas as employment, credit, education, divorce
and custody. Also contains appendixes on state
laws on discrimination in employment, education,
housing and financing for housing and other matters. Also give addresses and phone numbers of
over 115 sources of legal help and women's organizations. Send $3.95 plus $1 for postage and hand-
ling to: Literature Department, American Civil
Liberties Union, 132 West 43rd Street, New York,
NY 10036.

Publications available from the Women's Bureau,
U.S. Department of Labor, Washington, D.C. 20210.
(Enclose a stamped, self-addressed envelope.)

- A working Woman's Guide to Her Rights. ($2.75)
  Topics covered are helpful to men as well and
  include: employment, pay and sources of assistance.

- New Regulations to Help Open Nontraditional
  Jobs for Women - Explains the Department of
  Labor's new regulations on equal employment
  opportunities for women and minorities in the
  construction industry and apprenticeship opportunities.

- Protection Against Sex Discrimination in Employment

- Brief Highlights of Major Federal Laws on Sex
  Discrimination in Employment

Publications available from WORKING WOMEN, 1224
Huron Road, Cleveland, OH 44115

- Hidden Assets - a 25 page analysis of the
  status of women and minorities' employment in
  banks.

- Vanished Dreams - a 30 page documentation of
  age and sex discrimination faced by women
  office workers in employment.

- Pay Equity for Office Workers - a brochure
  examining the issue of equal pay for work of
  comparable value.

- How to Ask For a Raise

- Age Discrimination - brochure on the problems

faced by working women over 40 years of age.

HOW TO ACHIEVE THE LOOK OF SUCCESS

CLOTHES AND GROOMING

The Executive Look: How to Get It, How to Keep It by Mortimer Levitt (Atheneum)

Making the Man: The Insider's Guide to Buying and Wearing Men's Clothes by Alan Flusser (Simon & Schuster)

How to Dress Your Man by Charles Hix (Crown)

How to Dress Well: A Complete Guide for Women by Priscilla H. Grumet (Cornerstone)

How to Look Ten Years Younger by Adrien Arpel (Warner Books)

The Woman's Dress for Success Book by John T. Molloy (Warner Books)

Adrien Arpel's 3-Week Crash Makeover/Shapeover Beauty Program by Adrien Arpel with Ronnie Sue Ebenstein (Pocket/Wallaby)

Image Impact: The Aspiring Woman's Personal Packaging Program edited by Jacqueline Thompson (A & W Publishers) - discusses grooming, wardrobe, body language, self-assertion, business manners and other aspects of a woman's image.

COMMUNICATING WELL

How to Talk Well by James F. Bender (McGraw Hill)

Make the Most of Your Best: A Complete Program For Presenting Yourself & Your Ideas with Confidence and Authority by Dorothy Sarnoff (Doubleday)

CATALYST issues the following publications for women, also helpful to men. You can order them by writing to Catalyst, 14 East 60th Street, New York, NY 10022.

- Attitudes: Male/Female

- Assertiveness Training

KEEPING MENTALLY AND PHYSICALLY FIT

Kicking Your Stress Habits: A Do-It-Yourself Guide For Coping With Stress by Donald A. Tubesing (Whole Person Publications, 1981)

The Work/Stress Connection: How to Cope With Job Burnout by Robert L. Veninga and James P. Spradley (Little Brown and Co.)

How to Avoid Stress Before It Kills You by Matthew J. Culligan and Keith Sedlacek, M.D.

Anger: The Misunderstood Emotion by Carol Tavris (Simon & Schuster)

Anger: How to Recognize and Cope With It by Dr. Leo Madow (Scribners)

A New Beginning: How You Can Change Your Life Through Cognitive Therapy by Dr. Gary Emery (Simon & Schuster)

Stop Procrastinating: Do It! by James R. Sherman (Pathway Books)
How to Survive Getting Fired & Win! by Jerry Cowle

How To Live To Be 100 Or More: The Ultimate Diet, Sex and Exercise Book by George Burns (B. Dalton)

Jane Brody's The New York Times Guide to Personal Health by Jane Brody (Times Books, New York)

The Middle Years by Donald Donohugh, M.D. (Saunders Press, 1981) - comprehensive medical, emotional and live-life-to-the-fullest guide.

Making It Through Middle Age by William Atwood (An intensely personal account by the former president of Newsweek who has changed jobs 7 times since he was forty, survived polio and two heart attacks)
Old Enough to Feel Better by Michael Gordon, M.D. (Chilton Books, 1981) - guide to health and aging.

Adding Years to Your Life & Life to Your Years by Durk Pearson and Sandy Shaw (Warner Books, 1981) - describes how diet can reduce risks of cancer, heart attacks, and other ailments and control aging, improve learning and memory.

Pep Up Your Life: A Fitness Book for Seniors is a free booklet issued by Travelers Insurance Company. Write to Travelers Film Library, 1 Tower

Square, Hartford, Connecticut 06115.

Over 55: A Handbook on Aging edited by Theodore G. Duncan (Franklin Institute Press) Medical specialists explore the medical, economic and psychological aspects of aging.

Pathfinders by Gail Sheehy (William Morrow) Personal accounts by mature persons from all walks of life which will make you feel good about yourself.

Your Memory: A User's Guide by Dr. Alan Baddeley (Macmillan) - includes mnemonic techniques to improve your memory.

The Memory Book by Harry Lorayne and Jerry Lucas (Ballantine, 1975) - includes mnemonic techniques to improve your memory.

You can also obtain free literature on health and safety topics by writing to the NATIONAL HEALTH INFORMATION CLEARINGHOUSE, P.O. Box 1133, Washington, D.C. 20013.

UPGRADING YOUR SKILLS OR LEARNING NEW SKILLS

SOURCES OF INFORMATION AND HELP

NATIONAL EDUCATION ASSOCIATION OF THE UNITED STATES, 1201 16th Street, NW, Washington, D.C. 20036. Phone: (202) 833-4000. (general inquiries)

ADULT EDUCATION DIVISION of your local school board, or contact the school superintendent's office for information about adult education courses and services.

NATIONAL HOME STUDY COUNCIL
1601 18th Street, NW, Washington, D.C. 20009. Phone: (202) 234-5100. Send for their "Directory of Home Study Schools."

FEDERAL STUDENT AID PROGRAM
Box 84, Washington, D.C. 20044. Phone: (800) 492-6602 (Maryland); (800) 638-6700 (elsewhere)

NATIONAL ASSOCIATION OF TRADE AND TECHNICAL SCHOOLS, Office of Public Information
2021 K Street, NW, Washington, D.C. 20006. Phone: (202) 296-8892. Send for their "Directory of Accredited Private Trade and Technical Schools."

AMERICAN COUNCIL ON EDUCATION
Office of Educational Credit
One Dupont Circle, NW, Washington, D.C. 20036.
Send for a copy of "A Guide to Educational
Programs in Noncollegiate Organizations."

NATIONAL INSTITUTE FOR WORK AND LEARNING
1211 Connecticut Avenue, NW, Washington, D.C.
20036. Phone: (202) 466-2450. Sponsors the Center
for Education and Work, Center for Women and Work,

NATIONAL CENTER FOR EDUCATIONAL BROKERING
Projects include worker education and training
policies for mid-life and senior citizens.

CLEARINGHOUSE ON THE HANDICAPPED
Department of Education Services
Washington, D.C. 20202. Phone: (202) 245-0080

EMPLOYMENT AND TRAINING ADMINISTRATION
U.S. Department of Labor
Contact the regional office nearest you or write
to the headquarters for the address: 601 D Street,
NW, Washington, D.C. 20530. Phone: (202) 376-6270.

POST-SECONDARY EDUCATION PROGRAMS FOR DEAF AND
OTHER HANDICAPPED, U.S. Department of Education
Room 3121, Donohoe Building, 400 Maryland Avenue,
SW, Washington, D.C. 20201. Phone: (202) 245-9598.

YOUR STATE OFFICES, such as the following New York
State services, may be listed in the phone book
under the same or similar titles:

    Department of Labor
    University Without Walls
    Cultural Education Center
    Office of Independent Study
    Office of Apprenticeship Training
    Office of Vocational Rehabilitation
    Higher Education Services Corporation
    Higher Education Opportunities Program
    Office of Non-Collegiate Sponsored Education

or, write to the Bureau of Apprenticeship and
Training, U.S. Department of Labor for information
and applications to take examinations.

SUGGESTED READINGS

Guide to Independent Study Through Correspondence
Instruction by the National University Extension
Association. Order from Peterson's Guide, Book

Order Department, Box 978, Edison, NJ 08817

On-Campus, Off-Campus Degree Programs for Part-Time Students by the National University Extension Service. Order from Peterson's Guide

Tips on Home Study Schools issued by the Council of Better Business Bureaus. See your local BBB or write to the Council of Better Business Bureaus, 1150 17th Street, NW, Washington, D.C. 20036.

How to Get Credit For What You Know: Alternative Routes to Educational Credit- a free brochure issued by the Women's Bureau, U.S. Department of Labor, Washington, D.C. 20210.

How to Get Credit for What You Have Learned as a Homemaker and Volunteer published by the Educational Testing Service. Send $5 to ETS Publications Division, Princeton, NJ 08541.

Directory of Education and Career Information Services for Adults published by the National Center for Educational Brokering, 1211 Connecticut Avenue, Suite 301, Washington D.C. 20036 (If you get no response, ask your local librarian for a copy)

Re-Entry: A Handbook for Adult Women Students by Nancy Maes. Available from the Program on Women, Northwestern University, 1902 Sheridan Road, Evanston, ILL 60201

Learning Independently - lists over 3,000 tape recordings, correspondence courses, and programmed learning materials on over 400 subject areas. Valuable to those who want to upgrade their skills or learn new skills at home. See if your local library or college has a copy.

A Woman's Guide to Apprenticeship is issued by the Women's Bureau, U.S. Department of Labor. For women interested in training as skilled workers in the service trades, construction and manufacturing. How to apply; barriers you may face; your legal rights; sources of help. Send a check for $3 to the U.S. Government Printing Office, Pueblo, CO 81009.

Happier by Degrees: The Most Complete Sourcebook for Women Who Are Considering Going Back to School by Pam Mendelsohn (E.P. Dutton)

HOW TO STUDY AND PASS EXAMS

How to Pass Employment Tests by Arthur Liebers
(ARCO)

How to Master Test Taking by Fred A. Anderson
(Skills Improvement)

How to Prepare for the Scholastic Aptitude Test by
Lester Hirsch

How to Beat Test Anxiety and Score Higher on Your
Exams by James Divine and David Kylen (Barron)

How to Study by Ralph C. Preston & Morton Botel

How to Take and Pass Simple Tests for Civil Service Jobs by Solomon Wiener (Monarch Press)

Successful Student's Handbook: A Step-by-Step
Guide to Study Skills by Rita Phipps (University
of Washington Press)

Barron's How to Prepare for the College Board
Achievement tests by Jerome Shostak (Barron)

How to Prepare for the College Level Examination
Program (CLEP) by Evarts Prescott,Jr. (McGraw)

How to Prepare for the High School Equivalency
Examination by C. Jenkins, et. al. (McGraw)

HOW TO START YOUR OWN BUSINESS

SOURCES OF INFORMATION AND HELP

Small Business Administration (SBA)
Office of Consumer Affairs
Washington, D.C. 20416. Phone: (202) 653-6519
Look in the phone book under "U.S. Department of
Labor" for the nearest office.

American Entrepreneurs Association
2311 Pontius Avenue
Los Angeles, CA 90064. Phone: (213) 478-0437
For people interested in starting a business.
Research on new types of small businesses;
seminars; monthly magazine; conventions.

American Women's Economic Development Corporation
1270 Avenue of the Americas
New York, NY 10020. Phone: (212) 397-0880
Non-membership organization for women owning or planning to form a small business. Sponsors training and technical assistance program; provides management training and advisors who work in specific problem areas, assistance in preparing a business plan, and continued support after the program is completed. Also has a national telephone counseling service for women not enrolled in training program. Staff is made up of experienced business persons and specialists from university business schools and major corporations.

Women Entrepreneurs
3061 Fillmore Street
San Francisco, CA 94123. Phone: (415) 929-0129
Supporters include bank loan officers and venture capitalists. Provides access to vital information and resources, some in conjunction with the SBA, Mayor's Office of Economic Developmenbt, etc.

National Association of Companion Sitter Agencies and Referral Services
801 Princeton Avenue, SW, Birmingham, AL 35211.
Phone: (205) 785-5171

Elder Craftsmen
851 Lexington Avenue
New York, NY 10021. Phone: (212) 861-5260
Non-profit outlet for crafts persons over 60 years of age. Sells handiwork on consignment.

New York Exchange for Women's Work
660 Madison Avenue
New York, NY 10021. Phone: (212) 753-2330
Sales outlet for handiwork and foods made by women in their homes. Helps about 700 women earn a livelihood.

National Freelance Photographer's Association
60 East State Street
Doylestown, PA 18901. Phone: (215) 348-2990
Assists news media to obtain photographs. Maintains photograph file from members for industry. Publishes a variety of guides, directories, pamphlets.

Office of Small and Disadvantaged Business Utilization, U.S. Department of Agriculture
127 West Administration Building, Washington, D.C. 20250. Helps rural women with their businesses.

Include a brief description of your business (farm, motel, antique shop, etc.) along with a request for help.

National Alliance of Home-Based Businesswomen
P.O. Box 95-GH
Norwood, NJ 07648
Serves as an information network.

SUGGESTED READINGS

Worksteads: Living and Working in the Same Place by Jeremy J. Hewes (Dolphin Books)

Mind Your Own Business at Home, by Coralee Kern, is a newsletter for home-based entrepreneurs. Send $3 for a sample copy to C.S. Kern, 2520 North Lincoln Avenue,, Box 60, Chicago, ILL 60614.

Mail Order Moonlighting by Cecil G. Hoge (Ten Speed Press)

Mother Earth News Handbook of Home Business Ideas & Plans (Bantam Books)

Minding My Own Business: Modern Entrepreneurs Share Their Stories of Success by Marjorie McVicar and Julia Craig (Richard Marek Publishers)

How to Become Financially Successful by Owning Your Own Business by Albert J. Lowry (Simon & Schuster)

How to Earn Over $50,000 a Year at Home by Dan Ramsey (Parker Publishing)

184 Businesses Anyone Can Start and Make a Lot of Money by Chase Revel

Extra Dollars: Easy Money-Making Ideas for Retired People by Ray Hoffman (Stein and Day Publishers)

Consulting: The Complete Guide to a Profitable Career by Robert E. Kelley

Women Working Home: The Home Based Business Guide and Directory (how to market your service or product, tax deductions, free counseling, and more) Send $12.95 plus $1.25 postage to Women Working Home Press, P.O. Box 237-GH, Norwood, NJ 07648.

How to Run a Housesitting Business by Jane Poston. For information on how to order it, write to Ms. Poston at 1708 East 9th Street, Tucson, Arizona 85719.

Franchise Opportunities Handbook lists over 1,000 franchise businesses, how much you need to invest in each, what kind of financial and managerial help you can expect. Published by the Commerce Department. Send $10 to the Superintendent of Documents, U.S. Government Printing Office, Washington, D.C. 20402.

Everywoman's Bookshelf is a catalogue of publications for women entrepreneurs (crafts, franchises, marketing, money management, etc.) Send $1 for a catalogue of publications to Dept. WD, Box 104, Wilton, CONN 06897.

How to Pick the Right Small Business Opportunity by Kenneth J. Albert (McGraw Hill)

Jobs for Weekends by Roberta Roesch (Berkeley Publishing Co.)

The Complete Book of Money Making Opportunities by J.F. Straw (Frederick Fell Publishers, Inc.)

The following publications are available from McGraw-Hill Book Company, 1221 Avenue of the Americas, New York, NY 10020.

- How to Start and Operate a Mail Order Business by Julian Simon - (057417-0) $19.95.

- The Small Business Guide to Borrowing Money by Richard L. Rubin and Philip Goldberg (054198-1) $24.95

- Do-It-Yourself Marketing Research by George E. Breen and A. B. Blankenship (007446-1) $24.95

- The Small Business Legal Advisor by William A. Hancock (025979-8) $24.95

Tips on Mail Order Profit Mirages is free from the Council of Better Business Bureaus, 1150 17th Street, Washington, D.C. 20036. (The message is: look before you leap.)

Literature is also available from the Small Business Administration, for free or at low cost. The following is just a small sample of their numerous items. You can send for these and a list of other publications by writing to SBA, P.O. Box 15434, Fort Worth, TX 76119.

- Checklist for Going Into Business
- Selecting the Legal Structure for Your Firm
- Business Plan for Small Service Firms
- Association Services for Small Business
- Locating or Relocating Your Business
- Basic Budgets for Profit Planning
- Business Plan for Retailers
- Insurance Checklist for Small Business
- Marketing for Small Business
- Learning About Your Market
- Handcrafts
- Tax Guide for Small Business
- The ABC's of Borrowing
- More Than a Dream: Raising the Money
- Women's Handbook: How SBA Can Help You Go Into Business
- Advertising, Packaging, and Labeling.... ..$2.50
- Starting and Managing a Small Business of Your Own...............................5.00
- Starting and Managing a Small Service Business..................................4.50
- Handbook of Small Business Finance..........3.00

INDEX

Also consult the appendix
  and table of contents.